Discovering the
COLORADO PLATEAU

Discovering the
COLORADO PLATEAU

A Guide to the Region's Hidden Wonders

BILL HAGGERTY

FALCON®

Guilford, Connecticut

FALCON®

An imprint of The Rowman & Littlefield Publishing Group, Inc.
4501 Forbes Blvd., Ste. 200
Lanham, MD 20706
www.rowman.com

Falcon and FalconGuides are registered trademarks and Make Adventure Your Story
is a trademark of The Rowman & Littlefield Publishing Group, Inc.
Distributed by NATIONAL BOOK NETWORK

British Library Cataloguing in Publication Information available

Library of Congress Control Number: 2020950538
ISBN 978-1-4930-3715-5 (paper : alk. paper)
ISBN 978-1-4930-3716-2 (electronic)

♾™ The paper used in this publication meets the minimum requirements of American National Standard for Information Sciences—Permanence of Paper for Printed
Library Materials, ANSI/NISO Z39.48-1992.

Contents

Acknowledgments

I acknowledge community—and I am grateful for my family and friends. How would I ever explore without the purposeful support of all of you?

There are five individuals and a dog I am most thankful for in helping me with this book: the Haggerty Guide Service—i.e., JT (John) Toolen, wife Diane Smith, and their Bad-Ass Adventure Dog Raz. "We Guide Haggerty!" was their motto. And they did. All across the Plateau. I also acknowledge brother Tim and sister-in-law Bernadette. When life took a twist and I was stunned and overwhelmed, Tim said, "Take off, eh?! I've got your back." Bernie took care of everything else—AND provided moral and spiritual support. Hourly. Daily. Weekly. As needed. I am also indebted to my buddy Ray Pilcher, friend and geologist extraordinaire, who helped make sure I didn't screw up too much on rocks and such.

This book would not have happened without these and all the stouthearted outdoor crusaders who joined me on various jaunts across the magnificent Colorado Plateau, including Finnian Fulks, Nick Massaro, Steven Marshall, Ed Gibbons, Paul Chenault, Bill Elmblad, Joe Rudy, Peggy Pilcher, Ray Pilcher, Jubal Fulks, Dorothy Davis, Glenda Haggerty, Bridgette Haggerty, Austin Haggerty, Kevin Moore (deceased), Bruce Froseth, Guy Kelly, Denice Kelly, Marj McKenna, Larry McKenna, Joe McKenna, Greg Godbey, Julie Grode, Chris Belle, Dan Dekoven, Nancy Harbert, Robert Traylor, Laurie Rink, Dan Birch, Lori Martin, Ordy Ploehn, Lori Spence, Dr. Kim Spence, Jenn Logan, Scott King, Hanna Finn, Wade Finn, Gail Keeley, Mark Chiono, Dick Maschmeyer, Geoff Tischbein, and Kate Kellogg.

I know I missed someone, but I love you all. And now, I should be able to sell at least forty-five copies of this book—if you all buy your own copy! (Kevin doesn't have to.)

We all came into this world gifted with innocence, but gradually, as we became more intelligent, we lost our innocence. We were born with silence, and as we grew up, we lost the silence and were filled with words. We lived in our hearts, and as time passed, we moved into our heads. Now the reversal of this journey is enlightenment. It is the journey from head back to the heart, from words back to silence; getting back to our innocence in spite of our intelligence. Although very simple, this is a great achievement. Knowledge should lead you to that beautiful point of "I don't know." … The whole evolution of man [sic] is from being somebody to being nobody and from being nobody to being everybody.

—Sri Sri Ravi Shankar

Introduction

Tiny goldfinches, Say's phoebes, Bullock's orioles, mourning doves, and Gambel's quail all harmonize a final cacophonous good day to the sunset. In the near distance, a twilight coyote hunt evokes howls of delight from the newest generation of song dogs. The colors change rapidly across the Bookcliffs, from shadowed tan to pink to red to slate blue-gray, while the whispery white clouds floating above the Colorado National Monument turn first to a delicate pastel pink, then flame-colored crimson and gold.

This is where I live. This is where I play. This is where I write. This is where I pray—on the altar of the Colorado Plateau. At times, it seems to be an unrelenting country—full of droughts, dust, gnats, mountain bikes, and ATVs. Yet its beauty is insurmountable. Its delicate desert primrose and dazzling crimson red claret cup cactus, its inspiring monolithic towers, its trickling streams that shape great canyons, and its intriguing tributaries that become the mighty Colorado River itself. This land is stunning and beautiful in its barren openness.

The sprawling 140,000-square-mile Colorado Plateau has the highest concentration of parklands in North America. It is filled with breathtaking canyons, tremendous arches, spectacular vistas, intriguing spires, and beguiling hoodoos. There are 9 U.S. national parks, a national historical park, 28 national monuments, and 31 wilderness areas, along with millions of acres of national forest, Bureau of Land Management (BLM) lands, state parks, and other protected public properties.

This is sacred land to Native Americans, whose ancestors eked out a living on this high desert plateau 10,000 years before Christ. They continue to revere this land, pay homage to it, and celebrate its spirituality. It also is the chosen land of followers of Joseph Smith and Brigham Young, who moved west to escape religious persecution and establish their church based on the Book of Mormon in this broad and fractured country 170 years ago. While major fault zones delineate the geologic boundaries of the Colorado Plateau, it is this ethnic and religious divide that outlines its cultural boundaries.

In truth, this is sacred land to anyone who has ever experienced its majesty, its magnitude—and its emptiness. This is the country that the ancient Hopi called the Fourth World. It is what early Spanish conquistadors called El Malpais—the badlands. Modern cosmopolitan man sometimes refers to it as the stinkin' desert.

A great horned owl now roosts on the peak of the barn above my office, hooting a reminder that some people are very scared of this country. Some believe it is harsh, barren, boring, and dry, a stinkin' desert full of gnats, snakes, scorpions, and buzzards.

Some believe it's just a pile of rocks, as one visitor points out in chapter 8 on Canyonlands National Park. But what a story these rocks tell. It's the story of time itself. It's a story of when the infant earth was forming, shifting and shaking, chucking, jiving, and spinning into that bright oval sphere that sustains us today.

The Colorado Plateau is a relatively stable block of the earth's crust, set apart by major, ancient fracture zones in 550-million-year-old Precambrian basement rock. These faults helped dictate the location and orientation of the plateau. A fault is a fracture in the earth's crust along which movement has taken place. Basement fault zones outline the plateau and, on the surface, that outline is fuzzy for most of us.

The southern boundary lies adjacent to a fracture zone known as the Mogollon (pronounced mogo-YAWN) Hingeline and trends northwest to southeast across three-quarters of central Arizona. Along this topographic break are several volcanic features, including the San Francisco Volcanic Field near present-day Flagstaff.

The western border of the Colorado Plateau is the "orogenic" mountain zone that braces the stable Colorado Plateau against a more tectonically active severe uplift. Orogenic zones develop when a continental plate crumples and is pushed upward. At one time, this may have been the western edge of the North American continent. This mountain zone is interrupted in north-central Utah by the oddly east–west trending Uinta Mountains, which define the northern boundary of the Colorado Plateau Province.

The eastern edge of the province is the most arbitrary. The northwest-trending zone, the Uncompahgre (un-com-PÁ-gray) Uplift, would best define this boundary, but the San Juan Mountains of southwestern Colorado get in the way. Some authors believe the San Juans belong to the Southern Rocky Mountain Province. If that's the case, a subjective line must be drawn from the southern Uncompahgre Uplift to the northern edge of the San Juan Mountains. These are true mountains in every sense, with 14,000-foot alpine peaks composed of volcanic rock that punched through older rocks deposited by shallow seas. Perhaps those older rocks more closely resemble the Colorado Plateau. However, in an attempt at conformity, I sadly have excluded this beautiful and significant range from coverage here.

The southeastern boundary of the Colorado Plateau generally follows the Rio Grande, a noticeable fault-bounded valley extending from south of Albuquerque, New Mexico, to the north and west. From here, one must use considerable imagination to connect the Rio Grande Valley to the Mogollon Hingeline, completing the circuitous boundaries of the plateau.

As I say, the boundaries to most non-geologists are blurry. Generally, this is called the Four Corners region, where the states of Colorado, Utah, Arizona, and New Mexico meet, even though the Colorado Plateau reaches far into northwest Colorado near the Wyoming border. There are about 140,000 square miles of territory covered here—with some very notable exceptions: Arches, Bryce, Zion, Capitol Reef, Grand Canyon, and Mesa Verde National Parks. Hundreds of quality publications have been produced on these parks, and they need no more publicity. They already are being loved to death.

This book is a celebration of the lesser known publicly owned areas of the plateau. It touches on politics, recreation, geology, archeology, astronomy, religion, and culture. It is by no means a complete compendium of public places on the Colorado Plateau. For example, Cedar Breaks and Vermillion Cliffs National Monuments regrettably have been left out. That's because I got snowed out two years in a row. There are hundreds more areas that have been snubbed because of time, space, or weather—or I didn't want to reveal a favorite spot (even though I caved in chapter 6 on the Black Canyon).

This corpus, however, will get you off the interstate. For many visitors, the plateau's high-altitude semiarid desert environment is bleak and threatening, hot, dry, and miserable precisely because they never get off the interstate highways. Those roads were built along the flattest and most drab-colored strata imaginable for economic reasons. It's cheaper than building roads into spectacularly gnarly canyons and up multicolored, steeply inclined mesas.

Yet as I write about this marvelous place, I do so with much trepidation and quite a bit of self-admitted hypocrisy. I battle the demons of my own conundrum. While I sing "Take only pictures, leave only footprints," and rail against extractive industries chomping at the bit to rip up this little piece of heaven on earth, I drive a fossil-fuel-powered vehicle hundreds of miles to visit these sacred spaces. I've left a large carbon footprint. I lament the once open environs of such world-class parks as Zion and Arches, yet I write about the Grand Staircase or Bears Ears—only to watch more people come. Author and public lands advocate Amy Irvine writes in her excellent book *Desert Cabal: A New Season in the Wilderness*, "The minute there is a line drawn around these lands, a sign staked on their behalf, the masses come running. They come at full tilt, with their mountain bikes, ropes and GoPros."[1] Rick Moore from the Grand Canyon Trust goes further: "All evidence suggests that tourism is the greatest single threat to the archeological resources of the Colorado Plateau."[2]

But will those who have never heard the call of the canyon wren come to its aid? Will those who have never felt the ebb and flow of the Green River or experienced its stunning magnificence as it winds through Desolation and Gray Canyons ever write their representatives and tell them to keep it flowing freely? How can one feel the stillness of a star-filled night in Valley of the Gods without respectfully entering that valley? How can one experience the spiritual sensation of peering into an Ancestral Puebloan ruin without following in the paths of the ancient ones? How can special places like Bears Ears and Grand Staircase be protected without ever smelling the sweet fragrances of sage and pine and ephedra—Mormon tea—on a spring morning?

Maybe looking at nice photos and reading descriptions of the San Rafael Swell or Canyon de Chelly or Kodachrome Basin or the Bistí badlands will be enough. As Edward Abbey wrote in his seminal book *Desert Solitaire: A Season in the Wilderness*, "The love of wilderness is more than a hunger for what is always beyond reach; it is also an expression of loyalty to the earth, the earth which bore us and sustains us, the only home we shall ever know, the only paradise we ever need—if only we had the eyes to see."[3]

If you want to race across the plateau to get out of the heat or the dust or to avoid even a glimpse of abject poverty, please take the interstate. For the rest of us, linger. Meander. Stop often. Listen to the birds. Stay out of the midday sun.

This is public property. It belongs to you and me. Celebrate that fact—and tread as lightly as you can across its sensitive landscape. On reservation property, be respectful—and ponder the situation of those who live here. Then, act.

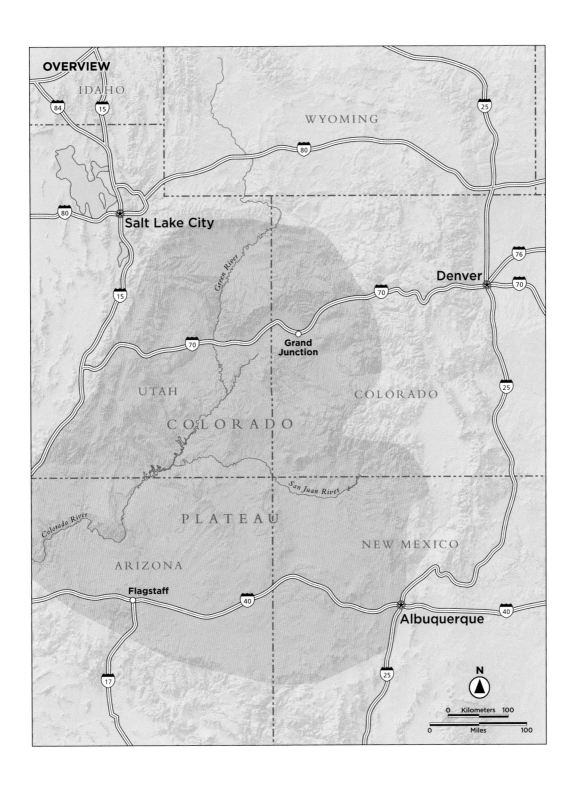

Little Grand Canyon of the San Rafael River

OVERVIEW

This is where our journey across the Colorado Plateau begins. Well, actually, this is where it ended 65 million years ago for the dinosaurs. This, however, is where John Wesley Powell began his journey down the Green and Colorado Rivers in 1869. He's the man who named this the Colorado Plateau Province. He was one crazy one-armed dude, floating these untamed and undammed rivers in wooden craft with oarsmen who had no idea what they were doing or what they were getting into. They were the first ones who floated the Grand Canyon—with Powell strapped to a chair on their wooden boat and barking out orders.

To Powell, the Colorado Plateau was actually a series of plateaus and mesas located on an immense basin surrounded by highlands. Today, we know that the plateau encompasses an area of about 140,000 square miles. The average elevation of the plateau is 6,352 feet, but elevational range of the plateau includes canyon bottoms at less than 2,450 feet and mountain peaks at 12,600 feet above sea level.

Billy, I need to get the hum of humanity out of my ears!
—Kevin Moore, philosopher, poet, and friend (1952–2019)

The geology of the plateau consists primarily of sedimentary rocks formed hundreds of millions of years ago. Sandstones, shales, and limestones are common. Unbelievably shaped rock formations molded by wind and water abound. Volcanic rocks also are common across much of the plateau, such as at El Malpais in New Mexico and Sunset Crater and the San Francisco Peaks near Flagstaff, Arizona.

Obviously, dinosaurs once roamed here. You can view some of their remains embedded in a mud and clay wall at the Dinosaur National Monument's Carnegie Dinosaur Quarry Exhibit Hall.

John Wesley Powell and his expedition floated the Green River through Gates of Lodore in the northern section of this national monument. The river flows into then out of Colorado on its journey to meet up with its grand sister river, the Colorado. The mighty river then blasts through the Grand Canyon and eventually trickles into the Sea of Cortez and Gulf of California in Mexico, dammed for a lifetime as the lifeblood of a thirsty southwest United States.

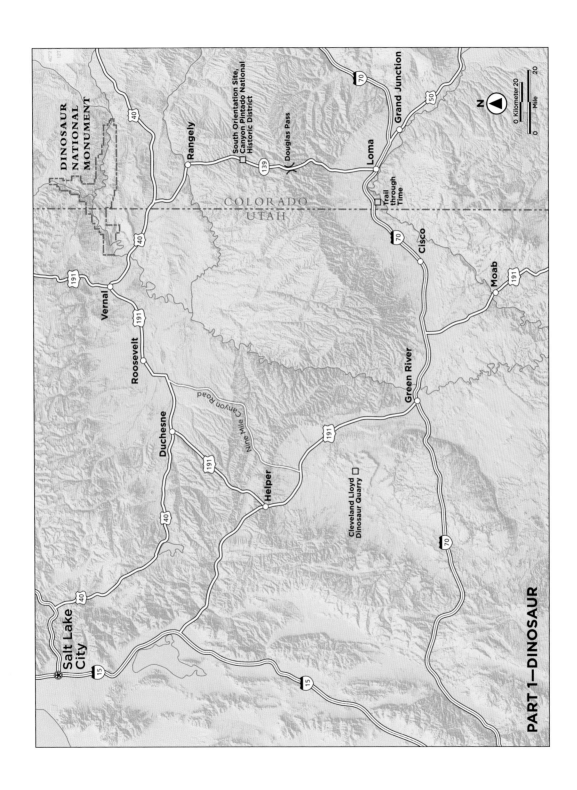

PART 1—DINOSAUR

CHAPTER 1
DINOSAUR NATIONAL MONUMENT

SIZE—210,000 acres along the Colorado-Utah border
YEAR ESTABLISHED—October 4, 1915, when President Woodrow Wilson dedicated the original 80-acre tract surrounding the dinosaur quarry—still one of the most extraordinary fossil sites in the world.
MANAGING AGENCY—National Park Service (NPS), Dinosaur National Monument
DOG-FRIENDLY?—While pets are welcome in the monument, they are not permitted on the trails or in the monument's backcountry. Due to extremely hot summer temperatures, do not leave pets in a vehicle for any amount of time.
FEES AND PERMITS—$25 per private vehicle, $20 per motorcycle, $15 per person (bicycle or walk-in) for a 7-day pass; annual pass, senior pass, access pass, and active duty military passes also accepted
NEAREST CITIES—Dinosaur, CO; Jensen, UT
NEARBY PUBLIC PROPERTY—Flaming Gorge National Recreation Area, Browns Park National Wildlife Refuge, Gates of Lodore, Desolation and Gray Canyons on the Green River, Canyon Pintado and thousands of acres of BLM property.
SPECIAL CONSIDERATIONS—Go to nps.gov/dino/planyourvisit/hours.htm, or call the park at 435-781-7700 for complete information on hours of operation for the Dinosaur Quarry.

OVERVIEW

This area was ravaged by drought about 150 million years ago. In fact, the entire western interior of North America was high and dry. Dinosaurs of all shapes and sizes gathered near a dwindling river in what is now eastern Utah—and eventually died of thirst or disease.

Over the next few million years, rain finally returned to the area. High waters and flash floods shoved dozens of dinosaur carcasses into a relatively small depositional area. And there they remained.

Dinosaurs went extinct 65 million years ago in the Tertiary period when tremendous uplifts altered this area from sea level to form mountains and valleys with large lakes. Massive erosion and river-cutting began carving the magnificent canyons we continue to marvel at today.

During this period, something really weird happened. The ancestral Upper Green River once flowed east to the North Platte River in what is now southeast Wyoming. However, erosion of the Lower Green River combined with the uplift of the Rocky Mountains and caused the entire river to change course, with its drainage now flowing south as it does today.

Uniquely, three physiographic regions—the Colorado Plateau, the middle Rocky Mountains, and the Wyoming Basin—all meet here. The movement of the river,

The Yampa and Green Rivers meet behind Steamboat Rock in Echo Park.

combined with the influences of the physiographic region known as the Great Basin to the west, greatly enhanced the biological diversity of this ecosystem. From dinosaur bones to major rivers changing course, this is one of the most unique—and remote—spots in North America.

Renowned paleontologist Earl Douglass discovered that pile of dinosaur carcasses in 1909. With funding from industrialist and philanthropist Andrew Carnegie and the Carnegie Museum of Natural History in Pittsburgh, Pennsylvania, the quarry was painstakingly excavated for 13 years. By then, President Woodrow Wilson had declared this site a national monument.

Today, you can still view that large pile of bones discovered by Douglass. It looks like the cross section of a gruesome mass grave, with gnarled bones and broken skeletons floating in a sea of gray-blue mud some 50 feet deep. Bone fragments and skeletons of allosaurus, diplodocus, and stegosaurus are dispersed randomly where they expired millions of years ago, throughout a thick layer of dried mud within the Morrison Formation. Some specimens were excavated by Douglass and cohorts a hundred years ago and are still displayed at the Carnegie Museum in Pittsburgh—including *Barosaurus lentus*, *Allosaurus fragilis*, *Stegosaurus ungulates*, and *Apatosaurus louisae*. (OK, that might not excite everyone, but as a boy growing up just a few miles from the Museum of Natural History in Denver, I have always loved that kind of stuff!)

Dinosaur National Monument was expanded from its original 80 acres in 1938 by a forward-thinking President Franklin Roosevelt, to 210,000 acres in Utah and Colorado. It now encompasses the spectacular river canyons of the Green and Yampa Rivers. While this is an outdoor museum for dinosaur fossils, it's also a museum of human history, with 12,000 years of recorded archeological data present here. In fact, this area contains one of North America's most complete records of cultural development. At least, that's what the ranger told us as we visited the world-renowned Carnegie Dinosaur Quarry Exhibit Hall, which was literally built onto that massive wall of Morrison mud.

Fossils and rock art are two great reasons to visit Dinosaur National Monument. Add to that 30 miles of marked hiking trails and a tour of historic Brown's Park in northwest Colorado, and you've got next year's vacation nearly planned.

There are no dinosaur fossils on the Colorado side of the monument. If you want to see dinosaur fossils, you must visit the Utah side of the monument, near Jensen, Utah. Because the largest collection of dinosaur fossils is protected within a secure structure known as the Carnegie Dinosaur Quarry Exhibit Hall, visits are allowed only during certain hours, but it's well worth the trip.

Bones in the wall of mud!

On the Colorado side, be prepared for desert hiking: Take a hat, sunscreen, and water—a minimum of two quarts of water per person is recommended in the summer; let someone know where you are going and when you are due back; wear comfortable shoes. Open-toed shoes are not recommended; use caution near cliffs and keep a close eye on small children; watch for afternoon thunderstorms during the summer.

One short hike extends from the end of the Harpers Corner Road, a 32-mile scenic drive that includes overlooks of the Yampa and Green Rivers. The road begins in Colorado, swings into Utah, and then goes back into Colorado. The Harpers Corner Trail (two miles out and back) at road's end offers great photographic opportunities of the Green and Yampa Rivers flowing toward Steamboat Rock, where they converge into a much larger Green River that flows downstream into Whirlpool Canyon.

ECHO CANYON CONTROVERSY!

In 1952, David Brower became the first executive director of the Sierra Club and joined the fight against the Echo Park Dam within the boundaries of Dinosaur National Monument. The battle was a crucial episode in conservation history.

In the years following World War II, the Bureau of Reclamation issued a blueprint for several large dams along the upper Colorado River and its tributaries, including the Green and Gunnison Rivers. Among the proposed dam sites were Flaming Gorge, Glen Canyon, and Echo Park. The storage capacity of the reservoirs created by these dams would help the upper basin states of Colorado, Wyoming, Utah, and New Mexico maintain their allotted share of the Colorado River as determined by the Colorado River Compacts of 1922 and 1948.

Brower and conservationists across America opposed the dam on grounds that it violated the National Park Service Act of 1916, which mandated that the parks and monuments be kept unimpaired for future generations. They argued that approval of the dam would make it easier to propose dams within other national parks and monuments.

The Sierra Club, along with the Wilderness Society, National Parks Conservation Association, Audubon Society, Izaac Walton League, and dozens of other smaller groups, publicized the remote and little-known monument in national newspapers and magazines. Brower also challenged the bureau engineers' argument that the dam and reservoir in the high and narrow Whirlpool Canyon would minimize evaporation. He insisted the engineers had neglected to subtract one key figure while calculating evaporation, a charge the engineers admitted to about three months later.

This solidified political pressure, and in 1955, the bureau removed the Echo Park Dam from the Colorado River Storage Project. In April 1956, President Eisenhower signed legislation authorizing dams at Flaming Gorge and Glen Canyon, along with a provision stating that no dam or reservoir could be located within any national park or monument.

Conservationists celebrated the end of their six-year campaign to block the Echo Park Dam and demonstrated Americans' growing devotion to wild areas throughout the United States,. However, the act signed by President Eisenhower also allowed for a much larger ecologically and environmentally damaging Glen Canyon Dam to move forward.

I saw eight of the tail bones of a Brontosaurus in exact position. It was a beautiful sight. . . . It was by far the best-looking dinosaur prospect I have ever found.

—Earl Douglass, on his first major find at what would soon be known as the Carnegie Dinosaur Quarry, August 17, 1909

Upstream from this spot, and on the northern side of the national monument—a 107-mile, 3-hour drive—Lodore was the first major canyon encountered by John Wesley Powell and his men on their 1869 expedition. It begins as the Green River departs Brown's Park in the northwest corner of Colorado, then carves its way through the Uinta Mountains in the southern portion of the Wyoming Basin. At Gates of Lodore, the river inaugurates an 18-mile journey through a maze of colorfully rugged slot canyons to its end at Echo Park and the confluence of the Green and Yampa Rivers.

The absolute best way to see this country is to float it, like Powell, only with better equipment. Both the Yampa and Green Rivers require permits to float. Permits for private operations are obtained through lottery. Go to recreation.gov for more information. Commercial raft companies can also accommodate those willing to take off a few weeks and travel to one of the most remote and unique parts of our nation—and of the Colorado Plateau.

SIGNATURE ACTIVITY: RAFT TRIP THROUGH DESOLATION AND GRAY CANYONS

On July 6, 1869, John Wesley Powell entered Desolation Canyon on his epic expedition down the Green and Colorado Rivers. By July 13, the expedition had rafted through more than 50 rapids in Desolation and Gray Canyons before passing present-day Green River, Utah. The expedition would soon careen through Cataract Canyon below the confluence of the Green and Colorado Rivers, and eventually through the Grand Canyon itself on the greatest first descent of all time.

Powell and his crew had already rowed a hundred miles in 43 days from Green River, Wyoming (near present-day Flaming Gorge), and through Gates of Lodore before reaching what Powell labeled "a region of wildest desolation." By then, one crewman had quit, one wooden raft had been destroyed, the flour was soaked, and the bacon was rancid. And they had a LONG way to go.

Thirteen modern-day river rats recently rowed 84 miles through Desolation and Gray Canyons from September 2 to 8, 2019—a day quicker than Powell. We bounced leisurely over rapids with names like Rattlesnake Rapid, Nefertiti Rapid, and Jack Creek Rapid, gleefully hooting and hollering all the way. Powell's crew was certainly hollering—out of pure fear! But hey, that rookie crew had a one-armed leader strapped onto a chair in a bulky, awkward wooden boat with broken oars made of driftwood, and the crew itself had never rafted through whitewater like this! We merry pranksters, on the other hand, bobbed and floated through desolate yet spectacular canyons on sweet modern rubber rigs with five large, contemporary coolers that kept food fresh and dry and beer semi-cold (although the ice still melted by the seventh day!). Furthermore, we rafted with expert oarsmen. Scott King from Carbondale, Colorado, for example, had rowed through here more than 30 times. Laurie Rink, from Grand Junction, had rafted this run too many times to remember.

The history of the Fremont culture, depicted in artifacts, ruins, and pictographs, written accounts of cowboys and desperados, and the diligent work of water conservationists all were important to King's understanding of this river ecosystem. "Today's trip is a privilege for us," he noted. "It's a privilege that should last. It should be something that we can pass on."

The serenity of the serpentine canyon contrasted sharply with the power of the river. At the same time, the seeming calmness of the river contrasted sharply with the jagged and steep canyon walls carved by this river over eons of time. In places, those walls loomed 5,000 feet above our bobbing heads. That's as steep and deep as the Grand Canyon.

Numerous Class II rapids thrill rafters in Desolation and Gray Canyons on the Green River, with a few Class III rapids that make boaters pay close attention.

King is not the only one who believes this river, this history, and this privilege should be preserved. In March 2019, the Emery County Public Land Management Act was signed into national law as part of the Dingell Natural Resources Act. It established 663,000 acres of wilderness in Emery County, Utah, and designated 63 miles of the Green River under the Wild and Scenic Rivers Act. This included more than 13 miles of Desolation Canyon as either "wild" or "recreational."

King's fiancée, Jenn Logan, is a fish biologist for Colorado Parks and Wildlife. She stalks fish for a living. This particular week, she was on vacation. Yet she suspected that a fish she'd stalked in western Colorado for years was close by. An electronic PIT (Passive Integrated Transponder) tag helps scientists like Logan track fish by

The river is very rapid and many lateral canyons enter on either side . . . crags and tower-shaped peaks are seen everywhere, and away above them, long lines of broken cliffs; and above and beyond the cliffs are pine forests, of which we obtain occasional glimpses as we look up through a vista of rocks. . . . We are minded to call this the Canyon of Desolation.

—John Wesley Powell

providing a reliable lifetime "barcode" for individual fish. A rare and endangered pikeminnow with PIT tag #475 had swum 135 miles from Colorado and into Utah over the past 30 days. She knew this because good ol' #475's PIT tag had pinged one of Jenn's antennas three weeks earlier. "Initially," she said, "it was tagged near the mouth of the Green River as a small fish in 2003. It's probably 19 or 20 years old by now."

Highlights for John Wesley Powell in this canyon included swamping and flipping his boat and spending grueling hours portaging or lining the remaining wooden boats around larger rapids. Highlights on our trip included great food, spectacular scenery, sandy beaches, abundant wildlife, and near-perfect weather . . . and the stars, and the toe painting, and the horseshoes, and the Paddy's Irish Whiskey, and

Five rafts, one paddleboard, thirteen people, and lots of gear to load . . . still a little easier than John Wesley Powell had it!

the Divine Dog Wisdom Cards—"designed to inspire and delight you while offering meaningful guidance for your day and your life."[4]

"I really liked sleeping on the sand, listening to the water at night, seeing the stars," said Marj McKenna, a retired teacher from Denver, now living in Grand Junction.

"Did anyone mention the weather?" added Larry McKenna, her husband, also a retired teacher living the good life, manning oars of a blue 16-foot Cataraft. The weather, indeed, was spectacular for a raft trip that saw somewhat gentle river flows at about 2,500 cfs (cubic feet per second), although the river can rage up to 50,000 cfs. (One cubic foot per second equals about 450 gallons per minute; 695 gallons per minute equals a million gallons per day. You do the math!)

Powell's route of exploration through the heart of the Colorado Plateau while mapping the Green and Colorado Rivers is very different today from what it was 150 years ago. Three major dams have flooded about 40 percent of that original route. Tens of thousands of rafters annually descend the other 60 percent of these rivers. The National Park Service, US Forest Service, Bureau of Land Management, and Native American reservations now protect vast segments of the route. Many stretches—like this section—require advanced lottery applications. It took our group a couple of years to finally land our permit for Deso/Gray through recreation.gov. You have to apply for the application between December 1 and January 31. You'll be notified if you draw by February 15. Then you can plan your own epic adventure. Or you can hire a professional outfitter. For a list of outfitters licensed to float this stretch of river, go to blm.gov/sites/blm.gov/files/uploads/Desolation-Lotteries-Desolation%20 Canyon%20Outfitter.pdf.

SIGNATURE ACTIVITY: FIELD TRIP TO THE DINOSAUR QUARRY EXHIBIT HALL

WHY GO?

Museums make you feel good. Museums make you happy. Museums make you smart and provide an easy environment to learn. Museums count as a day in school, and when you see a huge mud wall full of dinosaur bones, you'll be hooked on museums for good!

SPECS

ACTIVITY TYPE: Visiting the bone pile!
TRAILHEAD/PUT-IN/ETC.: At the doorsteps of the Carnegie Dinosaur Quarry Exhibit Hall, 7 miles north of Jensen, UT
DISTANCE/LENGTH: A few hundred feet
AVERAGE TIME REQUIRED: 1 to 3 hours
CONTACT/MANAGING AGENCY: National Park Service, Dinosaur National Monument
DIFFICULTY: Easy, wheelchair-accessible

SPECIAL CONSIDERATIONS: This is an indoor, temperature-controlled museum, but if you've left your pet in your vehicle, it may be deadly hot!

GETTING THERE
SHORT DESCRIPTION: Drive 7 miles north of Jensen, UT, to the Dinosaur Quarry parking lot.
GPS COORDINATES: 39°02′31″N, 108°37′47″W

OVERVIEW

Field trip! Field trip! A day away from school. One problem . . . most school districts can't afford to send their kids to Dinosaur National Monument on a field trip (or anywhere else, come to think of it). Sure, this is an incredible outdoor museum of fossils dating from 500 million years ago, when this area was marine and tropical, to 150 million years ago, when plant-eating sauropods and ornithopods and flesh-eating theropods roamed the earth. But it's really a long way from anywhere! (Well, it's not far from the oil patch of the Colorado Plateau, Vernal, population 10,000. Or Rangely, population 2,100, billing itself as "Way outside of Ordinary.")

Despite its remoteness, more than 300,000 people a year visit this famous dinosaur quarry because, as NPS Ranger Erin Cahill says, "Every family has a dinosaur nerd." So, you may not get to escape school for a field trip, but summer vacation, here we come!

Freely admitting she's the dino-nerd in her own family, Cahill and her cohorts provide hundreds of programs a year to visitors, schoolchildren, and adults, both at the museum and virtually—via an online program called "Skype in the Classroom."

Erin can take any English-speaking classroom in the world on a guided tour of the Quarry Exhibit Hall, all electronically via Skype. "We can handle up to four tours a day," she says. That's a lot of virtual tours.

"Yea, but look how many kids we can reach this way," she insists.

Visitors from around the world come here in person to check out the wall of bones. Like Erin says, there's a dinosaur nerd in every family. But they also come to see what wide open spaces really are, what gnarly canyons really look like, what a two-lane blacktop with no traffic feels like. It may feel weird to some. Some may not like it at all. However, as Erin Cahill, the sage ranger from Carnegie Dinosaur Quarry Exhibit Hall, says, "If you don't like the scenery and archeology and geology here, just go around the corner."

You'll find it there. And maybe even learn something on this field trip!

CHAPTER 2
DINOSAUR DIAMOND SCENIC AND HISTORIC BYWAY

SIZE—512 miles long

YEAR ESTABLISHED—The highway was designated a national historic byway in 2002, although Colorado and Utah both have different names for the same trip! Figures.

MANAGING AGENCY—State patrol, county sheriffs, city cops

DOG-FRIENDLY?—It's up to you. You have to drive 500 miles with the pet. Does it get carsick? Do you?

FEES AND PERMITS—Check gas prices. Gas was $2.75 per gallon in Green River and Price, UT, and $2.68 in Grand Junction in September 2019. Do you have a valid U.S. driver's license?

NEAREST CITIES—Grand Junction, Fruita, Dinosaur, Rangely, and Loma, CO; Moab, Green River, Jensen, Vernal, Roosevelt, and Helper, UT

NEARBY PUBLIC PROPERTY—Dinosaur National Monument, Flaming Gorge National Recreation Area, Ashley National Forest, Uinta National Forest, Manti–La Sal National Forest, Canyonlands National Park, Arches National Park, Colorado National Monument, McInnis Canyons National Conservation Area, White River National Forest, Uncompahgre National Forest, Grand Mesa National Forest, and extensive federal lands managed by the Bureau of Land Management

SPECIAL CONSIDERATIONS—The scenic byway can be driven year-round, but check weather reports, especially in winter. It can be nasty driving in the middle of a storm. In the summer, be prepared for heat! Watch behind you when you pull over.

OVERVIEW

The Dinosaur Diamond is a 512-mile-long national scenic byway coursing through eastern Utah and western Colorado—an area that has produced more dinosaur fossils and footprints than anywhere else on earth. It also bisects some of the most important cultural and archeological landmarks and destinations on the Colorado Plateau. Prehistoric petroglyphs and pictographs cover rock cliffs across this northern edge of the Colorado Plateau.

It's the dinosaur nerd in all of us that created the byway, which is known as the Dinosaur Diamond Scenic and Historic Byway in Colorado and the Dinosaur Diamond Prehistoric Highway in Utah.

Around 150 million years ago, a shallow, warm sea invaded the central part of North America. As it receded, thick mud from what's now known as the Morrison Formation covered the area. In the warmth of the Jurassic dry season, dehydrated dinosaurs blundered into the muck of this dying sea in search of a drink. Here, they got stuck in the mud—and perished. Some were very large. For example, the *Apatosaurus louisae* grew up to 69 feet long and ate plants. You may have heard it referred to by its scientifically incorrect name, brontosaurus.

Dinosaur bones from throughout this area rewrote the paleontology/history books over the past 125 years. Paleontologist Elmer Riggs and his assistant H. William Menke found the first known skeleton of the giant sauropod dinosaur *Brachiosaurus altithorax* in Grand Junction, Colorado, in 1900, at a spot now known as Riggs Hill. The next year they discovered an apatosaurus a few miles away on Dinosaur Hill in Fruita. The brachiosaurus continues to grace the entrance to the Museum of Natural History in Chicago.

Dinosaur track sites and bone trails can be found along the Interstate 70 (I-70) corridor two miles from the Colorado-Utah border, where an active dinosaur quarry continues to operate during the summer months at Rabbit Valley. Another active dinosaur quarry exists in the Bookcliffs near Price, Utah, at the Cleveland-Lloyd Dinosaur Quarry. Dinosaur bones and dinosaur track sites also may be found at more than seven sites near Moab, Utah. If that doesn't make the dinosaur nerd in you tingle, the entire route of the Dinosaur Diamond is laden with bones and tracks embedded in rocks deposited from a period of time that spans approximately 252 million years to 66 million years ago.

Our dinosaur tour begins at the Dinosaur Journey Museum in Fruita, Colorado, just west of Grand Junction. Here, dinosaur nerds of all ages will find life-size robotic dinosaurs, experience a simulated earthquake, and observe paleontologists at work in their laboratory. The hands-on interactive museum includes more than 15,000 fossil

Historians and biologists agree this great hunt probably took place in late November or early December, during the bighorn sheep mating season. It's the only time of year when rams, ewes, and lambs would be present in the same place at the same time.

specimens, a sandbox for making your own dinosaur tracks, and a "quarry site" where kids can uncover actual Jurassic dinosaur bones.

Following Dinosaur Journey would be visits to Riggs Hill in Grand Junction, Dinosaur Hill in Fruita, and a great little side trip to the McInnis Canyons National Conservation Area and a stop at the Fruita Paleontological Area. This world-class fossil site contains a prolific record of Jurassic micro-vertebrates. In fact, Grand Junction resident Wally Windscheffel discovered the *Fruitafossor windscheffeli* here in 1998. At six inches long, it was slightly longer and slimmer than a hairy-tailed mouse. This termite-eating mammal was a digger, hiding in burrows from larger dinosaurs.

Your next stop should be at exit 2 off I-70, two miles from the Colorado-Utah border at the Trail through Time. This short trail winds above an active dinosaur quarry where paleontologists and volunteers continue to uncover fossils from 80 million years ago—at least during most parts of the year. It's closed in the winter.

Next, take exit 214 in Utah off I-70 and hit the Upper Colorado River Scenic Byway (Utah Highway 128). It's also part of the Dinosaur Diamond and leads visitors through the drop-dead gorgeous Colorado River corridor between the old railroad siding town known as Cisco, to Moab. (OK, Cisco isn't much to look at, but the rest of it is! Check out chapter 7 on Fisher Towers Federal Recreation Area, located along the same road!) Continuing toward Moab, you'll find seven outstanding sites to view dino tracks. A visit to the Museum of Moab dinosaur exhibit also is well worth it.

From there, travel on U.S. Highway 191 back to I-70, then west to Green River, Utah. Mat saltbush, also known as matscale, is all that grows east of Green River between the Bookcliffs and the Colorado River. It's about as high as your Birkenstocks and is the only plant that can live in this salty shale environment.

When you see the "Gateway to the Wild" sign entering the town of Green River, question it. The Green River flows through here, for sure, and there are lots of wild places near Green River. The town itself? Not so much. However, it does have an outstanding museum—the J. W. Powell River History Museum. It's all about the men who first floated—and charted—this wild river. Crazy dudes, for sure!

Three great side trips can be found between here and the Utah State University Eastern Prehistoric Museum in Price, Utah, which displays a really cool woolly mammoth skeleton. The first is a trip through Huntington (population 3,121, the largest town in Emery County) to see the great Buckhorn Wash Petroglyph/Pictograph Panel. Several artists in two cultures separated by 1,000 years apparently created this rock art. People of the Barrier Canyon culture painted figures called pictographs at least 2,000 years ago. People of the Fremont culture pecked figures called petroglyphs into the rock face about 1,000 years ago.

The second side trip here leads visitors through Nine Mile Canyon, billed as the longest outdoor museum in the world. John Wesley Powell led a government expedition

Bill Elmblad from Grand Junction inspects one of the hundreds of rock art panels in Nine Mile Canyon.

through this portion of Utah in 1869. His topographer, F. M. Bishop, created a nine-mile triangulation drawing, which he named Nine Mile Creek. The canyon was subsequently called Nine Mile Canyon even though it is actually 40 miles long—thus the name/distance confusion.

Native Americans who made Nine Mile Canyon home as early as AD 300 were part of the Fremont culture. "Fremont" is considered a catchall term used to describe scattered groups of hunters and farmers. They also were artists and communicators who drew and pecked pictures all over these rock walls in Nine Mile Canyon, creating that feeling of traveling through an outdoor museum.

The third side trip is a one-hour drive from Price leading east to Jurassic National Monument and the Cleveland-Lloyd Dinosaur Quarry. This spot has the most concentrated collection of Jurassic-era dinosaur bones known anywhere, but the road may be impassible in the winter.

From there, head up the Price River to Vernal, Utah, on U.S. Highway 40. Vernal is the oil and gas patch of Utah—not very scenic unless you're really into power lines, gas wells, and oil rigs. However, I can't criticize since I drove here in my fossil-fueled vehicle.

Vernal is home to a great local brewery—the Vernal Brewing Company—and features more outstanding dinosaur displays at the Utah Field House of Natural History State Park Museum. What's more, Vernal and sister city Jensen are the gateway into Dinosaur National Monument and the world-famous Carnegie Dinosaur Quarry Exhibit Hall. (See chapter 1, "Dinosaur National Monument.")

DINOSAUR NAMES

Allosaurus, Apatosaurus, Barosaurus bones
Diplodocus, Dryosaurus, Stegosaurus tracks
Opisthias rarus, Dinochelys whitei
Glyptops plicatulus, Hoplosuchus kayi

Tongue twister? Not if you're into naming dinosaurs like Sir Richard Owen, who first coined the term "dinosaur" in 1842 to describe the fossils of extinct reptiles. *Deinos* in Greek means "fearfully great," while *sauros* means "lizard." Fearfully great lizards were found in spades in the area that encompasses the "Dinosaur Diamond" in northwest Colorado and eastern Utah, although most of them were much larger than lizards.

Most dinosaurs were named for the person who first discovered them. The *Apatosaurus louisae* from the Carnegie dinosaur quarry, for example, was a sauropod (long-necked dinosaur) and named *Apatosaurus*, or "false lizard," because of its unbelievably large size. The species, *louisae*, was named for industrialist/philanthropist Andrew Carnegie's wife, Louise. Carnegie financed most of the excavations of the Carnegie Dinosaur Quarry Exhibit Hall at Dinosaur National Monument. He had an *Apatosaurus* sent to Pittsburgh, Pennsylvania, near the turn of the century, where it still stands in the Carnegie Museum of Natural History.

From here, it's time to head back to Grand Junction over Douglas Pass and through Canyon Pintado—the Painted Canyon. The area was named by Franciscan friar Silvestre Vélez de Escalante, who along with Atanasio Dominguez was tasked by the Spanish empire with finding an overland route from Santa Fe, New Mexico, to their Roman Catholic mission in Monterey, California, back in 1776. Thousands of pictographs are found here, and the BLM has designated numerous roadside pullouts to display some of this artwork.

Some petroglyphs indicate prehistoric Barrier Canyon people occupied this canyon 11,000 years ago. Other rock art dates to the Fremont people and ancient Puebloans, from 1,300 to 600 years ago, and others still to the Native American Ute tribes since that time.

It's a long trip, this Dinosaur Diamond tour. There are dino tracks and bones galore. There are pictographs and petroglyphs, wildlife and big skies. It pays to take your time and ponder these larger-than-life things that ancient people and ancient critters have already pondered.

SIGNATURE ACTIVITY: THROUGH THE EYES OF A CHILD

WHY GO?

Have you ever witnessed the joy and curiosity of a six-year-old boy as he races through an animated dinosaur museum? Have you seen the delight on the face of a six-year-old girl as she pushes a button and a gigantic robotic dinosaur squirts water at her four-year-old brother? Pure delight!

SPECS

ACTIVITY TYPE: Take a kid to the dinosaur museum
TRAILHEAD/PUT-IN/ETC.: Parking lot at Dinosaur Journey, Fruita, CO
DISTANCE/LENGTH: A few hundred feet, turning into a couple of miles as the kids race back and forth
AVERAGE TIME REQUIRED: About an hour
CONTACT/MANAGING AGENCY: Museum of Western Colorado, 970-858-7282
DIFFICULTY: Easy, if you can handle the kids that long
SPECIAL CONSIDERATIONS: Beware: You exit through the gift shop!

GETTING THERE

SHORT DESCRIPTION: 550 Jurassic Court, Fruita, CO
GPS COORDINATES: 38°02'31"N, 108°37'47"W

OVERVIEW

Six-year-old Nathan Tucker was interested in the velociraptor, a bipedal, feathered carnivore with a long tail and an enlarged sickle-shaped claw on each hind foot. Those funny, clawed feet were used to tackle and disembowel prey.

"Was it really fast?" he asked his mom, Vicki Tucker. "Yes," she replied. "It was really fast."

"But it's not now," said the knowledgeable Nathan. "It's dead."

Then he raced to the next exhibit.

Velociraptor is one of the dinosaurs most familiar to the general public due to its prominent role in the *Jurassic Park* movies. In real life, however, it was about the size of a turkey.

Four-year-old Jackson Fix said his favorite thing at Dinosaur Journey in Fruita, Colorado, was the triceratops, but he really liked "all the animals that moved."

Chloe Fix, six years old, said the earthquake simulator was her favorite thing. "It was fun." But not in real life.

Dinosaur Journey is one of the best places in the world to see dinosaurs through the eyes of a child. Charlotte Tucker is three years old and her big brother Benjamin is five. They squealed with glee as mom Vicki Tucker, along with Chloe and Jackson's grandmother, Julie Grode, looked on, both smiling broadly.

Carrot Top meets triceratops: Six-year-old Nathan Tucker says Dinosaur Journey is "funny—and really scary!"

Kids from 3 to 103 enjoy this place. What's not to like? There are robotic T. rexes, flying pterodactyls, swimming long-nosed gar, and an earthquake simulator. There are real bones of a huge *Apatosaurus* that once grew to 80 feet long and stood 17 feet tall. There are microscopic views of fossilized beetles, birds, and crane flies. And you can watch as real paleontologists gingerly brush clay and rock to discover new dinosaur bones in a working laboratory, just like Elmer Riggs did back in 1900 when he discovered the very first apatosaurus not far from here.

Like Nathan said, "This place is funny. And really scary."

What more could you want?

Numerous towering monoliths
exist within Monument Canyon.

PART 2
GRAND JUNCTION/MOAB

OVERVIEW

The major population hubs on this end of the Colorado Plateau are Moab, Utah, and Grand Junction, Colorado. While the fast-flowing Colorado River drowsily wends through these two towns to supply 40 million people with water in the West, not many of them actually live on the plateau itself. That's because, in general, THERE'S NO WATER! It's a desert. It receives from 8 to 12 inches of rain per year, and when it comes, it comes in flash floods that wash downstream before your very eyes! It can be dry and hot in the summer, extremely cold in the winter, and windy in the spring. But the towns of Grand Junction and Moab offer respite.

Located on the Colorado River, both communities are WAY into the great outdoors. Mad Max Moab, as some locals have dubbed it, is loaded with jeep tours, jeep rentals, and Razor rentals. My neighbor once remarked, "It doesn't appear any of them have been anywhere near a razor." I pointed out that Razors are the latest in motorhead motion. They are off-road four-wheelers that seat two or more passengers—"the ultimate combination of power, agility and comfort," according to Polaris. For only $25,399 (MSRP), you could rip up some terrain in a 2019 Polaris RZR XP Turbo S Velocity side-by-side recreational sports vehicle with 32-inch tires and a 168-horsepower engine. This baby can create incredible washboard roads at about 145 miles per hour. And wouldn't you love to follow it across the hot, dry, dusty desert. If you don't want to pay that much though, you can always rent in Moab, a conflicted city suffering from the slings and arrows of outrageous misfortune—or, as Edward Abbey put it, "industrial tourism."

Moab is really a cross between Mad Max and eco-decked mountain biker. Driving Ford F-250 pickups with trailers that can carry four Razors, leather-bedecked motorheads with total eclipse sport utility masks chat amicably with Subaru-driving, Lycra-clad bicyclists and Vibrum-soled, CamelBak'd trail warriors as they all wait for seats at the numerous local watering holes, and there are some very good ones in this town.

Grand Junction, home of the National Junior College World Series, Colorado Mesa University, and world-renowned Enstrom's Candies, is historically a proud boom-bust community. Its chamber of commerce still clings desperately to the oil, gas, and coal industries, which naturally boom and bust every 6 to 10 years. In the meantime, a thriving fruit and wine industry, combined with incredible outdoor recreation opportunities and businesses, have really brought this community kicking and screaming into the 19th, if not the 20th century.

Whether you're into motorized or self-propelled sport, this red rock country is surrounded by public property, and outdoor recreational opportunities abound. There are thousands of miles of ATV trails out here and hundreds of miles of mountain bike, hiking, and equestrian trails. And there's the Colorado River. From Grand Junction to Westwater, Utah, through Ruby and Horsethief Canyons, the wide, flat river allows

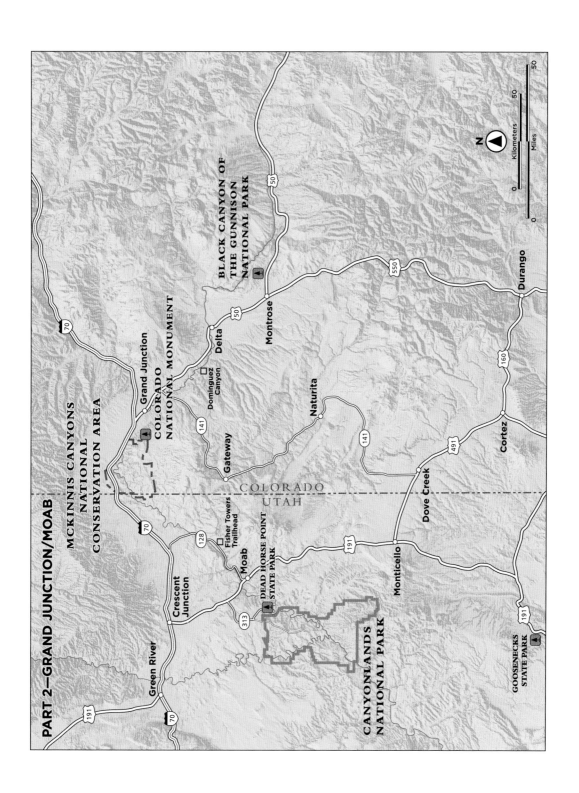

PART 2—GRAND JUNCTION/MOAB

MCKINNIS CANYONS
NATIONAL
CONSERVATION AREA

191

70

Green River

Crescent
Junction

70

313

DEAD HORSE POINT
STATE PARK

128

Fisher Towers
Trailhead

Moab

Grand Junction

COLORADO
NATIONAL MONUMENT

141

Dominguez
Canyon

Delta

50

70

BLACK CANYON OF
THE GUNNISON
NATIONAL PARK

Gateway

Montrose

Naturita

141

550

Durango

COLORADO
UTAH

CANYONLANDS
NATIONAL PARK

191

Monticello

Dove Creek

491

Cortez

160

GOOSENECKS
STATE PARK

191

N

0   50   0

Kilometers   50

Miles

0   50

A drive on the Old River Road through Professor Valley is spectacular.

recreationists of all ages to enjoy a cool float in the hot summer. The current is much swifter than it looks, and the water comes from snowmelt! Don't underestimate the power of the river! Westwater Canyon—below Ruby and Horsethief—offers what many consider the best one-day whitewater raft trip in North America. Be prepared for the Class IV "Skull Rapid" and "Room of Doom," an eddy in the river that eats 12-man rafts for lunch. Go with someone who's been there—and hang on tight! Yehaw! Downstream, the river opens up again into a relatively easy ride beneath Fisher Towers, through Professor Valley, and into Moab. You can relax and enjoy the spectacular scenery.

From Dominquez–Escalante National Conservation Area in west-central Colorado to the Canyonlands in southeast Utah, this red rock country is just waiting to be explored, and Grand Junction and Moab are great jumping-off points!

CHAPTER 3
COLORADO NATIONAL MONUMENT

SIZE—20,000 acres
YEAR ESTABLISHED—May 24, 1911, by President Taft, after 15 years of badgering by a local coot named John Otto, the monument's first full-time caretaker
MANAGING AGENCY—National Park Service, Colorado National Monument
DOG-FRIENDLY?—No dogs are allowed within national monument boundaries.
FEES AND PERMITS—$25 per private vehicle, $20 per motorcycle, $15 per person (bicycle or walk-in) for a 7-day pass; all other annual, interagency, and senior passes accepted
NEAREST CITIES—Grand Junction and Fruita, CO
NEARBY PUBLIC PROPERTY—BLM's Bangs Canyon/Tabaguache Trail system (world-class hiking, mountain biking), McInnis Canyons National Conservation Area and Black Ridge Wilderness, Little Bookcliffs Wild Horse Range, Grand Mesa National Forest, Uncompahgre National Forest, Kokopelli Trail, Rabbit Valley, and the Trail through Time active dinosaur dig
SPECIAL CONSIDERATIONS—Share the road! Bicyclists BELONG HERE! They pay taxes and entrance fees just like everyone else. Be patient. There will be a place to pass soon enough!

OVERVIEW

I am blessed and grateful to have a 20,000-acre national monument as my backyard. I live just outside the east entrance to the Colorado National Monument. I see it when I look out my window or drive into my driveway.

It's a major part of the reason I've stayed so long in the desert Southwest. It's part of the reason I love and respect and promote public lands on the Colorado Plateau.

I've enjoyed these canyons for more than four decades, and I know they don't belong just to me. They belong to all of us.

I've marveled at them, meditated in them, gained strength, and savored solitude in them. I've been eaten alive by gnats in them, been drenched by glaring hot sun in them, and been frozen to the bone from their frigid, wind-driven winter storms.

And I've enjoyed them even more.

I've hiked with biologists, geologists, rangers, ranchers, students, and tourists through these marvelous sheer-walled red rock canyons. Our collective senses have been overwhelmed, just as

Collared lizard: You want a piece of me?

John Otto's senses were overwhelmed when he first came here in 1906. "Some folks think I'm crazy," Otto wrote at the time, "but I want to see this scenery opened up to all people."

Otto single-handedly built many of these trails, raised money, penned newspaper editorials, badgered chambers of commerce, and wrote endless letters to Washington politicians in support of national recognition for these ancient canyons and towering monoliths. He eventually became its first caretaker when President William Howard Taft declared this a national monument in 1911.

Forming the southwest rim of the Grand Valley, where the largest population center on the Colorado Plateau resides (slightly larger than Flagstaff, Arizona—150,000 vs. 140,000), this monument records a colorful story of alteration. Formations here display mountain building, erosion, and climatic change over 1.7 billion years as the North American continent gradually shifted northward to where it currently lies.

Exposed at the base of this national monument is 1.7- to 1.5-billion-year-old Precambrian basement rock—gneiss, schist, and granites. On top of the monument lies a thick layer of Morrison Sandstone, about 140 million years old. In between are layers and layers and eons and eons of erosion, deposition, and constant change.

That natural change continues today. In January 2000, for example, a section of cliff suddenly dropped. After hanging on for 140 million years, a gigantic sandstone boulder from the Morrison Formation came crashing down on top of Rim Rock Drive, the scenic two-lane blacktop road following the rim of these canyons for 23 miles between the towns of Grand Junction and Fruita, Colorado.

Monument Canyon Trail takes visitors beneath many of the major spires and monoliths within this national monument.

WHEN TO VISIT?

Any time of year is a good time to visit the Colorado National Monument. In the winter, bring your Nordic skis. If there's not enough snow on the monument, there's more than enough on the Grand Mesa, on the opposite side of the Grand Valley. In the summer, bring your bike or your hiking shoes and binoculars. You also may want to consider mid-August to the end of September for a visit here, to combine your visit with the Grand Valley's fruit harvest.

The Palisade Peach Festival, in mid-August, is one of the original agricultural festivals in Colorado. Held each year just as the area's peaches reach their peak, it's Peach Mania. Satisfy your hunger for "local and authentic" with delicious peach products: from pies to ice cream, preserves to salsas, peach brandy and wine to virgin peach daiquiris, not to mention bushels of just-picked fresh peaches—all in a very scenic setting. Visit http://palisadepeachfest.com.

Colorado Mountain Winefest, in mid-September, is the largest wine festival in the state. The Winefest features 60 wineries from across Colorado. Highlights include wine tasting, chefs, artisans, live music, seminars, food, special VIP tickets, bottle sales, winery tours, and more. Visit https://coloradowinefest.com.

Autumn also features fall colors. The orchards in the valley change colors, and the cottonwoods in the bottom of No Thoroughfare Canyon in the national monument are spectacular. So are the quaking aspen on the side of 10,000-foot Grand Mesa.

This historic drive offers glorious views of impressive spires, imposing monoliths, deep red rock canyons, and crisp blue skies, through a forest of dark green piñon pine and juniper trees. In the background is the Grand Valley of the Colorado River, the unique Bookcliffs Mountain Range, and the largest flattop mountain in the hemisphere—the 10,800-foot Grand Mesa.

From any vantage point along Rim Rock Drive, the panoramic vistas looking across the Grand Valley show how sun and shadow can create a new and unique canvas all day long because of the aforementioned Bookcliffs. The low-slung mountain range, averaging about 8,000 feet in elevation, stretches nearly 200 miles from the town of Palisade at the east end of the Grand Valley to Price Canyon near Helper, Utah. It is the longest contiguous mountain range in the United States that orients from east to west instead of north to south. Because of this, the sun and shadows dance gracefully across its various canyons and crevasses throughout the day and glow scarlet at sunset. This is also home to the BLM's Little Bookcliffs Wild Horse Range, one of

Nonvenomous bull snakes fill a niche within this national monument.

the best-managed wild horse ranges in the arid Southwest, where wild horses can destroy habitat at an alarming rate.

Along Rim Rock Drive are 19 viewpoints and 14 trailheads. Hikes vary here from half a mile to 14 miles round-trip. The road also accesses the Saddlehorn Visitor Center and Campground. Located four miles from the west entrance of the monument near the town of Fruita, Saddlehorn offers the only established campground within the monument. There are no electrical hookups or showers in the campground, and there's virtually no water available in the backcountry, so plan accordingly. Backcountry camping also is permitted. A free backcountry permit is required and may be obtained at the visitor center.

One of the most popular hikes is Monument Canyon Trail as it winds its way beneath many of the park's major rock sculptures, such as Independence Monument, Kissing Couple, and the Coke Ovens, which tower overhead. It's best to leave a vehicle at each end of this hike and shuttle one vehicle back after the six-mile trek downhill.

From 1907 to the early 1930s, Otto built miles of the trails that still exist here, including Monument Canyon Trail. He also built Serpent's Trail, once dubbed "The Crookedest Road in the World," featuring more than 20 switchbacks. Otto envisioned this as the main route between Colorado and Utah. While that dream never materialized, Serpent's Trail today is a great—albeit strenuous—hike, rising 794 feet in 1.9 miles. Bicycles and motorized vehicles are no longer allowed on this trail, leaving it to foot-powered pedestrians only.

> I came here last year and found these canyons, and they feel like the heart of the world to me. I'm going to stay and build trails and promote this place, because it should be a national park.
>
> —John Otto, the Colorado National Monument's first custodian

In the 1930s, during the Great Depression, the men of the Civilian Conservation Corps (CCC), along with Park Service employees and skilled local workers, hewed Rim Rock Drive out of sandstone, largely with hand tools. It soon became the main road.

Auto touring along Rim Rock Drive remains the major tourist attraction for the monument, while the bicycle riding is world class! Individuals and small groups come from all over the world to pedal this historic road.

The ICON Eyecare Tour of the Moon is the only sanctioned group bicycle ride across the monument. (See "Signature Activity: Tour of the Moon.") The Park Service has discouraged major cycling events for safety and other mostly legitimate reasons. (The main reason is that the first four miles up Rim Rock Drive from the east side are narrow, twisting, and turning. It's also the main road to Glade Park, a ranching area with numerous 35-acre "ranchettes" on private property above the Colorado National Monument. There are a number of locals who commute up and down this section of road daily, and frankly, some just don't like bicyclists.)

Because of the unique and varied terrain of this national monument, wildlife is abundant. Don't be surprised to see mule deer and desert bighorn sheep, as well as Hopi chipmunks, rock squirrels, collared lizards, Gambel's quail, turkey vultures, golden eagles, red-tailed hawks, and even peregrine falcons, the fastest bird on earth, known to hit speeds of 200 miles per hour.

While I've enjoyed the monument for all these decades, it remains one of the least visited national monuments in the United States, with annual visitation hitting 375,000 in 2017. It's kind of like having my own personal national monument in my backyard, and I'm pretty grateful for that!

SIGNATURE ACTIVITY: TOUR OF THE MOON

WHY GO?

The ICON Eyecare Tour of the Moon is a dream ride through spectacular red rock country, with great views of steep canyons and the Colorado River and Grand Valley below. The first six miles up to the top of the monument are tough. After that, it's a remarkable ride!

SPECS

ACTIVITY TYPE: Group-supported bicycle ride
TRAILHEAD/PUT-IN/ETC.: Both start and finish are at Two Rivers Convention Center in downtown Grand Junction.
DISTANCE/LENGTH: 41- or 62-mile courses. You choose!
AVERAGE TIME REQUIRED: 2 to 4 hours
CONTACT: info@tourofthemoon.com
DIFFICULTY: Strenuous, especially the first 6 miles or so
SPECIAL CONSIDERATIONS: You're cycling at altitude. Grand Junction is at 4,583 feet, and the high point of the Colorado National Monument is 6,640 feet. Also, this ride occurs in late September. Usually the weather is drop-dead gorgeous, but it could rain or snow, so watch the forecast.

GETTING THERE

SHORT DESCRIPTION: The event begins and ends at Two Rivers Convention Center, 1st and Main Street, Grand Junction, CO.
GPS COORDINATES: 39°02′30″N, 108°37′47″W

OVERVIEW

Considered the premier road bicycle ride on the Colorado Plateau, the ICON Eyecare Tour of the Moon takes riders on a 41-mile or 62-mile route through the Colorado National Monument. Starting and ending in downtown Grand Junction, the breathtaking high desert scenery and red rock canyons provide an epic day of cycling.

The original "Tour of the Moon" was one of the most famous stages of the Coors International Bicycle Classic. Between 1980 and 1988, the Coors Classic was the largest men's and women's pro-am race in the world, attracting top teams and top riders such as cycling legend Greg LeMond, who won the Classic in both 1981 and 1985. In 1984, the film *American Flyers*, starring Kevin Costner, was inspired by the Tour of the Moon and filmed on-site in Mesa County.

Tour organizers are quick to point out that this is NOT a race anymore, as the supported ride celebrated its eighth year in 2019 with nearly 2,200 riders participating. Riders begin between 7:30 and 8:30 a.m. and can ride at their own pace. There are three or four aid stations along the way with water, energy drinks, snacks, fruit, and nutrition bars. Sag wagons drive the course with water and are available to assist riders experiencing mechanical difficulties or those who become too fatigued to finish.

The first six miles of both courses take riders up the east side of the monument, and it's a bit of a grunt! The elevation rises 2,000 feet in that stretch. The rest of the ride, however, offers smooth sailing along the twists and turns of Rim Rock Drive, where you may spy bighorn sheep or soaring golden eagles.

Those who choose the longer, 62-mile (100 metric miles for a century ride!) ride can cruise down the west end of the monument and enjoy a mostly flat ride through the farming country surrounding the town of Fruita. Others may say "enough" and opt for the classic 41-mile loop back to downtown Grand Junction.

CHAPTER 4
MCINNIS CANYONS NATIONAL CONSERVATION AREA

SIZE—123,460 acres (including 75,000 acres of Black Ridge Canyons Wilderness)

YEAR ESTABLISHED—Colorado Canyons National Conservation Area was created by congressional act in 2000. Controversy erupted in 2005 when it was renamed McInnis Canyons after then U.S. representative Scott McInnis in a congressional maneuver infamously called the "McInnis-as-god" bill.

MANAGING AGENCY—Bureau of Land Management, 2815 H Road, Grand Junction

DOG-FRIENDLY?—Dogs are allowed under control (see "Dogs in the Wild!" sidebar in chapter 29).

FEES AND PERMITS—Permits are required only to float and camp along the river.

NEAREST CITIES—Fruita and Grand Junction, CO

NEARBY PUBLIC PROPERTY—Colorado National Monument, BLM's Bangs Canyon/Tabaguache Trail system (world-class hiking, mountain biking), Little Bookcliffs Wild Horse Range, Grand Mesa National Forest, Uncompahgre National Forest, Kokopelli Trail, Rabbit Valley, and the Trail through Time active dinosaur dig

SPECIAL CONSIDERATIONS—Moisture of any kind can make these roads impassable, while summer daytime temperatures can exceed 100°F. Hiking is best done early in the morning at this time of year. Water sources are limited and unreliable any time of year, so pack your own water. Biting gnats can be nasty from May through August. Pack insect repellent.

OVERVIEW

McInnis Canyons National Conservation Area has the second-largest concentration of natural arches in North America. (The largest concentration is just down the road at Arches National Park near Moab, Utah, which also is located on the Colorado Plateau.)

This area is known for more than all those arches though. Internationally important fossils have been uncovered here during more than a century of excavation. Pictographs and petroglyphs abound, and the Old Spanish Trail runs through here. It is a recreation destination for world-class mountain biking.

Want more? There are 25 miles of the Colorado River winding its way through Horsethief and Ruby Canyons, home to mule deer, bald eagles, elk, black bear, desert bighorn sheep, hundreds of species of birds, and four very endangered fish—the Colorado pikeminnow, humpback chub, bonytail chub, and razorback sucker.

The BLM manages for multiple uses within this national conservation area (NCA). Cattle grazing is allowed on 663 acres within the NCA. In Rabbit Valley on the northwest edge of the area along the Colorado-Utah border, primary activities include motorcycle and ATV riding. Three paleontology trails exist here, along with numerous

hiking and horseback trails. Rafters, kayakers, and duck hunters utilize the Colorado River corridor, and motorized boat traffic is allowed in Ruby Canyon.

Rattlesnake and Mee Canyons provide outstanding opportunities for solitude and primitive recreation within Black Ridge Wilderness Area. The 75,550-acre wilderness forms the core of the NCA, which was designated as a "nationally significant area" by Congress in 2000.

Located south of the Colorado River, Black Ridge is situated on an east-west plain and is dissected by seven red rock canyons varying in length. Rattlesnake Canyon is one of the longer canyons slicing through the ridge, eventually spilling into the Colorado River near the Colorado-Utah state line. Rattlesnake Canyon Arches Trail is one of the most adventurous and fascinating trails here. Seven major sandstone arches display their age, majesty, and delicacy along this route.

Mee Canyon, also located within the Black Ridge Wilderness, offers another exciting hike in this high-desert country. With arches, windows, spires, and alcoves, the trek into this canyon is not recommended for inexperienced hikers. It steeply descends both Entrada and Wingate Sandstone layers with exposed cliffs and very

He talks to trees. He nukes weeds. He's the guardian of saplings. He's the Prince of the Cottonwood Gallery.

Troy Schnurr is the BLM's Lone Ranger on the Colorado River through Horsethief and Ruby Canyons on the Colorado-Utah border. He is the benevolent patron of the river corridor. He is the cottonwood whisperer.

With his aviator sunglasses and well-worn BLM ball cap pulled low, he flashes a sly grin from behind a bushy white horseshoe mustache and gently wraps another cottonwood sapling with protective wire to keep beavers at bay.

He plies his politics of goodwill to the Colorado River with a pair of pliers from the back of his trusty steed—a red, 16-foot Maravia rubber raft with yellow markings, fully loaded with safety, survival, and tree-planting equipment, and a silver 9.9-horsepower Honda outboard motor.

His slow drawl is smooth as silk, yet tough as need be with the duck-hunting crowd. At the same time, he can tell a gaggle of geeks they're dumb as stumps while they shake his hand, thanking him for enlightenment.

As the Bureau of Land Management's lead park ranger for McInnis Canyons NCA, Schnurr patrols a 25-mile reach of the Colorado River. His territory begins at the Loma Boat Launch, just off exit 15 from I-70, 13 miles east of the Colorado-Utah border. It ends at Westwater, about 10 miles into Utah. This permitted stretch of river receives heavy use because of its easy access from I-70 and because it is flat water, meaning "no rapids."

There are 34 campsites along Schnurr's golden stretch. The river attracts experienced rafters, kayakers, canoeists, and stand-up paddleboarders because of its sheer beauty, yet this reach also sees a considerable number of novice and party users.

While this may be flat water, it remains a powerful and fast-moving river. Everyone on the water must use caution, or Schnurr will have to rescue them too.

It's a big river, and he hasn't been around to help everyone. He has assisted in recovering bodies of drowning victims more than once in his 25 years patrolling this river. Most of that time, he was literally the lone ranger. In fact, in 2000 he was the first BLM ranger for the then Colorado Canyons NCA, patrolling all 123,400 acres—plus the 25-mile stretch of river. Now he concentrates on the river and whispers to the cottonwoods. He's happy that a paid permit system was put in place in 2013 to control the number of users on the river each day. "It was just getting out of hand," he said. "Too many people and not enough campgrounds. It was a mess."

Schnurr said all money generated from the permits goes directly back into managing the river. He now has enough funding to hire seasonal help, keep campgrounds clear, and restore the river's health by eliminating aggressive and non-native tamarisk, Russian olive, and Russian knapweed. All the while, he continues to protect native grasses, willows, and cottonwoods as they return to stabilize the banks of this ever-changing river.

"Had a bobcat here just the other day," he said nonchalantly as we floated the river and he sipped on his sweetened coffee. He was not talking about the white and red industrial grade compact loader. He was talking about a four-legged bobcat—you know, medium-size, secretive, ranges from southern Canada to central Mexico.

Fremont cottonwood trees have long been a key component of riparian life zones of the Colorado Plateau. Their roots hold banks and help slow erosion; their large branches provide excellent shade and shelter for hundreds of species of insects, birds, and wildlife.

The day we floated, we saw a great blue heron, a half dozen different species of ducks, geese, mule deer, and bald eagles, and we found unmistakable signs of beavers, river otters, desert bighorn sheep, and black bears.

"Since we've taken out all the non-native species, a lot of these cottonwoods are coming up on their own and the wildlife is coming back," Schnurr noted as he placed wire nets around young saplings to keep them from being eaten by those tree-loving beavers.

While many saplings have sprouted naturally since the tamarisk was taken out, Schnurr has planted more than 250 native Fremont cottonwoods here and has placed protective wire around 1,000 more. He seemed to know the names of each and every tree. "I planted that one over there in 2005," he said, pointing to a healthy 25-foot-tall cottonwood in full autumn glory.

Most of them would never have survived had Schnurr not combatted the tamarisk with biological control— the tamarisk-eating *Diorhabda* beetle (also known as the tamarisk beetle)— and chain saws. Miles and miles of shoreline are now available for native grasses, plants, and trees to regenerate—and for wildlife and human use as well.

Since the middle of the 20th century, humans have dramatically altered this and other western rivers and made it harder for native trees to compete. "We've built dams and diverted water," he said. "The floods we once saw here in these canyons used to sprout new willows and cottonwoods on their

Colorado River cottonwood gallery

own. As we engineered the rivers, tamarisk just took over." (See "Tamarisk and the Tamarisk Beetle" sidebar.)

The U.S. Department of Agriculture began searching for a biological control for tamarisk in the mid-1980s. By 2001, they'd launched the tamarisk beetle program along Schnurr's stretch of river, as well as nine other sites on the Colorado Plateau.

"They released that beetle here and started watching it and studying it and marked a lot of trees," he said. "I still have a few bugs down here. They continue to munch away," he said, pointing to numerous stands of healthy 150- to 200-year-old cottonwood "galleries" along the river corridor. He noted that others have been burned out by wildfires, intensified by the overgrowth of tamarisk. All seven wildfires he's documented on this river corridor since 1994 were caused by humans. (One 87-acre fire on private property in 2015 was actually started by sparks from the railroad that runs the length of these canyons.)

When he first started patrolling this river a quarter century ago, there was only one really good campground. It was located at an important ecological area known as Black Rocks, an outcrop of metamorphic bedrock 1.7 billion years old. Here, the river narrows and plunges to depths of 80 to 90 feet. It's the most dangerous stretch of the river, not because of its mild riffles, but because people keep jumping off those inviting rocks. "There are so many crosscurrents, they may never surface."

It's also home to the river's four endangered fish: the pikeminnow (formerly known as the squawfish), the bonytail chub, the humpback chub, and the razorback sucker. All were pushed toward extinction because of the damming and channelization of the river—which also encouraged tamarisk growth.

"The rest of this river corridor," the gentle river ranger continued, "was just overgrown with tamarisk. You couldn't even find a place to pull your boat over to stop between here and Westwater," he said. While cottonwoods struggled, tamarisk continued to survive wildfire and drought, and even thrived. Yet slowly, painstakingly, the lone ranger began making headway. He fought purple loosestrife, tall whitetop (a non-native pepperweed), musk thistle, Russian thistle, Canada thistle, kosha weeds, and Chinese elm trees along with tamarisk, Russian knapweed, and Russian olive. While coordinating hundreds of volunteers, it would take the river ranger about two years to clear enough ground to open up a new campground.

"Maybe in the future we can open up more campsites, but right now, our parking is limited at the Loma boat launch, so if we open more campsites, it means building another parking lot." That means money, something that's in short supply for government agencies such as the BLM these days.

Schnurr figures he's got another couple good years in him before he retires, so the cottonwoods can breathe a collective sigh of relief. Once he leaves, however, he is worried about one thing: "Once you wrap a tree, you've got to maintain it (so the tree won't be strangled)," he said. "Rewrap, rewire, unwire. I've got a lot of hardware down here. I sure hope they replace my position once I'm gone."

limited access. Directional signs and other evidence of human imprints are limited here. If you think you're up for it though, you'll crawl through a small window arch, shimmy down an old "Navajo-style" ladder, inch your way across a sandstone ledge, and finally enter one of the largest natural alcoves on the Colorado Plateau.

The southeastern edge of the NCA butts up against the Colorado National Monument. The western edge plunges into red rock canyons winding down the Colorado River corridor far into Utah. This is where the world-famous Kokopelli Mountain bike trail etches a crooked path between Loma, Colorado, 15 miles east of the Colorado-Utah border, and Moab, Utah, 150 miles to the southwest. Mountain biking enthusiasts come from around the globe to test their skills on terrain that varies from technical singletrack to pavement. The majority of the trail is on old jeep roads, so a sag wagon can follow bicyclists who have mechanical problems or who are just too pooped to continue.

Lone river ranger Troy Schnurr's trusty steed!

By the late 1990s, this area was already known for its diverse recreational opportunities. Mountain biking was gaining tremendous traction in local communities, especially Fruita, on trails like Mary's Loop, Western Rim, and Russler's Loop. The ATV crowd roared to life in the desert country surrounding the Grand Valley. Hiking was huge in the NCA's Devils Canyon, Flume Canyon, and Pollock Bench trails in what's called the "front country" of the NCA, just south of the river. Geology and paleontology buffs came from far and wide to explore here, while rafting, hunting, and fishing were all stable economic drivers in a boom-bust oil and gas economy. Grand Junction

Teach us what it means to be humble in a world where we take ourselves too seriously and where wisdom and truth are often scorned.

—Richard Baxter, pastor of the Presbyterian Church of North Carolina, opening the U.S. House of Representatives session the day the "McInnis-as-god" bill passed

The water-guzzling tamarisk, *Tamarix ramosissima*, is the only tree along vast swaths of western rivers. Also known as salt cedar, a 2005 U.S. Geological Survey study found that it's the third most prevalent riparian tree in the West.

This deciduous arching shrub came to the United States as a decorative plant in the 1800s. By 1930 it was used for erosion control but was soon maligned for sucking up too much precious water in the arid West. Research now shows it takes about as much water as native riparian trees like willows and cottonwoods. Yet it grows as a monoculture and eventually strangles everything else, depleting the soil and negatively affecting birds, wildlife, and humans.

In response to the tamarisk invasion that originated nearly 90 years ago, a few native bird species began nesting in tamarisk trees. The endangered Southwestern willow flycatcher (*Empidonax traillii extimus*), for example, really likes dense, woody growths along the waterways of the arid Southwest. This was taken into account in 2001 when the U.S. Department of Agriculture (USDA) allowed the release of the tamarisk beetle, as long as no release occurred within 200 miles of a known flycatcher nest.

The beetle has now been released in nine states (California, Oregon, Nevada, Utah, Wyoming, Colorado, Montana, New Mexico, and Texas), excluding those areas where the endangered southwestern willow flycatcher nests. Things went well until 2008, when an unsanctioned beetle release in southern Utah reached the Virgin River and the very western edge of the Colorado Plateau. That was flycatcher habitat.

In 2010, the USDA ended the program, but the bugs don't care. They work in large, migrating groups and produce multiple generations in a season. In some places, the bugs have died off. In others, they munch on. Yet as BLM river ranger Troy Schnurr notes, "No matter how many bugs you have, you're never going to eradicate tamarisk. But maybe you can tip the scale a little in favor of the natives."

and the surrounding communities were becoming known for a plethora of outdoor activities.

Thus, "through an unprecedented collaborative effort on the part of government land management agencies, local landowners, environmentalists, ranchers and tourism officials," according to the *Denver Post*, Colorado Canyons NCA was born in 2000. This was one of the very few nationally designated areas in the United States created with little or no rancor. Even the establishment of the Lincoln Memorial came with tension. (On May 30, 1922, a large crowd gathered for the dedication of the Lincoln Memorial. The seating was segregated by race.)

Rancor found this area four years later when the area was renamed.

A handful of U.S. representatives suspended House Rule XXI, Clause 6, which specifically banned House members from misusing the political process for their own personal gain and glorification—they couldn't name public structures or public land for themselves. Yet Colorado Canyons was to be renamed for sitting U.S. Representative Scott McInnis. Congressman Tom Tancredo of Colorado, McInnis's home state, likened it to putting themselves on "an almost god-like level."

Once the House rule was suspended, the "McInnis-as-god" bill—as it came to be known—was introduced on July 13, 2004, and passed quietly in an empty chamber. President George W. Bush signed it into law on October 30, 2004.

SIGNATURE ACTIVITY: I CAN CANOE A CANOE, CAN YOU?

WHY GO?

This scenic trip introduces many users to the pleasures—and sometimes pains—of rafting on rivers flowing through the Colorado Plateau. It's "flat water," meaning no rapids. You may have to paddle a bit, but there's nothing more rejuvenating than a gentle glide past millions of years of geology. It's a kaleidoscopic adventure through time and space.

SPECS

ACTIVITY TYPE: Float trip!

TRAILHEAD/PUT-IN/ETC.: Loma Boat Launch just off I-70, exit 15; takeout: I-70 to exit 227, Westwater

DISTANCE/LENGTH: 25 miles

AVERAGE TIME REQUIRED: It depends on the flow, but give yourself at least two days so you can enjoy a night of camping on the river!

CONTACT/MANAGING AGENCY: Bureau of Land Management, 2815 H Road, Grand Junction, CO 81506, 970–244–3000. For river permits, go to https://www.recreation.gov/permits/74466.

DIFFICULTY: Gentle Class I and sometimes Class II rapids, but a river is always dangerous. ALWAYS wear your life vest. Also, if the flow is low and the wind is high, you may be paddling quite a way. Be strong!

SPECIAL CONSIDERATIONS: No permit is required for day use. However, a River Permit is required to float the river; overnight camping permits also are required year-round, and both must be reserved in advance at recreation.gov/permits/74466.

GETTING THERE

SHORT DESCRIPTION: PUT-IN: Loma Boat Launch, Loma, CO. Take exit 15 (Loma) from I-70; turn south on Highway 50; turn west on 13 Road until you reach the parking lot. Continue down 13 Road until you reach the river. **TAKE-OUT:** Westwater Ranger station and boat launch, Westwater, UT. Take I-70

to exit 227, Westwater. Follow signs to the ranger station and boat launch ramp, about nine miles south of the freeway.
GPS COORDINATES—PUT-IN: 39°02′31″N, 108°37′47″W; **TAKEOUT:** 39°5′11″N, 109°0′0″W

OVERVIEW

Row, row, row your boat. Row a little more. This is a great stretch of water to learn how to canoe, raft, kayak, or stand up on a paddleboard. The river's gentle but strong flow takes beginners and experts alike past 1.7 billion years of colorful geology, miles of gorgeous 150-year-old cottonwood galleries, and an abundance of wildlife, from bald eagles and great blue herons to desert big-horn sheep and collared lizards.

A double arch on the Rattlesnake Canyon Arches Trail

While this is generally a gentle glide, always be aware that this is a big river, and you can get swallowed up quickly. No matter what the flow, which you'd better check before you float, ALWAYS wear your personal flotation device (PFD). Special note from the United States Coast Guard: "A PFD is designed not to ride up on the body when in the water. But, when a wearer's stomach is larger than the chest, ride-up may occur."

Just sayin'.

This is a wonderful trip in the summer, as it's a great way to escape the heat. It's nice for families to leave the hustle and bustle of everyday life and relax on the river, building memories that will last longer than hard times. Not only that, you can take the family dog as long as it doesn't chase wildlife. Remember, however, that the permit allows for "a maximum of 25 heartbeats per group, including adults, children and dogs (two dogs per group)."

Again, just sayin'.

CHAPTER 5
DOMINGUEZ–ESCALANTE NATIONAL CONSERVATION AREA

SIZE—210,000 acres surrounding the 66,280-acre Dominguez Canyon Wilderness

YEAR ESTABLISHED—Created by an act of Congress in 2009 to protect one of the "crown jewels" of the BLM, but also to serve as an economic engine for local communities

MANAGING AGENCY—Bureau of Land Management, 2815 H Road, Grand Junction, CO

DOG-FRIENDLY?—Dogs allowed under control and on-leash around other users and during spring lambing season for desert bighorn sheep (see "Dogs in the Wild!" sidebar in chapter 29).

FEES AND PERMITS—None

NEAREST CITIES—Grand Junction and Delta, CO

NEARBY PUBLIC PROPERTY—Uncompahgre National Forest, Grand Mesa National Forest, Colorado National Monument, McInnis Canyons National Conservation Area, Gunnison Gorge National Conservation Area

SPECIAL CONSIDERATIONS—Hot in the sun. Cool in the shade. Be prepared.

OVERVIEW

"I've always thought about these [Native American] guys, up here pecking out pictures on sandstone cliffs, and wondered, 'What would their spouses say when they got home?'"

"'Oh sure, you're out there drawing pictures on rock, while I'm back here slaving over a hot fire, taking care of your rowdy kids, and helping grandma chew the leather. This may be her last winter, you know.'"

Thus soliloquized old buddy Bill Elmblad as he led me to a marked site within Bureau of Land Management territory in Escalante Canyon in the Dominguez–Escalante National Conservation Area.

This was a site formerly inhabited by Native Americans for a thousand years.

The pictures on the rock made that pretty obvious.

Look up! You may discover pictographs or petroglyphs on the canyon walls high above you.

Elmblad lives close and visits here often. He knows that pictographs, petroglyphs, red rock canyons, sandstone bluffs, quiet solitude, and outstanding wildlife viewing opportunities all make this a very special place.

The Dominguez Canyon Wilderness is a 66,280-acre maze of incredibly picturesque canyons located in the heart of the 210,000-acre Dominguez–Escalante National Conservation Area.

Multiple uses are allowed in much of the NCA, including livestock grazing, off-highway-vehicle riding, mountain biking in designated areas, boating, hiking, and camping. The wilderness, however, is managed to maintain its primitive characteristics.

The NCA extends from the top of the Uncompahgre Plateau at 7,500 feet to the banks of the Gunnison River at 4,682 feet. It is named for two Franciscan friars, Silvestre Vélez de Escalante and Francisco Atanasio Dominguez, who were attempting to find a route from Santa Fe, New Mexico, to Monterey, California, in 1776.

The two friars never visited their namesake canyons, even though they came close. Members of the Hayden Expedition christened these canyons Dominguez and Escalante in 1874, nearly a hundred years after the good friars passed this way.

Nonetheless, Native Americans, ranchers, prospectors, railroaders, and outlaws have visited and lived here for a very long time. Archeologists believe these canyons have been sporadically inhabited for 13,000 years and intensively inhabited for the last 1,500 years. Archaic-style petroglyphs from 1000 BC include "carved deer and elk, bear paws and a variety of anthropomorphs, or human-animal figures," according to Andrew Gulliford, professor of history and environmental studies at Fort Lewis College in Durango, Colorado. "Ute-style rock art goes from 1600 to 1880, including shield figures and a bison hunting scene with Native Americans on horseback surrounding a bison dripping blood."

Gulliford noted that the Uncompahgre band, Weminuche band, and Grand River band of Utes may all have traversed this canyon.

"Certainly, outlaws did."

The McCarty Trail between Escalante and Dominguez Canyons was named for the family who used to live here. According to Gulliford, the McCarty brothers rode with Butch Cassidy when he robbed the San Miguel Valley Bank in Telluride in 1889. Four years later, Tom McCarty robbed the Delta Bank, only to be shot by a hardware store owner with a buffalo gun. Tom died before he hit the ground.

The canyons McCarty was attempting to escape into provided great hiding places for outlaws, but they also provide habitat for a wide variety of wildlife, and special plants have adapted over eons of time to survive. Dave Kauffman, former field manager for the BLM's Uncompahgre Field Office in Montrose, said that the original Dominguez Wilderness Study Area was primarily concerned with protecting sensitive, threatened, and endangered plants, including the rare and beautiful Colorado hookless cactus (*Sclerocactus glaucus*) and Grand Junction milkvetch (*Astragalus linifolius*) that were native to these canyons.

Current management concerns include allowing recreation without damage, improving wildlife habitat, interpreting the pioneer history of the canyon lands, and reducing fire fuels.

Desert bighorn sheep were reintroduced between 1983 and 1991 and have done fairly well. Bone fragments, petroglyphs, and pictographs provide evidence that herds historically occupied this area, although they hadn't been seen here since the late 1800s.

The sheep seem to tolerate our presence. However, studies show hiking off trails around the sheep increases their stress levels and hiking off trails with a dog dramatically increases their stress levels.

February through April is lambing season for the sheep. Do not approach them during these times.

Cactus Park Trail accesses Big Dominguez Creek upstream from Newspaper Rock, and, looking southeast toward the Grand Mesa and the West Elk Wilderness, offers stunning panoramic views.

Besides bighorns, don't be surprised to find sign of mule deer, turkeys, chukar (similar to Hungarian partridge), black bears, mountain lions, collared lizards, and golden eagles.

There are 115 miles of streams and rivers in this conservation area, and biologists believe there is habitat suitable for 52 protected species of animals and plants.

Archeological sites can be found in all these canyons. Many of the sites in Escalante Canyon, to the south of Dominguez, are quite accessible. This, of course, leads to problems.

Land managers do as much as they can to identify and protect native rock art throughout the Colorado Plateau, but it's a tough job. You'd have to have been there when "John Loves Mary, 2008" appeared on a rock in this canyon. Apparently "Rex was Here, April 5, 1972."

Much of the rock art that Elmblad led me to had been scarred by more recent etchings on the sandstone cliffs of Escalante Canyon. Some of it you may call art. Some of it you may call graffiti. Some of it simply was mindless vandalism.

Big Dominguez Creek, along with Escalante, Cottonwood, and Little Dominguez Creeks, drains the east side of the Uncompahgre Plateau. Here, you can plainly NOT see what geologists call "the Great Unconformity." It's the same thing John Wesley Powell saw in the Grand Canyon in 1869.

The bottom of Dominguez Creek exposes brittle blue-gray schist, some of the hardest and oldest rocks in the world at 1.4 billion to 1.8 billion years old. Yet the visible red rock cliffs of 300-million-year-old Chinle Sandstone surround you. There's a gap of several hundred million years between the two that you cannot see—the Great Unconformity.

According to Grand Junction geologist Ray Pilcher, the Great Unconformity in the Grand Canyon, in the Black Canyon of the Gunnison River upstream from here, and in this canyon shows "where the contacts between sedimentary strata and the crystalline strata of greatly different ages, origins and structure represent periods of geologic time sufficiently long to raise great mountains and then erode them away again."

That's a long time!

Some rock art was defaced by bullet holes. Last month? Last year? A hundred years ago? Were they attempts to erase traces of America's past, or just idiots with guns and booze?

Despite this, it's intriguing to glimpse our past, where three distinct petroglyph styles dominate native rock art. They include Barrier Canyon rock art (6000 BC–100 BC), Fremont Indian rock art (AD 600–AD 1250), and Ute Indian rock art (AD 1300–AD 1880).

Most of the rock art Bill and I discovered could be attributed to Ute Indians, who may have displayed some of their artwork directly on top of older Ute art, or perhaps Fremont Indian rock art.

Just like Rex in 1972, and John and Mary in 2008, there's a fine line between rock art and graffiti. Bill pointed to one beautiful outline of a horse. Neither Ute nor Fremont people left that etching. With lichens and mosses growing over this horse, it was artwork etched many decades ago, not many centuries ago.

Elmblad led me to three or four different spots accessible by vehicle, or within a couple-hundred-yard walk. A few spots could be photographed from the car. Others required a scramble up the hillside to find.

I'm not telling you where they are. You need to discover them on your own. That's part of the intrigue. When you find something that was put there 800 years ago, you can ponder how that artist got there, or why, or what he was trying to convey.

In the same way, when you find the newer sites, you can easily decipher the deep, deep meaning of modern-day man. It'll make you appreciate those original Native American artists who pecked out beautiful pictures on rock while their spouses were back home cooking, cleaning, or helping grandma chew the leather.

SIGNATURE ACTIVITY: HIKE AND WADE

WHY GO?
Breathtaking scenery, newspaper rocks bearing ancient petroglyphs, nimble desert bighorn sheep, waterfalls, and a cool-down swim in the Gunnison River toward the end of the hike. Why not go?

SPECS
ACTIVITY TYPE: Hike, then wade in the Gunnison River to cool down.
TRAILHEAD/PUT-IN/ETC.: Dominguez Canyon Trailhead at the end of Bridgeport Road
DISTANCE/LENGTH: 6.6 miles to Newspaper Rock, out and back
AVERAGE TIME REQUIRED: 2.5 to 4 hours, depending on how long you soak in the river
CONTACT/MANAGING AGENCY: Bureau of Land Management, Grand Junction office
DIFFICULTY: Easy, but it can be very hot in the summer! Be prepared! Carry extra water—and drink it all!
SPECIAL CONSIDERATIONS: Keep dogs on a leash, especially during spring lambing season for bighorn sheep!

GETTING THERE
SHORT DESCRIPTION: From Grand Junction, take U.S. Highway 50 South 17 miles past the Mesa County Fairgrounds to Bridgeport Road. Slow down as you approach the road at the top of the hill, as there is no exit lane. Turn right on Bridgeport Road and travel down this narrow yet well-maintained gravel road for 3 miles to its terminus at the Gunnison River. Go slow around single-lane blind corners.
GPS COORDINATES: 38°48'20.16"N, 108°18'28.8"W

OVERVIEW
Only 20 miles from Grand Junction, red rock canyons and sandstone bluffs provide breathtaking scenery and hold geological and paleontological resources spanning 600 million years. Cultural and historic sites from the past 10,000 years can also be found here amidst desert bighorn sheep clinging to precarious ledges along the canyon walls.

All the news that's fit to print! Newspaper Rock depicts desert bighorn sheep, bears, deer, lizards, snakes, and human figures.

This is a good hike year-round, but it can get especially hot in the summer, so go early. By the time you return to the river, you'll be ready to get your feet wet.

For the first mile of this hike, you'll follow Denver and Rio Grande Western Railroad tracks that parallel the Gunnison River. (The train still runs through here a couple times a day.)

Once you cross the river on a well-constructed pedestrian/equestrian bridge, the nature of the hike changes dramatically. As you stroll 0.3 mile along the cool banks of the Gunnison, you'll pass a handful of group camping sites for boaters floating down the Gunnison from Delta. In another 0.4 mile, you'll arrive at the mouth of Dominguez Canyon. Here, you'll leave the river and hike west, then south into the breathtaking Dominguez Canyon Wilderness.

In another mile, the canyon splits. To the right (west) is Big Dominguez Canyon; to the left (further south) is Little Dominguez Canyon. (Interestingly, Little Dominguez is much larger than Big Dominguez Canyon. Go figure.) This is a good place to look with binoculars for bighorn sheep.

Hike another 1.6 miles up Big Dominguez Canyon to Newspaper Rock, a freestanding sandstone rock about the size of a trailer that squats in the center of the trail. Here are fine examples of Native American petroglyphs, featuring pecked outlines of desert bighorn sheep, bears, deer, lizards, snakes, and human figures. Descendants of Native American Utes who once roamed here still consider this a sacred place.

Look up and to your right (north) from Newspaper Rock and you'll discover petroglyphs on the canyon walls high above you. There are many petroglyphs, pictographs, and other Native American artifacts like wickiups and arrowheads throughout this area. Remember, take only pictures, leave only footprints.

You could hike another quarter mile along this trail to a unique waterfall on the south side of the trail. In fact, you could continue another 6.3 miles to the top of the Uncompahgre Plateau at about 7,500 feet in elevation, but that would require an overnight stay. Or simply return the way you came, head to the river, take your shoes off, and soak those hot, stinky feet. They'll thank you for it. But be careful, especially if the river is up! It can be very slick and dangerous.

CHAPTER 6

BLACK CANYON NATIONAL PARK AND GUNNISON GORGE NATIONAL CONSERVATION AREA

SIZE—Black Canyon National Park is 30,750 acres; Gunnison Gorge National Conservation Area is 62,844 acres.

YEAR ESTABLISHED—President Herbert Hoover established Black Canyon National Monument in 1933. It was enlarged by 10,000 acres and became a national park through congressional act in 1999 to help protect the natural beauty and wildlife habitat, which was threatened with inundation by another dam. Congress also designated Gunnison Gorge a national conservation area in 1999.

MANAGING AGENCY—The National Park Service manages the park; the Bureau of Land Management, Montrose Field Office, manages the NCA.

DOG-FRIENDLY?—Dogs are not allowed in the park, but they are allowed under control in the NCA. Please note: Pets are endangered by being on the South Rim of the national park—even on a leash! Over the past few years, female deer have acted aggressively and even attacked park visitors walking dogs. A doe perceives a dog as a threat to her fawns. Several deer have been euthanized, and a visitor was nearly mauled to death. Needless to say, special regulations apply. Pets and pack stock are allowed in the NCA but must be under visual, audible, or physical control at all times.

FEES AND PERMITS—BLACK CANYON NATIONAL PARK: $25 per private vehicle; $20 per motorcycle; $15 per person (bicycle or walk-in) for a 7-day pass; annual passes, senior passes, access passes, and active duty military passes also accepted. **GUNNISON GORGE NCA:** $3 per day per person if hiking into the canyon from the rim; $10 per night for camping. There are no other fees in the NCA.

NEAREST CITIES—Montrose and Delta, CO

NEARBY PUBLIC PROPERTY—Grand Mesa National Forest, Gunnison National Forest, San Juan National Forest, Uncompahgre National Forest; Dominguez–Escalante National Conservation Area

SPECIAL CONSIDERATIONS—Don't hike down if you can't hike out!!

OVERVIEW

The Gunnison River through Black Canyon National Park drops an average of 95 feet per mile—one of the steepest descents of any river in North America. The Gunnison Gorge, managed by the BLM, is just downstream.

Steep though it may be, it is an angler's paradise. This is Gold Medal water, the highest designation of any fishery in Colorado, one of the finest trout fisheries in the Lower 48.

And it's so much more. To a geologist, this canyon is an angelic cathedral of metamorphic architecture; to the ardent nature lover, it is shocking in its suddenness; to

Painted Wall with West Elks
in background

A NAP BY THE GUNNISON

> Sleep, that knits up the raveled sleave of care,
> The death of each day's life, sore labor's bath,
> Balm of hurt minds, great nature's second course.
> Chief nourisher in life's feast.
> —William Shakespeare, *MacBeth*, 2.2.3

That chief nourisher in life's feast came to me in the summer of 2017, not at the death of a day, but midafternoon while napping along the banks of the Gunnison River, deep inside the Black Canyon.

I was anxiety-ridden, scared, conflicted, and inflicted with a dire set of ills. Besides the horrible mess our world was in, my own heart ached with personal turmoil. After a tough backpack trip deep into the bowels of this dark abyss, my knees hurt and my left shoulder was stiff. My eyesight, my hearing, and my memory were shot. I didn't remember this trail being so tough. Granted, I was 41 years younger the first time I ventured here, down Bobcat Trail, in 1976.

I laid on the sand and stretched my aching back under the single-leaf ash shading my favorite campsite. Within moments, I was lulled to slumber by a lung-cleansing freshness, the murmur of running water, and the sweet melody of wind whistling through one of nature's greatest canyons. The air was laden with the mingled perfume of ancient cedar and juniper, sagebrush and Gambel oak, desert mahogany, my single-leaf ash—and fresh running water.

A scientist may say water is odorless—that what you smell would be a composite of the dissolved minerals and detritus in the water.

Whatever.

I could smell and feel and taste the sweet, sensual dampness of this rich riparian zone with every bracing inhale. Every exhale purged the stagnant breath of rotted anxiety out of my body and mind and spirit.

I slept a deep, refreshing sleep while pure, rarefied air seeped through my bones. It may have been only for a few minutes, maybe an hour, I don't know.

When I awoke, I stumbled to my feet and lurched a few dozen yards across slick, rounded river rock, cast my fly line into the rushing water, and caught a large brown trout hiding behind a medium-sized rock on the current's edge.

I smiled broadly and whooped loudly, then gently released the orange-spotted, brassy brown back to its watery home.

Black Canyon from the North Rim

rock climbers, it is approached with somber countenance; to kayakers, it is difficult yet playful, ominous yet gleeful.

To anyone who would peer over its steep ledges on either North or South Rim, or ply its depths through a rigorous descent followed by a more rigorous ascent, or float through its wickedly rapid rock gardens on the river itself, this is a sacred place.

But then, that's what makes all public lands on the Colorado Plateau so special. They are all sacred in their own way. They have been set aside for a reason.

This national park includes 12 miles of the 48-mile-long Black Canyon of the Gunnison River. It also contains the deepest and most dramatic section—the gorge is 2,772 feet deep near Warner Point.

At its narrowest, the canyon is only 40 feet wide from rim to rim. That's one reason for the moniker "black": Direct sunlight is limited to nonexistent in the bottom of this fascinating geologic spectacle. The other reason is the 1.7-billion-year-old metamorphic rock that forms the sheer black walls of this chasm. This Precambrian gneiss and schist, called granodiorite, is an igneous rock that solidified after melting at a great depth beneath the surface of the earth.

In his book *The Black Canyon of the Gunnison—In Depth,*[5] Wallace Hansen describes a unique combination of geologic activities that created this formidable canyon—hard rock uplifted, then carved by fast-moving debris-laden water.

Hansen postulates that the river first set its course millions of years ago over relatively soft Mesozoic and Cenozoic volcanic and sedimentary rocks. It then cut down to harder, older crystalline rock of the dome-shaped Gunnison Uplift. Once entrenched in its course, it continued cutting, with turbid water carrying mud and debris, occasional rock falls from high cliffs, and the relentless movement of landslides into the depths. This process took about two million years.

Other more subtle processes, such as gullying, frost action, and chemical weathering (acid rain), continue to increase the material available for the river to wash away, according to the National Park Service's 2005 "Geologic Resource Evaluation Report."

The river within the canyon drops an average of 95 feet per mile. It's one of the greatest rates of fall for a river in North America. By comparison, the Colorado River through the Grand Canyon descends an average of 7.5 feet per mile.

This steep descent supplies the energy to propel a relentless stream of water and sediment. Though now well controlled by three massive man-made dams above, this water continues to carve and polish, providing incomparable scenery, a rich and diverse riparian zone, and deep pools that are home to great populations of hungry trout.

While it's an angler's paradise, it's also heaven for rafters and kayakers seeking Class III/IV rapids, and rock climbers will find 126 different routes ranging in difficulty from 5.7 to 5.13-R.

> Some are longer, some are deeper, some are narrower, and a few have walls as steep, but no other canyon in North America combines the depth, narrowness, sheerness and somber countenance of the Black Canyon of the Gunnison.
> —Wallace Hansen, *The Black Canyon of the Gunnison—In Depth*

Recreational activity is not restricted to hard-core risk-takers, however. There's plenty of wildlife watching: Elk, deer, bear, wild turkey, and bighorn sheep all roam through this area. Hundreds of varieties of birds live here, such as mountain bluebirds, canyon wrens, white-throated swifts, and the fastest hunter of them all, the peregrine falcon, reaching speeds of 200 miles per hour as it swoops to capture its prey.

Many other species travel through here twice a year. For example, don't be surprised to hear the trumpeting sound of sandhill cranes as they fly hundreds of feet overhead, migrating between Bosque del Apache, in New Mexico, to a stopover spot on the side of the Grand Mesa at Fruitgrowers Reservoir, a few miles northwest of here. Tens of thousands of the four-foot-tall primeval creatures will rest a few days before continuing to the northern Rockies, where they will nest and raise their young prior to their 800-mile return flight in the fall.

Numerous trails lead hikers along both North and South Rims, as well as down into the canyon itself. The toughest trails, with names like S.O.B. and Slide Draw, begin inside the national park. Others, such as Bobcat, Chukar, Duncan, and Ute Park Trails, descend into the Gunnison Gorge through the NCA downstream from the national park.

Within the NCA, motorized, mechanized, hooved, and Vibram-soled transportation is allowed in designated areas. Mountain bikers enjoy miles of trails, as do motorized ATVers. Beware: Roads here are natural surface, rocky, and generally impassable when wet. High-clearance and four-wheel-drive vehicles are recommended.

Pack animals are used to carry the load for river rafters down Chukar Trail, on the south side of the canyon between the towns of Olathe and Delta. There's also a great horseback trail along that South Rim through the NCA.

Camping is permitted in certain areas, but not in others, so you'd better check with the Park Service or BLM, depending on where you wish to stay and what you are looking for in your visit.

At first glance, this dark canyon seems deep, foreboding, and inhospitable. It certainly can be. The hikes down into the canyon—and back out—can be brutal. There's poison oak everywhere once you reach the river bottom, so long pants and long-sleeved shirts are important. It's hot down there in the summer, cold in the spring and fall, and inaccessible in the winter. The rock is unstable, the trails are overgrown, and at times the gnats can get nasty.

The truth is, it's been a mighty barrier to humans since the beginning of our existence. Yet once known and thoroughly explored, it becomes soothing and invigorating—a chief nourisher in life's feast.

SIGNATURE ACTIVITY: FISHING THE GOLD MEDAL WATERS OF THE BLACK CANYON

WHY GO?
World-class trout fishing combined with world-class scenery make this a trip to put on any angler's bucket list!

SPECS
ACTIVITY TYPE: Spin cast or fly fishing—no egg soaking or worm dunking allowed
TRAILHEAD/PUT-IN/ETC.: Too numerous to mention here. Get the maps and do your homework.
DISTANCE/LENGTH: A couple hundred yards from the East Portal parking area, to 4.5 miles one way on the Ute Park Trail
AVERAGE TIME REQUIRED: 1 to 2 days minimum
CONTACT/MANAGING AGENCY: Black Canyon National Park; BLM Gunnison Gorge National Conservation Area
DIFFICULTY: Yep, every trail is difficult here, but well worth it!
SPECIAL CONSIDERATIONS: Rugged hikes, big water, and wild-fighting rainbows and browns await the angler rough enough and tough enough to handle them!

OVERVIEW
Anglers are all alike—we're just a bunch of jerks on one end of a line waiting for a jerk on the other end! And this is a great place to indulge our own jerkiness.

Only 322 miles of Colorado's 9,000 miles of trout streams—and three lakes—carry a Gold Medal designation. The Gunnison River boasts 27 miles of that designated water. Special regulations apply in order to protect this fishery. And while there are more than 60 pounds of trout per acre—a large percentage more than 14 inches in length—it's not like fishing in a barrel. This is BIG water by Colorado standards. The only river larger in this state is the Colorado River, which it flows into about 70 miles downstream. And because of the rapid drop in elevation—95 feet per mile—it's movin'! You'd better be careful!

Joe Rudy with big rainbow

On golden days, one can expect to catch and release a dozen or more brown or rainbow trout in the 16- to 18-inch range, some much larger. On other days, you can get skunked. That's why it's called fishin', not catchin'.

The West River Trail begins at the bottom of the canyon, at the confluence of the North Fork of the Gunnison and the main stem.

At the far upper end, you can actually drive down the East Portal Road to a camping/picnicking/fishing area beneath Crystal Dam. The winding, steep (16 percent grade), paved but rutted road with hairpin curves is closed during the winter months.

There are four trails into the Gunnison Gorge below the main stretch of Black Canyon. They enter from the south side near the towns of Delta and Olathe: Chukar, Bobcat, Duncan, and Ute Park Trails. There are seven trails dropping to the river from within the national park, including S.O.B. and Slide Draw. All are very difficult.

You can float through the lower canyon if you're an experienced rafter/kayaker. Expect numerous Class III/IV rapids, possibly Class V depending upon the flows. You can also hire guides. Float-fishing through the canyon on a three- or four-day float is the only way to go—if you can afford it!

For a fee, there's an early morning jet-boat service from the confluence of the North Fork and the main stem that takes anglers upriver about four miles to the Smith Fork. Anglers can either float out (the jet boat will transport a dory or raft for an extra fee) or hike out, if they're in shape.

No matter—do your homework. Don't just stumble on down here. It is dark and foreboding, and it can chew you up. But if you know what you're doing, you'll survive—and have lots of Gold Medal stories to tell.

CHAPTER 7
FISHER TOWERS FEDERAL RECREATION AREA

SIZE—Approximately 1,190 acres

YEAR ESTABLISHED—It's been under federal control since before Utah statehood in 1896, and it's been under BLM management since then.

MANAGING AGENCY—Bureau of Land Management, Moab Field

DOG-FRIENDLY?—Yes, but under control at all times (see "Dogs in the Wild!" sidebar in chapter 29).

FEES AND PERMITS—No fee for use of the area; $15 per campsite (pay at campground; cash or check only)

NEAREST CITY—Moab, UT

NEARBY PUBLIC PROPERTY—Colorado Riverway Recreation Area, Canyonlands National Park, Arches National Park, Westwater, McInnis Canyons National Conservation Area, the Bookcliffs

SPECIAL CONSIDERATIONS—It's HOT here in the summer. Come prepared! Also, campgrounds can get crowded. Check with the BLM in Moab.

OVERVIEW

Utah Scenic Byway 128, known as the Old River Road by locals, is one of the most breathtaking drives slicing through the Colorado Plateau. The road connects the crowded, hustling, bustling, bicycling, four-wheel-driving, too-hip-to-be-cool town of Moab, Utah, to the I-70 corridor. To the east is Fruita and Grand Junction, Colorado; to the west is Green River, Utah.

The 45-mile-long two-lane blacktop follows the Colorado River through breathtaking red rock canyons with beautifully manicured ranch resorts and past lofty mesas with incredible rock formations such as Fisher Towers. Driving east past the towers from Moab, the road and river flow through more gorgeous red rock canyon before the road leaves the river, heading northeast to travel through scenic Cisco, Utah, and eventually to I-70. Cisco was a saloon and water-refilling station for the Denver and Rio Grande Western Railroad in the 1880s. It now sits nearly abandoned and eternally trashed—a monument to a sad scene from the "Old Southwest" of a scarred landscape created by man-made follies on a parched high-altitude desert. Yet some life and humor remain, with handmade signs and spray-painted graffiti pointedly admitting this is not a tourist destination.

The towers, however, draw hard-core rock climbers and scenery-seeking photographers from around the world. Looming 900 feet above the Colorado River as it flows through Professor Valley, the towers were named for a miner who lived near here in the 1880s.

A 2.2-mile hiking trail through this area leads to 360-degree panoramic views, but climbers can cut off and head up toward the Corkscrew.

Every reference to Fisher Towers I found declares that they "are isolated remnants of a 225-million-year-old floodplain deposit."

OK. So, how did that happen?

When the Colorado Plateau was uplifted from tectonic activity while North America was forming about 20 million years ago, salt deposits underlying this region buckled, warped, and collapsed. Subsequent erosion caused the formation of large valleys and steep cliff escarpments. Water, wind, and time did the rest. Those elements continue to work 24/7, year after year, millennium after millennium.

Because of its gnarly spires, peaks, and points, Fisher Towers has become a mecca for hard-core rock climbers, despite their sandstone exterior. As one muddy climber put it on a rainy afternoon, "I learned the difference between climbing on sandstone and climbing on granite today!" The Cutler Sandstone that created the towers is actually very hard and does not fracture into continuous crack systems like most other sandstone. The rock here also is covered with a thick layer of mud, which makes the climbing dirty, difficult, and sometimes very dangerous.

Whole body aching from long days of big-wall hauling. Tiny tents, bivy sacs, snow caves lashed by hurricane sleet. Frozen fingers and toes. Migraines and altitude malaise. Not knowing what's to come. It doesn't have to be fun to be fun.

—Rock-climbing legend Jeff Lowe, 1950–2018

Nonetheless, it's incredibly scenic—a photographer's dream—and the hiking is fantastic. At least as many, if not more, people come here for the hike and scenery as they do for the climbing. In fact, the trail through here was designated a National Recreation Trail in 2007 and meanders for 2.2 miles one way, climbing from 4,717 feet in elevation to 5,550 feet and a stunning 360-degree view of the Colorado River through Professor Valley, Castle Rock, Castle Valley, and the high mesas of the Bookcliffs north of the river. The trail provides an opportunity to see the forces of geology that are characteristic of the Colorado Plateau up close and personal. You can feel it with your hands, slip on it in your hiking shoes, and take a little bit of it home in your socks. If it's windy, you may take a little more home in your hair and your eyes and your nose and your ears as well.

Nearby, that same river flows through an incredible canyon/valley/canyon area where thousands of rafters, kayakers, and canoeists play each year. A side canyon just downstream from Fisher Towers that's worth checking out is Onion Creek, 3.5 miles southwest of Fisher Towers. The Onion Creek Bench Trail is as sweet as a Vidalia onion, especially during college spring break, when most campgrounds along the Colorado River are chock-full of spirited outdoor enthusiasts who are chock-full of distilled spirits. When all those other areas are full of tourists, you won't spot another soul/sole on the Onion Creek Bench Trail.

The Old River Road takes visitors past Fisher Towers and Professor Valley.

The shadows of Fisher Towers provide a stunning location for camping, yet there is only room here for a small, five-site, tent-only campground. Numerous designated camping spots may be found at one of 11 different campgrounds along the Colorado River corridor or at Onion Creek. They're all pretty busy from spring to fall to accommodate the rafting crowd. Numerous rafting companies in Moab can oblige your every need. A calm-water half-day trip from Hittle Bottom, across the road from Fisher Towers, gives families, couples, or groups plenty of time to soak in the geology of the Colorado River as it flows through broad mesas and impressive red rock canyons on its way to Moab.

Whether you like the river, the climbing, the hiking, the scenery, or the serenity, Fisher Towers is public property well worth a visit. Heck, just the drive along Utah Scenic Highway 128 is worth the visit. Don't forget to slow down in Cisco. It's not abandoned, you know.

SIGNATURE ACTIVITY: CLIMBING ANCIENT ART

WHY GO?

This is a great place to hike, it's a great place to photograph, it's a great place to sit in silence and listen to the wind. It's also a fabulous place to climb—if you are an adrenaline junkie and like living on the edge!

ACTIVITY TYPE: Hard-core rock climbing
TRAILHEAD/PUT-IN/ETC.: Fisher Towers Campground and Parking Area (elevation at trailhead: 5,286 feet)
DISTANCE/LENGTH: 1.1 miles, then straight up
AVERAGE TIME REQUIRED: All day
CONTACT/MANAGING AGENCY: Bureau of Land Management, Moab Field Office, 82 East Dogwood, Moab, UT 84532, 435–259–2100
DIFFICULTY: YES!
SPECIAL CONSIDERATIONS: Get daily climbing weather reports at climbing weather.com/Utah/Fisher-Towers.

GETTING THERE
SHORT DESCRIPTION: Head north from Moab on U.S. 191N for 2.5 miles to UT 128E. Turn right and continue for 21 miles to the Fisher Towers Road. Turn right and travel 2.1 miles to the parking area and trailhead at the end of the road.
GPS COORDINATES: 38°43′31.2″N, 109°18′32.9″W

OVERVIEW
Do you like mountaineering, traditional climbing, top roping, bouldering, aid climbing, big wall scrambling, or just canyoneering? It's all available to hard-core rock climbers on the Colorado Plateau. However, there's one place in particular that attracts climbers from around the globe—Fisher Towers.

Make no mistake. Climbing is dangerous. All climbers must assume that their most trusted piece of protection is their ability NOT to fall. Nonetheless, at Fisher Towers there are more than 50 documented climbing routes, all rated above 5.4, with most in the 5.8 to 5.13 category. That's gnarly, in climbing terms. Most of us probably couldn't handle a 5.0 to 5.7 climb, which is considered easy for real climbers. A climb of 5.8 to 5.10 is getting tough, 5.11 to 5.12 is really difficult, and 5.13 to 5.15 is reserved for a very elite few.

Soaring 900 feet above the plain, the Titan is the largest tower here, but the most popular climbing is at Ancient Art—a multi-summited tower below the taller Kingfisher and Titan Towers. Within the Ancient Art structure lies Stolen Chimney on the Corkscrew Summit, the most popular route that supports traditional, sport, and top-rope climbing. It's rated at 5.10.

Both sport climbing and traditional climbing are a form of lead climbing. That means the first climber to go up is not protected by a rope from above. Top-roping involves a climber securely attached to a rope that then passes up through an anchor system to the top of the climb and down to a "belayer" at the foot of the climb. The belayer, another climber at the bottom, hangs on to that rope, taking up slack when

In April 2018 a world-renowned climber named Erik Weihenmayer returned to Fisher Towers for a climb. It had been 20 years since he last "touched the crumbly sandstone of the classic desert route 'Ancient Art.'"

Erik is blind. His climbing companions back in 1998 included Mark Wellman, who was paralyzed, and Hugh Herr, a double leg amputee. They reached the top of the Corkscrew on Ancient Art and started dreaming of creating a movement that eventually became No Barriers USA. It's a program that "empowers people of all walks of life and abilities to overcome obstacles, live a life of purpose and give back to the world." Check them out at https://nobarriersusa.org.

I have two good legs, I can see, I'm not paralyzed, and I am in awe when I look up at Eric and friends on top of the Corkscrew at Ancient Art.

needed and letting out rope when needed, so that if the climber were to lose her hold, she would not fall more than a short distance.

Many novice climbers start with top-roping. It's safer, psychologically easier, and less physically demanding—but this remains a sport for adrenaline junkies, so be prepared, and always go with experienced climbers who have been there and done that. You know they've safely survived for another day of climbing!

According to mountainproject.com, a heavily used website for rock climbers supported by outdoor equipment retailer REI, "rarely enough for the serious and scary Fishers, Stolen Chimney is a cruise that protects very well."

Yeah. Right.

Barrel cactus in bloom

CHAPTER 8
CANYONLANDS NATIONAL PARK/WHITE RIM BICYCLE RIDE

SIZE—337,598 acres

YEAR ESTABLISHED—President Lyndon B. Johnson established Canyonlands National Park on September 12, 1964, against the wishes of those who proposed a much larger national park of nearly 4.5 million acres.

MANAGING AGENCY—National Park Service, Canyonlands National Park, Moab, UT

DOG-FRIENDLY?—Yes and no. As the Park Service says, "Pets are welcome in the park, but there are limits on where you can take them." In some places dogs are allowed on-leash. In other places, like White Rim, they're not allowed at all. Check first.

FEES AND PERMITS—Yes and yes. Entrance fees are required, and permits, many of them free, are required in some places. Most campgrounds must be reserved and cost extra. In general, here's the deal: $30 per vehicle entrance fee (15 passenger capacity or less), $25 per motorcycle, $15 per person with no car (usually a bicycler). National annual passes ($80) and interagency senior passes ($80 for life) also are accepted.

NEAREST CITIES—Moab, Green River, and Monticello, UT

NEARBY PUBLIC PROPERTY—Arches National Park; Glen Canyon National Recreation Area; Goblin Valley State Park; Natural Bridges National Monument; Hovenweep National Monument; Capitol Reef National Park; Manti–La Sal National Forest; the new San Rafael Wilderness, including Labyrinth Canyon, Muddy Creek, and Desolation Canyon

SPECIAL CONSIDERATIONS—Drink lots of water, don't rely on cell service, respect nature, don't stand out in a thunderstorm, and leave drones and ATVs at home—they're illegal here.

OVERVIEW

The red rock canyonlands of southeast Utah are incredible for their ruggedness, beauty, and tranquility. Canyonlands National Park is the heart of it. Two of the three great rivers of the Colorado Plateau—the Green and the Colorado—converge here, splitting the park into three major districts: Island in the Sky, the Needles, and the Maze. The third great waterway of the plateau, the San Juan River, empties into the Colorado River at Lake Powell, just downstream from here.

No roads connect these remote areas to each other. You won't find any services, so bring everything you need for a visit to this craggy, colorful country. Make sure you gas up in Green River, Moab, or Monticello—and carry plenty of water. And unless you're in your father-in-law's sedan, don't bring a regular "car" down here. You'll need something with high clearance.

Most national parks on the Colorado Plateau are overrun with people. I just can't write about them anymore. In fact, that's part of my mutually agreed-upon contract

Canyonlands National Park preserves 527 square miles of colorful canyons, mesas, arches, and buttes along the Green and Colorado Rivers in southeast Utah.

with Falcon Press: nothing on Arches, Bryce, Zion, Capitol Reef, or the Grand Canyon. There are too many fine publications already available on those fabulous national parks. There also are too many people who love those parks to death. I pray the places I'm writing about in this book don't become overrun as well. But I can't write about the White Rim (see "Signature Activity: Ride the Rim") unless I write about Canyonlands National Park, even though two great books, *Best Easy Day Hikes, Canyonlands and Arches National Parks* and *Hiking Canyonlands and Arches National Parks*,[6] from author Bill Schneider have already been published by Falcon Press.

Despite its past publicity and notoriety, this remains a fabulous park to write about, to photograph, to investigate, to visit, and to cherish. That's because it's hard to get here and difficult to get around once you do get here. I've spent years exploring the Maze District. I became enamored with this wild land in the early 1970s, and it's just as its name implies—an incredible maze of canyons sprawling from beneath squirming ridges like Medusa's hair! It offers some of the finest backcountry camping I have ever experienced—but it's real easy to get lost!

A man could be a lover and defender of the wilderness without ever in his lifetime leaving the boundaries of asphalt, power lines, and right-angled surfaces. We need wilderness whether or not we ever set foot in it. We need a refuge even though we may never need to set foot in it. We need the possibility of escape as surely as we need hope; without it the life of the cities would drive all men into crime or drugs or psychoanalysis."

—Edward Abbey, *Desert Solitaire*

The Harvest Scene in the Maze is one of the finest examples of rock art remaining from the Archaic people who lived here 8,000 to 2,000 years ago. The larger-than-life scene depicts faded ancient people harvesting rice grass, an important food of the native tribes. The Doll House, also found in the Maze, is an incredible rock structure hiding the Dollhouse Granary, an ancient grain bin that remains from those Archaic people. Most people today find this by floating the mighty Colorado River, then hiking upstream. Not far from there is Water Canyon. Whoa. It's one of the most delightful canyons I've ever hiked because of its twists and turns, its rock structures and sandy alcoves, its deep red jasper—an impure variety of silica highly valued by ancient Puebloans—and its water, the most precious commodity of all in the desert.

But here's the deal: The four-wheel-drive roads leading into the Maze are the toughest kidney-busting rides I know of. It takes four hours of hard four-wheel-driving from Green River just to get to the Maze Overlook. Is it worth it? Heck yes! You should see it, experience it, be mesmerized by it, and be humbled by it. But I've been there, done that, got the T-shirt. My kidneys just can't handle that road anymore.

How about the Needles district? Named for the colorful spires of Cedar Mesa Sandstone that spring out of the desert floor with amazing irregularity, the Needles forms the southeast corner of the Canyonlands. Hundreds of pillars and spires stretch southward for miles, forming a jumbled and at times hostile landscape. Yet this area also has many fascinating arches, domes, canyons, and signs of ancient Puebloan life such as ruins and rock carvings. There are more

Towers and canyons stretch to the horizon along the White Rim Trail.

The White Rim Road is an unpaved four-wheel-drive road that traverses the top of the White Rim Sandstone formation beneath Island in the Sky Mesa in Canyonlands National Park. It has become the classic long-distance mountain bike ride of the entire red rock region of southeast Utah. However, the Atomic Energy Commission built this and numerous other roads in this part of the country in the 1950s so prospectors could reach their uranium mining claims. Uranium was used for nuclear weapons production during the Cold War, a period of great tension between the former Soviet Union and the United States following World War II. The mines along this road produced very little uranium, and all of them have since been abandoned. Nonetheless, these mining roads opened up the Canyonlands to tourism as more people learned about the area's geologic wonders.

than 60 miles of interconnecting trails here. Fifty more miles of rugged backcountry roads lead to natural geologic structures and cultural antiquities, trailheads, and campsites. My favorite hike here is the Chesler Park Loop/Joint Trail, a somewhat strenuous 11-mile jaunt that offers great panoramas of the Needles before winding through deep, narrow fractures in the rock.

Then there's Island in the Sky. I will never forget one of my first visits to the spectacular Green River Overlook here. The day was sunny but windy, and as we exited our vehicle and held on to our hats, we heard a nasally, high-pitched whine pierce through the breeze. "Oh sure, Morey. You forget the camera," wheezed a short, squat woman with a thick New Jersey accent and a snarl as deep as the canyon on her furrowed face. "What are we here for? YOU forget the camera. What is this, Morey? A bunch of rock. Who am I? Just the mother of your children, Morey. Who am I? You can't take MY picture, the mother of YOUR children, in front of THESE rocks because YOU forget the camera."

Lovely views though, and memories to last a lifetime.

It's great to take in the panoramic views at Green River Overlook from the top of this Island in the Sky, but it's an entirely different scene beneath the island. That's why the 100.7-mile-long White Rim bicycle ride is so popular. (See "Signature Activity: Ride the Rim.")

Some activities in Canyonlands National Park—such as backcountry travel and river trips—require a permit. That's because this is a fragile environment. Too many people doing too many stupid things can really cause long-term damage. Well-prepared visitors need a permit for all overnight trips into this extraordinary backcountry. Day-use permits also are required for four-wheel-driving or mountain biking. And, of course, permits are required for world-class self-propelled boating opportunities on the mighty Green and Colorado Rivers.

While many national parks offer numerous amenities to make it easy for tourists to visit, this is one national park where you really have to take care of yourself. It's remote and it's rugged, but it's also quiet and sublime, surreal and comforting. And don't forget your camera. Even though Morey's wife may not be around, there are still plenty of rocks to take pictures of!

SIGNATURE ACTIVITY: RIDE THE RIM

WHY GO?
While the red rock country along the Colorado–Utah border offers numerous classic mountain bike rides as well as many multiday rides, this is considered Utah's ultimate multiday bike ride. It's rough, tough, and drop–dead gorgeous.

SPECS
ACTIVITY TYPE: Long-distance mountain biking
TRAILHEAD/PUT-IN/ETC.: Schafer Trailhead
DISTANCE/LENGTH: 100.7 miles; Elevation: 6,183 feet at the top, 3,948 feet at the river; Ascent: 5,949 feet; Descent: 5,937 feet
AVERAGE TIME REQUIRED: 4 days
CONTACT/MANAGING AGENCY: Canyonlands National Park, 435–719–2313, nps.gov/cany/index.htm
DIFFICULTY: Strenuous. Hard. Difficult. Tough. But a real gas!
SPECIAL CONSIDERATIONS: Groups of up to 15 are allowed only 3 sag wagons, so pack carefully! Plus, this is a rugged four-wheel-drive road, so make sure your sag wagons and their drivers are prepared for it.

GETTING THERE
SHORT DESCRIPTION: Travel 11 miles northwest from Moab, UT, on U.S. Highway 191 to UT Highway 313. Turn left (west). In 15 miles, this road becomes Island in the Sky Road. In another 5.8 miles, turn left (south) onto the South Fork Road. Travel 3.3 miles to the trailhead parking area.
GPS COORDINATES: 38°27'33.4"N, 109°47'41"W

OVERVIEW
I must broach a sensitive topic that is rarely discussed in books such as this: Specifically, my perineum is really, really sore after a 100-mile bicycle ride on the White Rim beneath Island in the Sky at Canyonlands National Park.

Oftentimes, authors will beat around the bush. "My butt's sore," they'll pen, or "This ride is tough on the rear." But that's not my issue.

Sure, I could have ridden more miles on my mountain bike than I did in preparation for this gargantuan four-day saddle (sore) ride. I could have been in better shape. I could have purchased a new bicycle seat. Better yet, I could have adjusted that seat to better suit my needs on this arduous bicycle ride through America's Canyonlands. But no matter how you cut it, it's not my butt that's sore. And I'm now sitting on my nice, comfortable office chair and eliciting fond memories of a great ride with great people through spectacular country in early April.

The cottonwood trees were just beginning to bud along both the Colorado and Green Rivers as we rode downstream above the Colorado, then upstream next to the Green. These two mighty rivers converge just downstream from here, and both were just beginning to swell with the spring runoff of a

Greg Godbey, front, from Littleton, Colorado, and Joseph McKenna from Santa Fe, New Mexico, cycle along a typical stretch of road on the White Rim.

healthy wet winter in the Henry Mountains, the Abajos, the La Sals, and the majestic Rocky Mountains themselves.

The White Rim is considered THE classic long-distance mountain bike ride in the Moab, Utah, area. It's 100.7 miles long and is usually done in a four-day ride—with the support of a sag wagon to carry food, water, camping gear, bike parts, and beer. Because this is such a popular ride, obtaining $30-per-night camping permits here is difficult. All designated campgrounds on this rim are by reservation only, and you must begin your quest for permits four months in advance at reserveamerica.com. Good luck with that!

The best time to be here is spring and fall. It's really hot in the summer and really cold in the winter. Yet at any time of year, great riding and spectacular scenery draw mountain bikers from around the world to this little island of heaven on the Colorado Plateau.

CHAPTER 9
DEAD HORSE POINT AND GOOSENECKS STATE PARKS

DEAD HORSE POINT STATE PARK

SIZE—5,362 acres
YEAR ESTABLISHED—San Juan County donated the land to the State of Utah in 1959, recognizing its scenic qualities but not having the funds to protect it.
MANAGING AGENCY—Utah Division of State Parks and Recreation, Moab, UT
DOG-FRIENDLY?—Dogs are allowed on a maximum 6-foot leash. No pets are allowed on the Intrepid Trail System.
FEES AND PERMITS—$20 per vehicle up to 8 passengers, valid for 3 days; $15 for seniors 62 and older; $10 per motorcycle; $4 pedestrian or cyclist (biking into park)
NEAREST CITY—Moab, UT
NEARBY PUBLIC PROPERTY—Arches National Park, Canyonlands National Park, Colorado River Corridor Recreation Area, Fisher Towers
SPECIAL CONSIDERATIONS—Safety concerns include the relative isolation of the park (30 miles to food, gas, and medical care), lightning danger, and unfenced cliffs. Watch the kids closely.

GOOSENECKS STATE PARK

SIZE—10 acres of incredible scenery!
YEAR ESTABLISHED—Opened as a state park in 1962 because the county couldn't afford to maintain it
MANAGING AGENCY—Utah Division of State Parks and Recreation Bluff, Utah
DOG-FRIENDLY?—Dogs are allowed on-leash; do not leave your dog in the vehicle. It can be intensely hot here in the summer!
FEES AND PERMITS—$5 day-use fee per vehicle with up to 8 people; $2 per person fee for bus tour groups; $10 per night per campsite
NEAREST CITIES—Mexican Hat and Bluff, UT
NEARBY PUBLIC PROPERTY—Valley of the Gods, Cedar Mesa, Grand Gulch, Natural Bridges National Monument, Canyonlands National Park, and Lake Powell
SPECIAL CONSIDERATIONS—Safety concerns include the relative isolation of the park, lightning danger, unfenced cliffs, and intense heat in the summer. Watch the kids closely.

OVERVIEW

Meanders are curves in a river. Goosenecks are extreme incised meanders that create a series of curves, bends, loops, and turns in a river channel.

With the La Sal Mountains in the background, the Colorado River meanders 2,000 feet below Dead Horse Point.

There are two state parks in southeast Utah that feature these extreme incised meanders—Dead Horse Point State Park and Goosenecks State Park. While both are situated in the southeast portion of the state, they are 157 miles apart and are located on two different rivers. It takes about three hours to drive between them on U.S. Highway 191. The northernmost one, Dead Horse Point State Park near Moab, looms 2,000 feet over the Colorado River. The second, Goosenecks State Park near Bluff and Mexican Hat, towers 1,000 feet over the San Juan River.

Though they are situated on two different rivers (the San Juan eventually flows into the Colorado River at Lake Powell), the similarities are consistent with the terrain of the Colorado Plateau. Millions of years ago, these rivers meandered through a relatively flat landscape. Then, an intense uplift period occurred, raising the Colorado Plateau high above the Basin and Range geologic province of Nevada, southern Arizona, and southern New Mexico. The rivers cut through this uplift over millions of years as the water of the rivers swung from side to side, shifting in their channels and flowing through their respective floodplains.

Now, immense vertical cliffs meet with deep canyons sculpted from water and wind to create a kaleidoscopic masterpiece of color, shape, and sheer space.

DEAD HORSE POINT

Dead Horse Point got its name in a rather grisly fashion. According to legend, early ranchers in this area would use the peninsula as a horse corral by allowing the natural cliffs to serve as a fence. Cowboys would round up wild mustangs living on the mesa and push them to the end of the peninsula, which is only about 30 yards wide. They would block the escape with branches and brush, and then would select the best horses. Usually they would let the rest go. One time, however, some of the animals were allegedly left in the corral and died as a result of the lack of water on the peninsula, within view of the mighty Colorado River 2,000 feet below.

Historic evidence shows humans have used this area for at least 10,000 years. A few stone tools and some rock art are all that remain of those early inhabitants of the Paleo-Indian culture. By AD 500 both the Ancestral Puebloan and Fremont peoples had settled here. Both cultures disappeared from this area prior to 1300. Oral tradition suggests the Ute and Paiute cultures may have arrived here as early as AD 800. These ancient people certainly used Dead Horse Point to hunt for and capture wild game to eat.

Navajo apparently migrated to the area after 1300. Utes, Paiutes, and Navajo all were living here when Spaniards visited in the late 1500s, searching for a travel route to the Spanish missions in California.

The first Anglo-American settlement to the area came when Mormons attempted to establish the Elk Mountain mission in 1855. Conflicts with the Utes chased them out of the territory. In 1878, however, settlers and farmers established the community of Moab, 30 miles from here.

Today, much of this area is in white man's mechanized hands. Hundreds of miles of motorized ATV trails exist on BLM property around here. There's even a jeep trail beneath Dead Horse Point overlook. You'll have to inquire in Moab about that, since this book is mainly about self-propelled activities across the plateau.

While Moab was established as a ranching and farming community, tourism has dominated the economic scene since the mid-1980s. Moab is Utah's mecca for the outdoor-oriented crowd for both mechanized and self-propelled sports. ATVs and four-wheel-drive vehicles race through thousands of miles of Forest Service and BLM property while speedboats, skidoos, and houseboats motor on Lake Powell. Moab is loaded with four-wheeler Razors and two-wheeled mountain bicycles that cost nearly as much. You know you're in Moab if you're behind a toy hauler with two ATVs on Main Street, and next to you is a beat-up Subaru with two bicycles on top that are worth more than the car.

Generally, public land managers around here are quite cognizant of the fact that outdoor users here have very different needs. Thus, mechanized enthusiasts coexist but are normally separated from the mountain biking, hiking, rafting, and equestrian crowd.

GOOSENECKS STATE PARK

A vault toilet, a picnic area, and an incredible overlook are the only amenities found at Goosenecks State Park. Don't expect to find any hiking trails, ranger-led activities, or much of anything else. Not even a tree! One hiking trail—the Honaker Trail—begins outside state park boundaries along the paved road, Utah Highway 316, leading into the park. The highway is a great bicycling road since there is very little traffic, but it's short, only 3.5 miles from the turnoff to the state park. That's it for pavement out here!

A small campground here is as barren as the park. There are eight designated sites with picnic tables and fire pits, but the campground looks more like a dispersed camping area WITH NO SHADE! Nonetheless, it is situated on the rim of the Goosenecks Overlook and offers incredible views of the meandering San Juan River, 1,000 feet below.

This is a fabulous place to soak up the broad, expansive scenery of the Colorado Plateau. Eroded by water, wind, frost, and gravity for 300 million years, this area's incredible geologic activity carved and shaped the sinuous path of the San Juan River. From the overlook, visitors can barely see the dark volcanic intrusion of Alhambra Rock as a tiny speck in the distance. The buttes and spires of Monument Valley peak over the land to the southwest. To the north is Valley of the Gods. To the west lie the

One thousand feet below Goosenecks State Park flows the San Juan River, on its way to Lake Powell to meet the Colorado River.

Broad, expansive views await visitors to Dead Horse Point State Park.

Canyonlands. Below, the river twists and turns for a distance of more than 6 miles while advancing only 1.5 miles west on its way to Lake Powell.

At an elevation of 4,500 feet, this is an arid, high-altitude desert. Sightseeing, photography, and stargazing are popular activities here, especially if you camp. Keep in mind, however, that it can get really hot and there is NO SHADE for miles. So, if your travel plans allow, visit in the spring or fall for perfect weather, or winter for low sun angles and great photographic opportunities (even though it can get quite cold here too).

SIGNATURE ACTIVITY: BICYCLING, ON ROAD OR OFF

WHY GO?
You are miles and miles from anywhere, and you really need to get out of the vehicle and stretch a bit! Get going!

SPECS
ACTIVITY TYPE: Road biking, then mountain biking at Dead Horse Point; road biking at Goosenecks

TRAILHEAD/PUT-IN/ETC.: For the Dead Horse Point road bike ride, leave your vehicle near the intersection of U.S. 191 and Utah Highway 313; for the Goosenecks State Park trip, leave your vehicle at the intersection of Utah Highway 261 and Highway 316.

DISTANCE/LENGTH: 23 miles one way to Dead Horse Point; there are eight mountain bike trails inside the park, from short to long, easy to difficult; the road bike trip to Goosenecks State Park is 3.5 miles.

AVERAGE TIME REQUIRED: 1 to 2 hours to Dead Horse Point; a little less to Goosenecks State Park

CONTACT/MANAGING AGENCY: Dead Horse Point State Park, PO Box 609, Moab, UT 84532, 435–259–2614, stateparks.utah.gov/parks/dead-horse; Goosenecks State Park, 435–678–2238, stateparks.utah.gov/parks/goosenecks

DIFFICULTY: Easy road biking to both parks; mountain biking at Dead Horse Point varies from easy to very difficult.

SPECIAL CONSIDERATIONS: It's hot as Hades here in the summer, at both of these parks. Ride early in the morning or late in the evening if you're here at that time of year!

GETTING THERE
DESCRIPTION—RIDE TO DEAD HORSE POINT: Drive 11 miles north from Moab on U.S. Highway 191 and turn left (west) on UT State Route 313. Park here and pedal 20.3 miles to the park. That's 40.6 miles round-trip! Ride to **GOOSE-NECKS:** Drive 4 miles on U.S. 191 to U.S. 163 north; turn right and continue 17 miles to UT State Route 261; continue for 0.9 mile to UT State Route 316.

Park here and ride 3.5 miles into the park (7 miles round-trip).
GPS COORDINATES—DEAD HORSE POINT: 38°40'02.90"N, 109°41'14.76"W; **GOOSENECKS:** 37°11'55.61"N, 109°52'44.62"W

OVERVIEW

There's no Wi-Fi and cell service is spotty out here, so what the heck—you might as well get out of the vehicle and stretch a bit! Both of these roads are lovely bicycle rides because there's very little traffic, and you can see for miles and miles in all directions. It's hot in the summer, so you may want to ride early in the day or toward sunset. However, if you're here, that means you've driven hundreds and hundreds of miles from somewhere. You probably need to get out of the car and straighten up for a little bit, anyway.

There are a couple extra things you should think about if you're going to ride

The La Sal Mountains loom over the Colorado River.

out here. First, don't ride alone. It's a long way from anywhere, and the traffic is sparse. ALWAYS carry plenty of water, protect yourself from the sun, make sure your bike is well maintained and dependable, and remember there are lots of thorny plants out here in the desert. You may want to think about using a tire sealant in your inner tubes, even if you detest that green ooze coming out of your tube stem. Finally, know your own limitations in the heat and dry desert terrain.

Bicycles are allowed only along the paved road into Goosenecks State Park; however, eight well-defined mountain bike trails exist at Dead Horse Point State Park. It's a pretty short ride to Goosenecks (7 miles round-trip). You could stretch this out by riding your road bike from Bluff, 25 miles away. It's a pretty long ride to Dead Horse Point. You could shorten it by parking closer to the park or by simply driving to the park and then riding the mountain bike trails from there.

Inside Cutthroat Castle,
a once formidable establishment.

OVERVIEW

It's 60 miles from Cortez, Colorado, to Monticello, Utah. Surrounding these two metropolises is an incredible outdoor cultural museum. Mesa Verde National Park lies 10 miles—13 minutes—east of Cortez. A couple of good old boys from Mancos, Colorado—Richard Wetherill and his brother-in-law Charlie Mason—discovered "Cliff Palace" in Mesa Verde while searching for lost cattle in the winter of 1888. You can read a little more about that in chapter 15 on Chaco Canyon, since Wetherill and his wife Marietta ran a trading post there from 1998 until Richard was murdered in 1910.

Situated between Monticello and Cortez are Canyons of the Ancients and Hovenweep National Monuments. Archeologists believe there may have been 20,000 people who lived and farmed here 800 years ago. Maize (corn), beans, and squash were the main cultivated crops. They still are. In fact, you should treat yourself to some gourmet Anasazi beans from Adobe Milling Company in Dove Creek, not far from here. These pinto-like beans are fabulous!

Aztec National Monument lies 78 miles southeast of Cortez and 36 miles south of Durango, just inside the New Mexico state line. It's not far at all from Chimney Rock National Monument. At one time, the massive Aztec ruin contained more than 500 rooms and was obviously a major cultural center from AD 1050 to 1300. Aztec lies directly north of Chaco Canyon. Think they're connected?

Bears Ears National Monument, the La Sal Mountains, and Manti–La Sal National Forest also surround Monticello, Bluff, and Blanding, Utah. This area contains more cultural artifacts than anywhere else in North America. An absolutely fabulous museum, the Anasazi Heritage Center in Dolores, not far from Cortez, features artifacts from Ancestral Puebloan and other native cultures in the Four Corners region. The visitor center, which also doubles as the Canyons of the Ancients visitor center, is operated by the BLM and is situated on the point of two 12th-century archeological sites that were once home to ancient Puebloans. The museum is wheelchair-accessible, features permanent exhibits and special exhibits, curates extensive research collections, and houses a research library and an artist-in-residence program. It's a must-visit for anyone interested in our past.

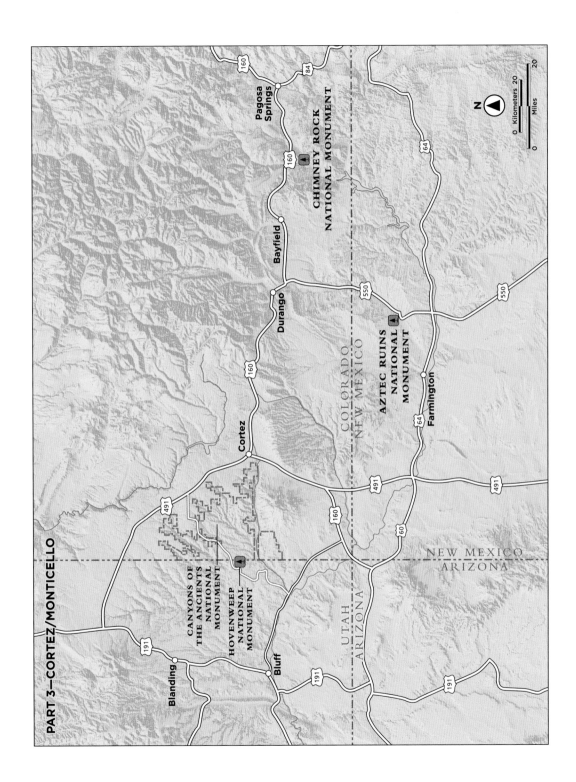

PART 3—CORTEZ/MONTICELLO

CHAPTER 10
CANYONS OF THE ANCIENTS

SIZE—171,000 acres

YEAR ESTABLISHED—Designated a national monument in 2000 by President Bill Clinton following broad-based local activism to protect one of the highest densities of archeological sites in the United States

MANAGING AGENCY—Bureau of Land Management, 27501 Highway 184, Dolores, CO 81323

DOG-FRIENDLY?—Dogs are allowed on-leash only. Keep dogs out of archeological sites and springs, and bring a plastic bag to scoop the poop.

FEES AND PERMITS—None

NEAREST CITY—Cortez, CO

NEARBY PUBLIC PROPERTY—Mesa Verde National Park, Hovenweep National Monument, Bears Ears National Monument, Manti–La Sal National Forest, San Juan National Forest

SPECIAL CONSIDERATIONS—This is sacred ground to Native Americans and it is their ancestral home. All cultural resources, structures, and artifacts are protected by federal law—and by the spirits of the Ancient Ones. Entering structures and some canyon interiors is not permitted.

OVERVIEW

A hike through Sand Canyon is a hike through the Great Sage Plain—an area between Cortez, Colorado, and Monticello, Utah, where deep soils hold winter moisture and have been used for dryland farming since the time of the Ancestral Puebloans, more than 800 years ago.

Several thousand acres of mesa and canyon farmland would have been required to support a population of 20,000 on the Great Sage Plain in AD 1270. They grew corn, beans, squash, and other crops in small fields and terraces, using small check dams for irrigation. They used solar calendars and astronomy to calculate growing seasons. They also hunted and tended to large flocks of turkeys. These weren't Butterballs. They still could fly.

Indeed, Ancestral Puebloans knew a lot of stuff about a lot of stuff. Look at their architecture; look at their farming practices, where "check" dams allowed them to grow crops on a plateau 5,000 feet above the sea and solar calendars directed planting seasons; look at their pottery. It's not just artwork, although the artwork is magnificent. They were stylish, distinctive, and functional.

There's a broad swath of the Colorado Plateau, from Mesa Verde National Park near Cortez, through Canyons of the Ancients and Hovenweep National Monuments, to Cedar Mesa and Bears Ears, where the spirits of the Ancient Ones still dwell. That's the belief of the Ute Mountain Utes, the Navajo, the Ute Indian Tribe of Utah, the

Sunny Alcove Pueblo once included eight rooms and a kiva.

Hopi, the Zuni, and all Native Americans who trace their heritage to Ancestral Pueb-loans 800 to 1,200 years ago.

There are more ancient artifacts in this zone than anywhere else in North America. While preservation would seem obvious here, controversy swirled briefly around the designation of this monument. Some users felt as though land that belonged to them was taken away, yet it had already been under BLM control, and the BLM's management plan did not change the land use. ATV trails that existed in the area prior to its designation as a national monument remain open, and grazing allotments have not changed. Yet indiscriminate trampling of ancient ruins has dramatically decreased.

In the late 1990s, former Colorado senator Ben Nighthorse Campbell tried to get Congress to act to protect this area and failed. A year later, a large coalition of local citizens, from ranchers and farmers to water and energy interests and local businesses around Cortez, Colorado, convinced naysayers of the value of the new designation in 2000. By 2008, economic data from a previously stagnant Montezuma County (where Cortez and Canyons of the Ancients lie) showed population growth up 5 percent and job growth up 10 percent. Natural resource extraction outside the monument's boundaries continued, while travel and tourism grew steadily.

In her "History and Intent of the Proclamation for Canyons of the Ancients National Monument,"[7] National Park Service historian Kristina L. Woodall wrote: "In the late nineteenth century and early twentieth century, a progressive movement extolling the responsibilities of a centralized government over the assets of the nation, and a conservation movement deeply concerned about the endangered prehistoric ruins of the American Southwest, combined and called for the Federal government to protect the best of the West. The collective consciousness of the American people, and their representative government, shifted from that of settling and developing every square inch of public lands for the benefit of individuals, local communities, and commodity-based businesses to that of setting aside spectacular untouched lands for the benefit of all Americans before their unique and irreplaceable values were forever lost."

What was at stake? This 171,000-acre national monument protects more than 100 archeological sites per square mile in some locations and includes 6,000 distinct structures, primarily from the pre-Puebloan era. In Sand Canyon alone, several well-preserved ruins can be viewed within 2.5 miles of a vehicle parking area in McElmo Canyon. The parking area is less than 15 miles southeast of Cortez, easily accessed, and therefore much in need of protection. (See "Signature Activity: Hiking to Ancient Ruins.") At the upper end of Sand Canyon, about 19 miles northwest of Cortez, lie the ruins of Sand Canyon Pueblo. Estimated to have been a 420-room complex with 100 kivas and 14 major towers, it would have been more than three times the size of Cliff Palace, the largest complex in Mesa Verde National Park. (Cliff Palace consisted of 123 rooms and 23 kivas.) This area was designated a national monument in 2000 by President Bill Clinton, partially because of the work done here. A number of rooms in this pueblo were excavated between 1983 and 1993. By then, most of the outer walls had crumbled since it was built on an open site with little protection from weather. What was excavated was then backfilled to protect

> With an emphasis on conservation, protection and restoration, the National Landscape Conservation System and Canyons of the Ancients National Monument represent a new era of management for the BLM. After 130 years of exploration and research identifying tens of thousands of irreplaceable and fragile archaeological sites, we know that Canyons of the Ancients represents the best of our cultural heritage. Using an army of volunteers who contribute on the ground services and applying the principles of balanced management and science-based decision-making, this crown jewel preserves ancestral homes and landscapes for Native American citizens and for children and communities throughout the United States."
>
> —Secretary of the Interior Ken Salazar, 2009

standing walls and preserve the site. Today, it appears as a pile of rubble about 0.2 mile west of the parking area near the upper Sand Canyon trailhead.

However, the Sand Canyon Pueblo Project, a partnership between the BLM and Crow Canyon Archaeological Center, has created a detailed account of this ancient village and its residents. All artifacts found during the excavations at Sand Canyon Pueblo are curated at the BLM Canyons of the Ancients Visitor Center and Museum in Dolores, Colorado (formerly known as the Anasazi Heritage Center).

Start your trip to this area with a visit to the center to discover the different opportunities to explore, to see what an ancient village actually resembled, and to learn about safely traveling across this beautifully rugged landscape.

CULTURAL CHRONOLOGY FOR SOUTHWEST COLORADO		
DATES	**PERIODS**	**DISTINCTIVE CHARACTERISTICS**
AD 776 to present	Euro-American	Homesteads dating from as early as the 1880s, camps, rock art and inscriptions, water control features, animal pens, mining claim markers, and roads.
Undetermined date to present	Ute	A mobile lifestyle based on seasonal rounds of hunting and gathering. Later, there were farms in McElmo Canyon. Early sites were represented by wickiups, rock art, and brown-ware pottery.
AD 1300 to present	Navajo	Seasonal use of the area for livestock grazing and resource gathering; hogans, sweat lodges, and distinctive pottery.
AD 1150 to AD 1300	Pueblo III	Large pueblos and a shift in settlement from mesa tops to canyon rims in some areas, with a dispersed pattern in others; high kiva-to-room ratios, cliff dwellings, and towers; corrugated gray and elaborate black-and-white (B/W) pottery; red or orange pottery (red ware) in some areas. There was a mass migration from the area by AD 1300.
AD 900 to AD 1150	Pueblo II	A Chacoan influence; Great Houses, great kivas, roads, etc., in many but not all regions; strong differences between Great Houses and surrounding unit pueblos composed of a kiva and small surface masonry room block; corrugated gray and elaborate B/W pottery as well as decorated red ware.

DATES	PERIODS	DISTINCTIVE CHARACTERISTICS
AD 750 to AD 900	Pueblo I	Large villages; unit pueblos of proto-kiva plus surface room block of jacal or crude masonry; great kivas; plain and neck-banded gray pottery; low frequencies of B/W and decorated red ware.
AD 500 to AD 750	Basketmaker III	Habitation in deep pit houses, plus surface storage pits, cists, or rooms; dispersed settlement with occasional small villages and occasional great kivas; plain gray pottery; low frequencies of B/W pottery. The bow and arrow replaced the atlatl; beans were added to the diet.
AD 50 to AD 500	Basketmaker II (late)	Habitation in shallow pit houses, plus storage pits or cists; dispersed settlement with small, low-density villages in some areas; campsites were important as well; gray pottery; atlatl and dart; corn and squash, but no beans; upland dry farming in addition to floodplain farming.
1500 BC to AD 50	Basketmaker II (early)	Long-term seasonal use of caves, rock shelters, and alcoves for camping, storage, burial, and rock art; San Juan anthropomorphic-style pictographs/petroglyphs; limited activity sites in open. There were baskets, but infrequent gray pottery; atlatl and dart; corn and squash, but no beans; cultivation was primarily floodplain- or runoff-based.
7000 BC to 1500 BC	Archaic	Subsistence based on hunting and gathering of wild foods; high mobility; low population density; shelters and open sites; atlatl and dart; use of baskets, but not pottery.
8000 BC to 7000 BC	Paleo-Indian	Big-game hunting and wild food procurement; high mobility; low population density; large, unfluted lanceolate projectile points; use of baskets, but not pottery.

Source: Adapted from Lipe et al., 1999.[8]

SIGNATURE ACTIVITY: HIKING TO ANCIENT RUINS

WHY GO?

A visit to numerous 800-year-old archeological sites fascinates, intrigues, and energizes those who wander here. The Sand Canyon Trail is 6.5 miles (one way) from Sand Canyon Pueblo to the lower trailhead in McElmo Canyon. A vehicle shuttle is recommended. Or go to the lower trailhead and hike up the canyon. Besides the largely backfilled Sand Canyon Pueblo at the upper trailhead, most of the viewable archeological sites are within 2.5 miles of the lower trailhead.

SPECS

ACTIVITY TYPE: Hike to the ruins

TRAILHEAD/PUT-IN/ETC.: From upper trailhead at Sand Canyon Pueblo

DISTANCE: 6.5 miles one way

AVERAGE TIME REQUIRED: 3 to 4 hours

CONTACT/MANAGING AGENCY: Bureau of Land Management, 27501 Highway 184, Dolores, CO 81323, 970–882–5600, blm.gov/visit/anasazi-heritage-center

DIFFICULTY: Easy to moderate

SPECIAL CONSIDERATIONS: If you don't shuttle vehicles and are not up to a 13-mile round-trip hike, start at the lower trailhead, as most of the major ruins are within 2.5 miles of the McElmo trailhead parking area. That still leaves you with a 5-mile hike in the desert. Take water!

GETTING THERE

SHORT DESCRIPTION—TO REACH THE MCELMO CANYON (LOWER) TRAILHEAD: From the intersection of Highway 491 and Highway 160 in Cortez, head south on Highway 491. In 2.5 miles, turn right (west) on County Road G at the signs for the airport and Hovenweep National Monument. Go 12 miles on this paved road. Trailhead parking is an unimproved slickrock surface on the north (right) side of the road. No water, toilet, phone, or other services are available.

TO REACH THE SAND CANYON (UPPER) TRAILHEAD: From the intersection of Highway 491 and Highway 160 in Cortez, drive north for 10.5 miles on Highway 491, then turn left (west) on Montezuma County (MC) Road P. This road eventually winds to P.5 road. In 4.5 miles, turn left at 18 Road. In 0.5 mile, you're back on P Road, which will turn right (west). Go another 1.5 miles to 17 Road. Turn left as the road becomes N Road. You'll lose the pavement here, but it's a well-maintained dirt road. Continue for 2 miles to the trailhead, marked with a small "Canyons of the Ancients" sign on the left-hand side of the road.

GPS COORDINATES—MCELMO CANYON (LOWER) TRAILHEAD: 37°20'29.30"N, 108°49'03.80"W; **SAND CANYON (UPPER) TRAILHEAD:** 37°23'58.60"N, 108°46'30.69"W

OVERVIEW

With 420 rooms, 100 kivas, and 14 towers, the Sand Canyon Pueblo was about three times the size of Cliff Palace, the largest pueblo in Mesa Verde National Park, 50 miles to the east. Information kiosks at the northern trailhead lead you about 0.2 mile from the parking area west to the original pueblo and discuss what happened here. The best standing ruins, however, remain along the lower stretch of this hike, so backtrack to the parking area and main trailhead, and head south.

Despite the lack of architectural "awe," the upper reach of the trail is charming in its own right. You are hiking through the Great Sage Plain, where deep soils hold winter moisture and have been used for dryland farming since the times of the Ancestral Puebloans.

From the trailhead, hike about 0.1 mile before dropping into a side draw of Sand Canyon. Follow this side draw for another two miles before it drops into the main gorge. By the time you reach the bottom of the canyon, you'll have descended about 700 feet, down 30 switchbacks.

At 2.9 miles, you'll reach the first of the major ruins, called "House with Standing Curved Wall." You can see a 38-foot-long curved wall under a massive sandstone overhang, with a couple windows and other supporting walls nearby.

Not far from "House with Standing Curved Wall" is "Sunny Alcove." In 1965, researchers found corncobs, pottery sherds, and fragments of grinding stones. On the inside of these remarkably sophisticated double-layered stone walls are well-preserved wall niches—little built-in shelves.

Today, many Native Americans consider this place their ancestral homeland. They don't consider this area abandoned. Rather, it's a living part of culture. Modern tribal people maintain close ties to the spirits of their ancestors who are buried on this landscape. Sites are often visited, and blessings are made on a regular basis.

As you continue down the canyon on this well-marked trail, you'll find at least six other ruins. Some, like Double Cliff House, were built in two ledges of an alcove. Others, like the Saddlehorn Pueblo, about a mile from the lower trailhead, have rooms in the alcove and structures on a pinnacle high above the alcove.

At 5.9 miles, you can see the McElmo Canyon Road and verdant farms adjacent to the lower trailhead. Many more ruins are protected on private property in this area.

At 6.2 miles, a spur trail leads to Castle Rock Pueblo, the last archeological site on the trail. It was built and occupied from around AD 1250 to the 1280s. In another 0.3 mile, you'll reach the lower trailhead, with the spirit of the Ancient Ones smiling upon you.

CHAPTER 11
HOVENWEEP NATIONAL MONUMENT

SIZE—784 acres
YEAR ESTABLISHED—1923, by President Warren Harding, to protect it from "cattlemen, ranchmen, rural picnickers and professional collectors"
MANAGING AGENCY—National Park Service, Hovenweep National Monument
DOG-FRIENDLY?—Pets are allowed on trails and in the campground. They are not permitted in the visitor center. Pets must be on a 6-foot leash at all times.
FEES AND PERMITS—There is no entrance fee. There is a campground fee of $15 year-round; $7 for holders of valid federal land passes such as the senior pass or access pass.
NEAREST CITIES—Cortez, CO; Blanding and Bluff, UT
NEARBY PUBLIC PROPERTY—Anasazi Heritage Center, Yucca House National Monument, Canyons of the Ancients, Manti–La Sal National Forest, Natural Bridges National Monument, Mesa Verde National Park, San Juan National Forest
SPECIAL CONSIDERATIONS—Hovenweep can experience large temperature fluctuations, sometimes more than 40 degrees in a single day. Be prepared!

OVERVIEW

Food. Water. Shelter. Space. All in an arrangement suitable for survival. That's what the ancient Puebloans were seeking when they built their towers at what is now known as Hovenweep National Monument.

Hovenweep is a Ute/Paiute word for "deserted valley." It straddles the Utah-Colorado border between Blanding, Utah, and Cortez, Colorado.

In the waning days of a remarkable civilization, skilled masons toiled for thousands of hours on the construction of impressive towers—still partially standing despite weathering, erosion, and vandalism more than 700 years later.

These towers, some as tall as four stories high, were set atop canyon outcroppings and canyon heads overlooking the few meager water sources remaining in this drought-stricken, high-altitude desert.

While some structures were built for housing and food storage, many were built for celestial and religious ceremonies. Although their actual

A sentry keeps watch over the canyons of Hovenweep.

functions remain a mystery, it appears all of them were designed for protection and defense of water.

Hovenweep structures, of all shapes and sizes, overlook canyons that were "essentially natural urban drainage systems," says Robert Traylor, an archeologist and retired attorney who spent five years in the 1970s uncovering artifacts for the National Park Service between Mesa Verde and here.

Distant mountains surround Hovenweep: 9,827-foot Sleeping Ute Mountain is directly to the east, with Mesa Verde just behind that; the 14,000-foot San Juan Mountains loom to the east and northeast in Colorado; the La Sals and the Abajos lie to the north and northwest in Utah; and the Chuska Mountains, including the Lukachukai and Carrizo Mountains, can be seen to the south. None of these mountains, however, drain onto this plateau. It's high, and it's dry.

"Questions show the mind's range, and answers its subtlety."

—Joseph Joubert, French moralist and essayist, 1938

Around 1200 to 1275, the entire Colorado Plateau experienced a tremendous drought. This urban drainage system was evaporating, and most of the people who once lived here migrated away. Those few stout beings who remained clung to the rare tiny natural springs of water that hadn't completely dried up.

Perhaps the top tower was used for defense and/or for celestial observations. Was the lower space for living?

Protecting the water source was literally a matter of life or death. Drastic measures of survival were needed against anyone who would dare try to take their water. The tops of these castles could be seen from the tops of other castles in the area. And their expert masons built thick walls.

Protection? Communication? Celestial viewing? Religious undertaking? Questions only partially answered.

The area was designated a national monument in 1923 by President Warren Harding. That was two decades after a report in 1903 by surveyor T. Mitchell Pruden, who wrote, "Few of the mounds have escaped the hands of the destroyer. Cattlemen, ranchmen, rural picnickers and professional collectors have turned the ground well over and have taken

If you want to know more about the Ancient Ones, or see some of the artifacts found in this area, go to the Canyons of the Ancients Visitor Center and Museum, also known as the Anasazi Heritage Center. Operated by the BLM, it's located outside Dolores, 11 miles north of Cortez, Colorado. An excellent museum, it focuses on Ancestral Puebloan, Native American, and historic cultures in the Four Corners region. There are also two 12th-century archeological sites just outside the museum doors. Its research collection of more than three million artifacts and records is impressive, and its research library of archeology and anthropology resources is excellent.

out much pottery, breaking more, and strewing the ground with many crumbling bones."

Little actual archeological excavation was done here until the 1970s. Many of the remaining artifacts that Traylor and his cohorts uncovered are now housed in the Anasazi Heritage Center and Museum in Dolores, Colorado, 43 miles east of here.

While other native tribes were hunters and gatherers, these ancient Puebloans resided in permanent communities. They grew maize (corn), beans, and squash on terraced fields, formed catch basins to hold water, built check dams to retain soil that would otherwise wash away, and diverted water to edible wild plants that grew in these drainages.

Archeologists believe there may have been as many as 20,000 people who lived and farmed in the Montezuma County, Colorado, area (about 2,000 square miles). It's estimated that each person required about 1 acre of land to harvest up to 40 bushels of corn per year. That's a lot of corn.

There were probably never more than 2,500 people who called Hovenweep home. Besides maize, they raised beans and squash, hunted deer and rabbits, and gathered wild berries and piñon nuts. Yet when the drought persisted, most of these Ancient Ones were forced to move—or starve. Some people migrated south and east to the Rio Grande Valley in New Mexico. Others moved south and west to the Little Colorado River Basin in Arizona. The Hopi of Arizona and the Puebloans of the Rio Grande Valley both claim these Ancient Ones as their ancestors.

The national monument protects six prehistoric villages built between AD 1200 and 1300. Talented masons balanced multistory towers on irregular boulders perched on canyon rims that have survived here for more than 700 years.

Similarities in pottery, masonry, and architecture indicate that these people were associated with, if not related to, groups from Mesa Verde and other nearby sites.

The six major Hovenweep site groups are located within a 20-mile drive of each other. They vary greatly in size. The largest is the 400-acre Square Tower Group, located next to the ranger station on the Utah side of the monument. Cajon Ruins also is located in Utah. The Holly Ruins, Hackberry Canyon, Cutthroat Castle, and Goodman Point ruins are located on the Colorado side of the monument.

A trail system leads visitors to all of the sites, which are open to the public, although their remote locations may be difficult to reach. The easiest is the Square Tower group, adjacent to the visitor center and campground. It features an interpretive trail. It's a great place to stare and ponder what life was like 800 years ago as you enjoy an incredible sunset over an intriguing land.

SIGNATURE ACTIVITY: HIKE TO CUTTHROAT CASTLE

WHY GO?

This short trail leads to the mighty ancestral ruins of Cutthroat Castle and a glimpse of Puebloan life in the arid southwest 800 years ago. You'll find tall towers overlooking a natural urban drainage system, built by skilled masons who spent thousands of hours constructing them.

SPECS

ACTIVITY TYPE: Hiking
TRAILHEAD/PUT-IN/ETC.: Cutthroat Castle parking area
DISTANCE/LENGTH: 1.4 miles round-trip
AVERAGE TIME REQUIRED: 1 hour
CONTACT/MANAGING AGENCY: National Park Service, Hovenweep National Monument
DIFFICULTY: Easy
SPECIAL CONSIDERATIONS: This is sacred ground to Native Americans, and it is their ancestral home. All cultural resources, structures, and artifacts are protected by federal law—and by the spirits of the Ancient Ones. Please, take only pictures. Leave only footprints. Entering structures or some canyon interiors is not permitted.

GETTING THERE

SHORT DESCRIPTION: From Cortez: Drive north on Highway 491 for 19 miles to Pleasant View. Turn left (west) on Montezuma County (MC) Road BB and continue for 6 miles to MC Road 10. Turn left (south) and continue on MC Road 10 for 11.3 miles to the Cutthroat Castle/Painted Hand turnoff, Road #4531. Turn left (southeast) on this rough dirt road and continue 3.1 miles to the Cutthroat Castle upper trailhead. You will pass two pull-ins for the

Some structures were built for religious ceremonies or celestial observation. All of them, however, appear designed for protection and defense of the most precious commodity in the arid Southwest—water!

Painted Hand Pueblo. (Visit it on the way out!) Most SUVs can make it to the upper Cutthroat trailhead. Hard-core four-wheel-drivers could drive to the lower trailhead, but then you wouldn't get much of a hike!

GPS COORDINATES: 28°26′38.04″N, 108°58′40.79″W

OVERVIEW

By the time you arrive at this trailhead, you'll want to get out of the vehicle and hike around. It's only 35 miles from Cortez, but it seems longer because of the last 3.1 miles of rugged road to get here.

Immediately this trail drops through some large cuts of easily navigable sandstone rock that kids of all ages will enjoy. The trail then traverses through piñon and juniper woodlands, intermixed with sagebrush and Mormon tea (*Ephedra nevadensis*). That's the shrub consisting of erect, segmented green twigs that age to a dull, cracked gray-green. In the springtime, it will produce yellow pods. Ancestral Puebloans drank a tea brewed from this plant to fight colds, kidney disorders, and other medical issues, as did early Mormon explorers who rediscovered this area in the 1800s.

The trail is easy to follow, and soon you'll travel through an area of black-crusted cryptogamic soil. As a living ground cover, these biological soil crusts are communities of living organisms consisting of fungi, lichens, cyanobacteria, bryophytes, and algae. Cryptogam is the foundation of high desert plant life.

About 0.6 mile into the trip, you'll find a really cool rock ledge the kids can hide under as they pretend to walk the paths of the Ancient Ones. You'll also get your first glimpse of the Cutthroat Castle complex in front of you and to your left.

Imagine ancient hunter-gatherers, initially mobile, taking temporary shelter beneath canyon overhangs and in shallow alcoves as they searched for food. They began cultivating corn, and eventually beans and squash, and then built more-permanent structures closer to their crops in valleys and on mesa tops.

Then, they vanished. Poof. Just like that.

The trail ends just below the largest structure at 5,794 feet above sea level. Check it out! Why did they come here? Why did they build such large structures? Why did they leave?

Archeologists know a lot, but mysteries still remain.

CHAPTER 12
AZTEC RUINS NATIONAL MONUMENT

SIZE—318 acres

YEAR ESTABLISHED—January 24, 1923, by President Warren G. Harding to prevent extensive looting of invaluable antiquities by greedy Anglo-Americans. It was listed on the National Register of Historic Places on October 15, 1966. It was declared a World Heritage Site in 1987.

MANAGING AGENCY—National Park Service, Aztec, NM

DOG-FRIENDLY?—Dogs are allowed in the picnic area adjacent to the monument. Dogs are not allowed in the visitor center or on the walk through the archeological site.

FEES AND PERMITS—This is a fee-free park!

NEAREST CITIES—Aztec, Farmington, and Bloomfield, NM; Pagosa Springs and Durango, CO

NEARBY PUBLIC PROPERTY—Chaco Culture National Historical Park, Mesa Verde National Park, Yucca House National Monument, Bistí De-Na-Zin Wilderness, Angel Peak Scenic Area, Salmon Ruins, San Juan National Forest, Chimney Rock Archaeological Area, Navajo Lake State Park

SPECIAL CONSIDERATIONS—Be careful. There's cell service here! That limits your chances of looking at or seeing anything!

OVERVIEW

Looking and seeing are often quite different. While some people saw only a pile of weeds, archeologists at Aztec Ruins National Monument found ancient pottery by looking closely in those weeds for potsherds (pronounced pot-SHARD)—small pieces of broken pottery. It may be in the weeds or on a hill of rock that they'll discover a piece of apparent rubble with black decorations on a stark white background—a sherd distinct in color, shape, design, and finish. Then they can see how it fits with other pieces with similar markings in a timeline associated with the Aztec Ruins Great House culture that thrived here from AD 1050 to 1300.

This once massive ruin featured more than 500 rooms, including a Great Kiva, numerous other ceremonial buildings, large public buildings, smaller structures, and tons and tons of earth-moving work. While some archeologists had their noses to the ground, looking through weeds and rocks for potsherds, others looked at the preserved wood that remains embedded in the walls of these ruins by people who lived here 1,000 years ago. The wood from ponderosa pine, chopped and dragged more than 40 miles from the San Juan Mountains to the north, was used in the construction of this planned community that rivaled Chaco Canyon, 55 miles due south (see chapter 15, "Chaco Culture National Historical Park").

Aztec rivaled Chaco Canyon in size and population.

Most of us learned in elementary school that counting the number of rings on a tree trunk tells the tree's age. Dendrochronology takes us to graduate school: It's a method of scientific dating based on tree-ring growth patterns. Where I just look at the number of tree rings as years, they see "annual historical ecological information." Whew. Dendrochronologists can see dry years, wet years, colder seasons, forest fires, insect outbreaks, nutrient availability—all from a tree core sample about the size of a pencil.

Because of its highly preserved wood, the Park Service believes "Aztec Ruins has more original wood than any other site in the Southwest."

Tree samples showed archeologists that Aztec Ruins was built in two phases—one around AD 1111 (even though people had inhabited the area since at least 1050), and the next around 1118. While those were the two largest building phases here, those same tree samples showed the Great Kiva wasn't completed until 1130. Tree samples also showed that the ancient Puebloans who lived here experienced two really serious droughts: One drought began the year the Great Kiva was completed in 1130 and lasted 50 to 60 years; the second major drought began around 1276 and persisted at least 24 years. That may have finally driven people away. Even

AZTECS NEVER LIVED HERE

Early Spanish explorers traveling north from Mexico called every ancient site they ever discovered "Aztec." Anglo-American settlers continued using the term in the 1800s. Wrong! Ancestral Puebloans lived in and built this ancient city. Their descendants now populate areas throughout the Southwest. The Aztecs were a Mesoamerican culture that flourished in central Mexico from 1300 to 1521. This site predates the Aztec culture by 300 years.

though the Animas River flows through here, it may have dried up, and without water, you're done on the Colorado Plateau. Your crops fail, wild game dies out, and other natural resources are depleted rapidly—like wood for fire and building. People get grouchy because they're hungry and thirsty, and erosion increases the dirt blowing in their eyes and ears and noses. That could drive anyone crazy—or at least away!

Dendrochronologists are pretty sharp. Those archeologists looking for sherds are pretty sharp too. They can describe the style of pottery vessels found here and discuss how that pottery reflected changing cultural influences. Aztec's first inhabitants made or traded for pottery similar to that found at Chaco Canyon. Items found in later deposits were made throughout the San Juan River basin after 1200.

Then there are the geologists—the folks who study rocks. In 1859, geologist Dr. John Newberry was the first apparent Anglo visitor to Aztec. He found the West Ruin here fairly well preserved. At one time, hundreds of rooms centered on an open plaza, including the Great Kiva, a round, subterranean structure with a diameter of 48 feet used for community ceremonies. Newberry discovered walls 25 feet

> The illiterate of the 21st century will not be those who cannot read and write, but those who cannot learn, unlearn and relearn.
>
> —Alvin Toffler

high in places and many rooms undisturbed. Good thing he recorded all he found. Anthropologist Lewis Morgan investigated the site in 1878 and estimated that in the 14 years since Newberry visited Aztec Ruins, settlers had carted off a quarter of the pueblo's stones for their own building material. A few years later, a local teacher and his students discovered rooms that had been untouched for centuries, including one room used for human burials. Most of it soon vanished. It wasn't until 1889, when the area passed into private ownership, that it was somewhat safe from looting. Finally, in

The Great Kiva at Aztec was restored in 1934 to what University of Colorado–educated anthropologist Earl Morris thought it would have looked like.

1923, eight months prior to his death, President Warren G. Harding set it aside for protection as a national monument.

Anthropologist Earl Morris headed the first dig at Aztec Ruins in 1916 in an attempt to understand the past. He returned in 1934 to supervise the reconstruction of the Great Kiva. It has been maintained by the Park Service ever since, and it is the only fully covered example of what a Great Kiva may have looked like 1,000 years ago. Watch your head as you enter. Either those ancient Puebloans were short or they stooped a lot!

As we look over Aztec Ruins today, it's hard to imagine life 1,000 years ago, but because of the fine work of archeologists, geologists, anthropologists—and dendro-chronologists—we can see a lot more!

SIGNATURE ACTIVITY: LEARNING TO LOOK, LOOKING TO SEE

WHY GO?

Sometimes we get bored walking down the same street, sitting at the same desk, going to the same grocery store. If questioned, we may find we're totally unaware of the existence of certain objects, colors, sounds, and textures. Well, wake up, Sparky! Here's a chance to enhance your observation skills.

SPECS

ACTIVITY TYPE: Learning to look, looking to see
TRAILHEAD/PUT-IN/ETC.: Aztec Ruins Visitor Center

DISTANCE/LENGTH: A half-mile walk
AVERAGE TIME REQUIRED: A couple hours
CONTACT/MANAGING AGENCY: Your mind
DIFFICULTY: Pretty difficult
SPECIAL CONSIDERATIONS: You have to make a game of it or you'll never pay attention.

GETTING THERE

SHORT DESCRIPTION: FROM ALBUQUERQUE OR BLOOMFIELD, NEW MEXiCO, follow U.S. Highway 550 north into the city of Aztec, turn left at the "T" intersection onto Highway 516, drive 0.75 mile and turn right, crossing the Animas River onto Ruins Road. Drive 0.5 mile to the monument. **FROM DURANGO, COLORADO,** follow U.S. Highway 550 south into the City of Aztec. Highway 550 becomes 516. Follow this and turn right immediately after crossing the Animas River on Ruins Road. Follow Ruins Road 0.5 mile to the monument.
GPS COORDINATES: 36°50'12.57"N, 108°00'03.85"W

OVERVIEW

Sometimes, as we walk through our neighborhoods, or walk through life, we look only at the sidewalk because we don't want to trip. We may not see a community of ants in its cracks, even though we're looking at them. We may look up at the sky and totally miss the soaring hawk. We may walk in the woods to look closely at a lovely quaking aspen tree, but miss the wildflower we just trampled. But we can train ourselves to see, just like the archeologist trains herself to see the glint of a potsherd. It only takes three things: (1) to learn to be a careful observer, even if we do not have sight through our eyes, since "seeing" also may involve touching, listening, and smelling; (2) to be aware of our surroundings; and (3) to recognize any part of our environment as being part of a larger whole.

That's how the ancient Puebloans survived—by paying attention to their environment: food, water, shelter, and space, all in an arrangement suitable for survival. They were part of it, not outside it. They knew they needed air, water, soil, plants, and animals but understood that once something was out of balance, life would be even more difficult.

How are your observation skills? Before you enter the visitor center, step out of the car and, without peeking back, list the objects that remain in the vehicle. Where

Original thatch, wood, mud, and brick are displayed on a tour through Aztec Ruins.

Left: T-shaped doorways were typical of Chacoan architecture. They were designed for ventilation, as well as access for native people carrying wide loads on their backs. Right: Windows for light and ventilation were placed purposefully by expert masons 1,000 years ago.

is your phone? How about your sunglasses? What's on the floor in front of the passenger seat? What's that in the middle of the console? Where's the gum? Is there dust on the dashboard? Are there fingerprints on the windshield? What's in the side panel of the car door? List everything you think is there. Then open the car door and look. Did you miss anything? Don't forget your keys.

Now, go inside. Keep a mental note of what you see and discuss it among yourselves when you hit the picnic area for lunch. Did you see the black-and-white pottery piece from 1150? Did you see that man from Illinois with the weird polka-dot shorts and black socks pulled up to his knees? Did you see the map of the major Basketmaker sites from 1000 BC to AD 200 in the Four Corners area? The map also marked Basketmaker sites from AD 200 to 750, FYI. Did you hit your head on the short doorway into the kiva? Were the fires lit? Were the stairways leading into the kiva lit? What was the ceiling structure made of? Were the pillars round or square?

After you've discussed what you all saw over a picnic lunch, talk about how the ancient Puebloans would have lived. What was important to them? What were they looking for? What did they see?

Aztec Ruins, with its kivas, public buildings, and 500 rooms, was a major commercial area 1,000 years ago.

As you practice this activity, you'll understand that looking and seeing are often quite different.

(*Note:* This exercise was adapted from one with the same title in an outstanding 1983 education program called Project WILD, sponsored by the Western Association of Fish and Wildlife Agencies and the Western Regional Environmental Education Council. As John Denver wrote in the introduction, "Its goal is to develop awareness, knowledge, skills and commitment which will result in informed decisions, responsible behavior and constructive actions concerning wildlife and the environment upon which all life depends.")[9]

PART 4
CHACO CULTURE

Sunset on the cracked eggs in
Bistí De-Na-Zin Wilderness

OVERVIEW

What would it take to pick up and leave? Would you be chasing a dream, chasing a woman, running away from a bad dream, running away from a bad relationship?

If you were a boy who lived in a working-class pueblo with about five other families, and one of them had a cute little girl you were sweet on, and there were three other boys your age in the same pueblo, and she was always flirting with them, would you leave?

Would you be so mad and depressed that someone cut down the tree you used to climb in your youth, a tree you saw your grandchildren climb in years later, just to make room for another grain bin or another room for another cliff-dweller, that you just couldn't take it anymore? Would you just leave?

What would it be like to live in the Chaco culture of AD 1100?

There's a 70-year-old woman in Grand Junction, Colorado, who clung to the tree her father planted 63 years earlier, in 1956. Police had to remove her bony hands from the bark of the old tree, and she cried and cried. She was brokenhearted. That tree was sacred to her. But the developer was waiting.

Would that have been enough for a family of Ancestral Puebloans to just pick up and leave? Was their sacred tree cut down to make room for another cliff-dweller, or to burn to keep the pueblo warm for another cold winter night? Maybe.

How about an entire community? What would make them so mad, or redirected, that they would all just up and leave?

Drought? Famine? War? Religion? Bad politics? Poor resource management?

All of the above? None of the above?

"All we really know for sure is that they came, they lived here for a while, and they left," said Hillary Grabowska, then a three-year veteran park ranger at Chaco Culture National Historical Park. She grinned a shy grin, pushed her straight blond hair behind her left ear, straightened her back in her forest-green Park Service ranger uniform, and in her most park ranger-ly manner, refused to be baited into the philosophical discussion of whether people left this area for religious reasons, environmental reasons, political reasons, or something else.

There are no written records of why people built such a magnificent cultural center over a period of a couple hundred years, then just left. Also, there are no cemeteries, no gigantic trash piles from people living here for so long. Nothing. They just up and left.

Ranger Hillary, however, engaged in a little pondering of her own. "What if it was like the Beijing Olympics? A bunch of workers came here and built this wonderful city, where there would be an opening ceremony, similar to the opening of the Olympics, perhaps religious, then there were games and celebrations for people from all

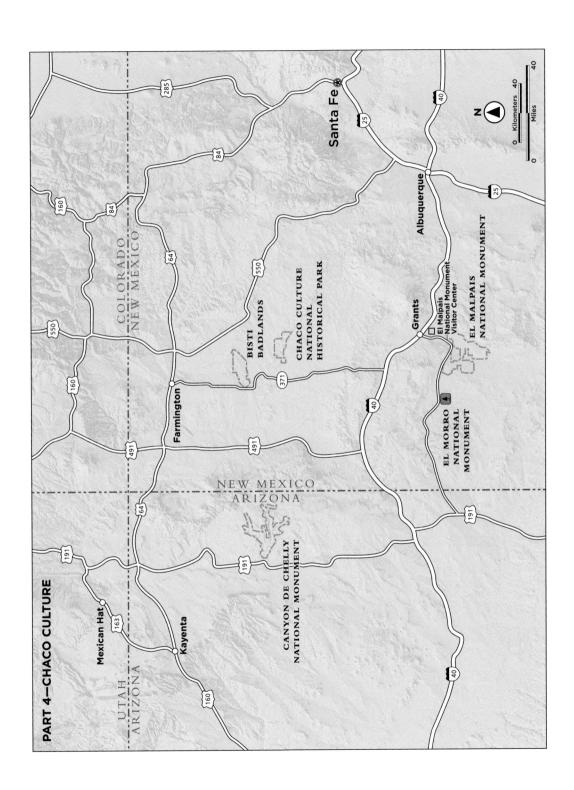

PART 4—CHACO CULTURE

While the stonework was distinctive, many researchers believe the walls may have been covered with a plaster derived from local clay soils.

regions, where cultures intermingled, traded wares, traded stories and histories. Then they left."

Huh.

Everyone's got a theory. Yet, as Hillary says, all we really know is that they came here, they lived here, and they left.

Chaco Canyon, and the history and archeology of Chacoan culture, have long fascinated us. There are hundreds of articles and books written on this place and its place in history.

Here's another one of them!

CHAPTER 13

EL MALPAIS NATIONAL MONUMENT AND NATIONAL CONSERVATION AREA

SIZE—The national monument consists of 114,000 acres; the national conservation area surrounding it consists of another 262,000 acres.

YEAR ESTABLISHED—Both were established by an act of Congress in 1987 and signed into law by President Ronald Reagan because of the nationally significant features found here.

MANAGING AGENCY—National Park Service, Malpais National Monument, manages the monument; BLM manages the national conservation area.

DOG-FRIENDLY?—Dogs are allowed on-leash; however, lava rock is sharp! It will destroy tender dog paws!

FEES AND PERMITS—This is a fee-free area!

NEAREST CITIES—Albuquerque and Gallup, NM

NEARBY PUBLIC PROPERTY—El Morro National Monument, Zuni Mountains, Bluewater Lake State Park, Cibola National Forest, Cebolla Wilderness Area, Chaco Culture National Historical Park, Pecos National Historic Park, Petroglyph National Monument, Salinas Pueblo Missions National Monument

SPECIAL CONSIDERATIONS—Wear good, sturdy boots and gloves; leave the pets at home because it's too hot and too tough on paws!

OVERVIEW

El Malpais means "the badlands," a moniker that Spanish conquistadors gave this area a few centuries ago. It accurately describes ancient lava flows that once ran as rivers of fire. Most commonly pronounced "el mal-pie-EES," the national monument and conservation area lie on the southeastern edge of the Colorado Plateau in northwest New Mexico.

Early geologists believed these massive, jagged lava flows emanated from nearby Mount Taylor, an extinct composite volcano active about 2.5 to 3.7 million years ago. Scientists from nearby Los Alamos National Laboratory, however, can now date flows using potassium-argon and carbon-14 methods, which indicate that molten lava also flowed here from 74 younger volcanoes erupting about 200,000 to 3,000 years ago.

Impressive buff-colored sandstone ridges tower over sensuous volcanic flows. These outcrops are remnants of a shallow sea that periodically covered this area from 63 to 138 million years ago. Erosions and eruptions, wind and water have continued to paint this portrait. This vast, arid expanse between the Zuni Mountains, Cebollita Mesa, and Horace Mesa is canopied by infinitely clear blue New Mexican skies punctuated with powder-puff clouds.

Collectively, Mount Taylor and the 74 other volcanic eruptions that formed basalt cones, cinder cones, and shield volcanoes are scattered in the distance. Lava found here—a'a and pahoehoe lava—is similar to that found in Hawaii. A'a, formed by fast-moving lava flows, is rough, broken, gnarled, and nasty. It will shred tender feet, hands, or paws. "Ah, ah, don't walk here!" Pahoehoe lava, (pronounced puh-HOH-ee-hoh-ee) with its ropy, coiled texture, was formed as the lava cooled on top and was pushed from a slow-moving underlying flow. It was still pliable when the flows beneath ceased.

Wind, rain, and freezing water continue to sculpt the hardened lava, while unique vegetation slowly conceals the flows. Flora and fauna are highly adapted to this specialized environment. Bonsai-type ponderosa and piñon pines may appear to be young trees because of their small size. Some, however, may be hundreds of years old but were twisted and stunted due to the harsh environment.

Evidence of prehistoric nomadic cultures dating back 12,000 years has been unearthed in the El Malpais region. Stone and bone tools from the Paleo-Indian period, 10,000 years BC, are all that remain. During the Archaic period (5500 BC to AD 400) residents appear to have "exhibit[ed] a growing dependence on agriculture," according to Park Service documents. From 400 to 1600, the people who survived in this arid landscape with about 10 inches of annual rainfall were chiefly farmers. They lived in stationary villages and established permanent architecture. A thousand years ago, ancient Puebloans built villages housing thousands of people. They have since migrated away, but remains of their homes may still be seen.

While scant few trails traverse its interior, native tribes constructed specific routes through this contorted field of solidified lava. They filled wide gaps with boulders and lava cinder to create pathways between the pueblos of Zuni and Acoma (ACK-a-ma). Nearly impossible to discern through the undulating flows of lava that look the same in all directions, the native people lined their trails with tall rock cairns to mark the way. As Spanish and Anglo-American explorers arrived in this country, they rarely followed those paths, reluctant to take horses across such jagged and sharp basaltic rock.

Similarly, today's travelers would rather drive or hike around than go through these badlands. Even the Continental Divide Trail that runs from Canada to Mexico takes a detour around El Malpais before continuing its route along the spine of North America. One small reach of this significant multinational trail, however, actually follows the old Zuni-Acoma Trail. New Mexico Highway 117 travels along the eastern side of the area. Highway 53 skirts the north and northwest. No road cuts across.

There are other trails and hikes around and through this badland for those daring few. Adventure and travel writer Nancy Harbert discussed this jagged landscape and a hike to a volcanic crater in her acclaimed book *New Mexico* in 1992: "The volcanoes that once spewed blistering hot lava still brood above the scene. The crater of one of them, Bandera Crater, can be seen at the end of a half-mile-long trail carpeted in soft cinder. Peering down 800 feet into the extinct volcano . . . all that remains are

La Ventana Natural Arch, on New Mexico Highway 117 on the eastern edge of the national monument, was formed by daily temperature swings of more than 50 degrees on the rock's surface for millions of years. Sandstone expanded in the day and cracked at night under the stress. The base and center failed first. Over time, an arc grew.

rust-colored scree walls with an occasional ponderosa pine stretching for the sun. A ghostly silence is disturbed only by a dislodged basalt pebble tumbling toward the crater's center." [10]

The lava flows of El Malpais have intrigued yet intimidated visitors for thousands of years. As the Park Service warns, "Their twisted and gnarled formations not only entice curiosity, but also demand a healthy respect from hikers and explorers."

Tenderfoots that we are, modern hikers need tough boots with good soles to trek through here. A good pair of gloves helps—just in case you stumble. One can only imagine how Native Americans carried water and wares barefoot or with handmade yucca-rope sandals through this inhospitable country. Hiking over this craggy, harsh terrain is not for inexperienced hikers. Many routes are marked by the same rock cairns that the Acoma and Zuni followed hundreds of years ago, yet they remain difficult

CAVES AND CRATERS!

An easy and interesting side trip here is a visit to the "Ice Cave" and Bandera Crater. Located on New Mexico Highway 53, the Ice Cave Road between El Morro and El Malpais, they're actually on private property. Nonetheless, since you saved so much with the two fee-free national monuments, it's worth 12 bucks to stop and see a fascinating collection of artifacts in an old-time trading post, take 70 steps down into the Ice Cave itself, and then visit Bandera Crater. (It's half price for kids.)

The trading post was built in the 1930s as a saloon and dancehall. This is where they kept their beer cold! Today, it operates as a tourist attraction, dealing in jewelry, pottery, rugs, and other contemporary Native American arts. Most of the ancient artifacts on display here were found in the adjacent lava fields and date back 800 to 1,200 years.

Located in a collapsed lava tube, temperatures in the ice cave never get above 31°F. As rainwater and snowmelt seeped into this cave, the ice floor thickened. It's about 20 feet thick now, with the deepest ice as old as 3,400 years, or so they say. That's not certain, but we do know that the green tint on the ice is caused by an Arctic algae and that in 1946, when ice removal was stopped, the ice wall was nearly 12 feet high.

Once you climb the 70 steps back out of the Ice Cave, take the half-mile hike (one way) to the Bandera Volcano overlook. This volcano exploded with a vengeance about 10,000 years ago in two stages; first, it blew so high that lava broke into cinders in midair, creating the cinder cone. Then, a massive lava flow broke out of its side and flowed nearly 23 miles. The crater is 1,400 feet wide at the top and roughly 800 feet deep. Elevation at the overlook is 8,036 feet. Elevation at the rim is 8,367 feet. Take your time. It's a 40-minute hike round-trip, maybe longer if you're not used to altitude. But it's one of the best views inside an erupted volcano in the country, and one of the most accessible.

to track. Stop at the visitor center and make sure you have the proper maps. If you have a GPS system—and *really know* how to use it—use it. (Keep in mind a magnetic compass may not be reliable because of iron deposits in the lava flows.) Then hike to one cairn and look for the next before proceeding. Remember that aboveground in El Malpais, everything looks like a pile of rocks—because it is! (No disrespect meant to the stunted yet majestic ponderosa pine!)

However, there's more than meets the surface here. In excess of 400 lava tube caves have been discovered beneath these lava flows. In fact, caving—or lava tubing—is a major recreational activity at this national monument and recreation area (see

"Signature Activity: Lava Tubing"), even in the hot summer, because lava tubes keep underground temperatures quite cool.

Most of the largest caves are closed, especially in winter, to protect hibernating bats. At least 14 bat species are found here. Most depend on these lava tubes for shelter, reproduction, or hibernation. In fact, one spot with the catchy name of Bat Cave is home to a summer colony of 40,000 Brazilian free-tailed bats. It's the only colony of its kind for hundreds of miles.

Bats in North America are really struggling right now. That's not a good thing for any of us. Bats eat millions and millions of night-flying bugs, which means they don't bug us. Many of those nocturnal insects are serious crop or forest pests, or can spread disease to humans or livestock. Bats pollinate plants, spread seeds, and play a significant role in science and medicine. Studying bats has aided with advancements in hearing, sonar, and vaccine development; bats have even—for you bloodthirsty devotees of Count Dracula—helped scientists figure out how blood coagulates.

The Ice Cave Trading Post has jewelry, pottery, and rugs as well as a cool ancient artifacts display—but no gas!

Bats are in peril from white nose syndrome (WNS), a white, fuzzy growth on the nose, ears, and wings of some affected bats. It's caused by a cold-loving fungus, *Pseudogymnoascus destructans*, that thrives in low temperatures (40°F–55°F) and high humidity—conditions common in caves and mines where bats hibernate.

So, before you trek into a cave, check with the visitor center first and make sure it's safe for the bats—and for you.

SIGNATURE ACTIVITY: LAVA TUBING

WHY GO?
You haven't lived until you've cruised through a lava tube! You can explore fascinating geology and hidden ice formations underneath lava flows at El Malpais—with a free caving permit and proper equipment, of course!

SPECS
ACTIVITY TYPE: Some would call it caving, but that somehow implies spelunking. This is simply a rough, bumpy hike through a very dark lava tube!
TRAILHEAD/PUT-IN/ETC.: Big Tubes Area leading to Big Skylight Cave, Giant Ice Cave, Sign Junction, and Four Windows Junction
DISTANCE/LENGTH: One to several miles

Lava tubing is chilly in summer or winter.

AVERAGE TIME REQUIRED: 2 to 4 hours
CONTACT/MANAGING AGENCY: El Malpais Visitor Center, 505-783-4774, nps
.gov/elma
DIFFICULTY: Strenuous and difficult, especially since it's really dark inside
these tubes!
SPECIAL CONSIDERATIONS: Although normally accessible in a passenger car,
these roads can be impassable during wet weather, even in a four-wheel-
drive vehicle.

GETTING THERE

SHORT DESCRIPTION: Take County Road 42 to the Big Tubes Road (NPS Road
#300) and travel 4.5 miles to the parking area.
GPS COORDINATES: 34°56'40.5"N, 108°6'24.8"W

OVERVIEW

About 11,000 years ago, steaming hot magma broke through the earth's crust near
what's now known as the Big Tubes Area. This liquid rock, under great pressure,
spewed into the air to form a lava fountain hundreds of feet high. Some of the lava
cooled and separated in the air, falling to the ground as cinders that accumulated and
built Bandera Crater.

Hot fluid lava flowed from the base of this loosely constructed cinder cone in a series
of flows that lasted several years. As the outer layer of lava cooled and hardened, it
insulated the fluid lava flowing within. Eventually that stopped flowing too, emptying
downhill and leaving behind a 17-mile-long lava tube system, one of the longest in
the continental United States.

At least 14 bat species are found at El Malpais. They depend on lava tubes for shelter, reproduction, and hibernation.

You can cruise through these caves—if you have good sturdy boots, a tough pair of gloves, a really good headlamp, a hard hat, and a free permit from the visitor center. Several caves in the Big Tubes Area can be explored with this permit, but you must first talk with a ranger for the latest caving information and the free caving permit. The ranger will let you know which caves are open and which are closed, either because they're hazardous, they contain delicate rock formations, or they house colonies of bats.

Don't do this alone! Group exploration is much safer. Also, dress appropriately for caves. Ambient temperatures in most caves are around 42°F (6°C) year-round. Some are colder. Cave ceilings are sharp—and may be low. The hard hat really comes in handy here! Each lava-tuber should carry three light sources and extra batteries and pay attention to the route. Remember junctions and landmarks.

If you see a bat, stop talking, keep your light pointed away, leave quietly, and report the sighting to a ranger. Finally, know your limits! If you're disoriented or tired, tell someone!

If you're prepared and heed all warnings, the Big Tubes Area will certainly have something to delight and captivate adventurous visitors of all ages.

CHAPTER 14

EL MORRO NATIONAL MONUMENT

SIZE—1,278 acres

YEAR ESTABLISHED—December 6, 1906, by President Theodore Roosevelt to prohibit further carving on the cliff; it was included in the National Register of Historic Places in 1966.

MANAGING AGENCY—National Park Service, El Morro National Monument

DOG-FRIENDLY?—Dogs allowed on designated trails, in parking lots, and in camping area on-leash only!

FEES AND PERMITS—This is a fee-free area!

NEAREST CITIES—Grants and Gallup, NM

NEARBY PUBLIC PROPERTY—El Malpais National Monument, Zuni Mountains, Bluewater Lake State Park, Cibola National Forest, Cebolla Wilderness Area, Chaco Culture National Historical Park, Pecos National Historic Park, Petroglyph National Monument, Salinas Pueblo Missions National Monument

SPECIAL CONSIDERATIONS—Hot in the summer, cold in the winter. Be prepared! Dress appropriately.

OVERVIEW

"Pasó por aquí" . . . Passed by here.

You can tell.

It seems like everyone who passed here—from at least three separate cultures—left their mark. Ancient Native Americans pecked desert bighorn sheep and bear paws, little stick men, and swirling geometric forms. Later, Spaniards and Anglo-Americans etched names and tales of adventure all over Inscription Rock, adjacent to the great yet tiny water hole that has always filled in this parched piece of high-altitude desert in northwest New Mexico. It's on the very edge of the Colorado Plateau, but no one called it that back in 1896, or 1786, or 1250.

The Spaniards named this rock "El Morro," meaning headland or cliff, usually one looming over a sea. That was in 1692, the same year as the Salem witch trials, yet people have been carving their piece of history into this rock since man first roamed the area. They came here because of the water. They found it by following a "cuesta," a long rock formation that gently slopes upward, then drops straight down, in this case some 200 feet. A fresh pool of runoff and snowmelt lies at the base of this cliff. In the shadow of El Morro, this pool was a true oasis in the desert for travelers passing this way. It was the only reliable water source for 30 miles in any direction. It was the only water between the pueblos of Acoma (ACK-a-ma) and Zuni. Etchings at water level show that the pool used to be surrounded by a grassy sandbank. Humans enlarged the pool at some point. It contains about 200,000 gallons of water now. Yet from the

El Morro is a cuesta, a rock formation that gently slopes upward and then abruptly drops—about 200 feet in this case!

In 1868, the Union Pacific Railroad ran a survey through here. While the Santa Fe Railroad rerouted travelers 25 miles to the south, "U.P.R." workers had plenty of time to stamp their own marks on this place.

beginning it contained water, the true essence of life in this harsh high desert at 7,296 feet above sea level.

There is a major prehistoric village with more than 500 rooms on top of this majestic questa. Prior to AD 1200, the people of this region were scattered throughout the valley, farming and learning new techniques in making pottery and new ways of building homes. Then, tree-ring dating shows that around 1275, they began to leave their small, scattered villages and gather into large towns such as "A'ts'ina," the dwelling on top of El Morro.

The Mesa Top Trail, a two-mile loop trail, takes modern-day visitors to the site that was excavated beginning in the late 1950s. A double line of single-story rooms surrounded the square plaza of this preplanned town. A double line of two-story rooms was formed outside the single-story rooms. A blank wall then surrounded the perimeter of the village with access via ladders. Most archeologists believe this was built for defensive purposes. The village stood intact for perhaps two generations.

Ancestral Puebloans then migrated from the village on top of the rock to the nearby pueblos of Zuni and Acoma. The first recorded foreign expedition to the area was by Spaniard Antonio de Espejo on March 11, 1583, whose journal noted that they camped at "El Estanque del Peñol," or "the pool by the Great Rock." They refrained from inscribing the rock, but in 1598 the self-referential Don Juan de Oñate, with almost 1,000 fellow settlers and 7,000 head of livestock, plodded north and planted the first Spanish settlement in what is now the southwestern United States, near present-day Santa Fe. That same year, he visited El Morro, which he called "Agua de la Peña," Water of the Rock.

Oñate led another expedition to the Gulf of California, where he declared he had discovered the South Sea. On the return trip, his expedition camped near the rock on April 15, 1605, fifteen years before the Pilgrims landed at Plymouth Rock. Oñate or someone in his party inscribed the following on the rock: "Pasó por aq(u)í el adelantado don Juan de Oñate del descubrimiento del Mar del Sur el 16 de abril de 1605." (Here passed by the Governor-General Don Juan de Oñate, from the discovery of the South Sea, the 16th of April, 1605.)

"Pasó por aquí." Passed by here. That phrase was inscribed into this rock face in a number of places at different times over the next three centuries. It's become the catchphrase of El Morro and has found its way into the title of numerous articles and books, including *Pasó por Aquí*, by Eugene Manlove Rhodes (see "Signature Activity: Read *Pasó por Aquí* by Eugene Manlove Rhodes). The book later became a motion picture titled *Four Faces West* in 1948, starring Joel McCrea as hero Ross McEwen.

In 1846, the forces of America's Manifest Destiny (see chapter 33, "Pipe Spring National Monument") marched west. The war with Mexico began and General

At 7,296 feet in elevation, El Morro can be chilly in the winter, but the sunsets are always grand!

El Morro—the great rock with its hidden waterhole!

Stephen Watts Kearny led his U.S. Army down the Santa Fe Trail. Two years later, the war was over. Much of present-day Texas, New Mexico, California, Arizona, Utah, and parts of Colorado and Wyoming were purchased by the United States as part of the Treaty of Guadalupe Hidalgo, which ended the Mexican-American War in 1848. It was managed by the General Land Office until the creation of the Bureau of Land Management in 1946.

Wasting little time consolidating its holdings, the U.S. Army surveyed the area, and Lieutenants J. H. Simpson and R. H. Kern inscribed their names on this rock on September 17, 1849.

A tremendous number of inscriptions that included a "U.P.R." moniker were carved in 1868, the year the Union Pacific Railroad sent a survey party past El Morro. The railroad never came through here, but that didn't stop the survey crew from etching their mark on the great stone travelers' register.

By 1906, El Morro was dedicated as a national monument and federal law made it a crime for people to inscribe anything more on the rock face. Park employees attempted to delineate some of the original markings with charcoal, but that practice was soon discontinued as well.

Eventually, time, wind, and water will erode these etchings of man, but as a historical and cultural dateline, El Morro was unique. It was an outdoor history book, and it remains so today.

SIGNATURE ACTIVITY: READ *PASÓ POR AQUÍ* BY EUGENE MANLOVE RHODES

WHY?

Written in 1925, this book, one of the first true "American Westerns," was titled for inscriptions at El Morro. It's a quick, easy read and a great primer for visiting this very edge of the Colorado Plateau where many cultures have passed, including Native Americans, Spanish conquistadors, and real American cowboys!

ACTIVITY TYPE: Reading
TRAILHEAD/PUT-IN/ETC.: In your mind!
DISTANCE/LENGTH: Mind expanding, or just pure escapism?
AVERAGE TIME REQUIRED: No one is timing you! Read at your own pace!
CONTACT/MANAGING AGENCY: Your brain
DIFFICULTY: You can do it! Come on, you can do it! We can all do it!
SPECIAL CONSIDERATIONS: Like a 14,000-foot peak, if you've never bagged a "Western," it can be intimidating! This is a nice easy one to get your juices flowing.

GETTING THERE

SHORT DESCRIPTION: It's about people who have passed by here.
GPS COORDINATES: The GPS coordinates to the Inscription Trail leading to the water and Inscription Wall are 35°02'22.6"N, 108°20'42.4"W. Who knows what the GPS coordinates of your mind are. I don't even know mine!

OVERVIEW

Wait a minute . . . a Western with no fistfight in the saloon or shoot-out on Main Street? This is a Western with a twist, and it was the first book on the syllabus for an upper-division English literature course I took at the University of Colorado back in the early 1970s. The course, titled "Cowboys, Spies and Spacemen" (this was Boulder, after all), was one of the best literature courses I've ever taken. It was all about uniquely American literature, and that begins with the Great American Western.

Back in 1925, there was no better writer of the American Western than Eugene Manlove Rhodes, who took the title for his book from Juan de Oñate's carving in the living rock of El Morro. Rhodes created his own memorial to the "decent people of (his) world who had passed this way without fanfare."

> "Your precious New Mexico! Sand!" she said. "Sand, snakes, scorpions; wind, dust, glare and heat; lonely, desolate, and forlorn!"
>
> —Jay Hollister, heroine of *Pasó por Aquí* by Eugene Manlove Rhodes, 1925

Picture a scene of a cowboy fleeing from a posse on a brindle steer (think Alex Karras in the Mel Brooks classic, *Blazing Saddles*.) Rhodes himself rode a steer for seven miles, fleeing from an irate sheriff, until his bovine mount "sulled" on him. His hero in the book *Pasó por Aquí* also rides a steer to escape from the law at one point. Two other major themes in the book deal with diphtheria, one of the most feared diseases in the isolated West, and cross-cultural ties between Hispanic and Anglo cultures. That cultural theme remains significant today.

Rhodes's classic Western is 125 pages long. You can read it while the rest of your party treks up to the A'ts'ina dwelling on top of El Morro. Then, as you're driving over to El Malpais and Chaco Canyon, it's their turn to read!

CHAPTER 15
CHACO CULTURE NATIONAL HISTORICAL PARK

SIZE—33,977 acres

YEAR ESTABLISHED—March 11, 1907, by President Theodore Roosevelt to protect it from theft, looting, and development in order to preserve one of the most important pre-Columbian cultural and historical areas in the United States. It was listed on the National Register of Historic Places in 1966; it became a U.S. National Historical Park in 1980; it was named a UNESCO World Heritage Site in 1987.

MANAGING AGENCY—National Park Service, Chaco Culture National Historical Park, Nageezi, NM

DOG-FRIENDLY?—Pets on a 6-foot leash are allowed on trails and in Gallo Campground. They are not allowed near any of the archeological sites.

FEES AND PERMITS—Vehicle entrance fee: $25 for 7 days; motorcycle entrance fee: $20 for 7 days; individual entrance fee: $15 for 7 days; all interagency passes also accepted. Gallo Campground costs $15 per night per campsite. Campers with interagency senior or access passes pay $7.50 per night per campsite. Reservations for campsites must be made at least three days in advance. To reserve a campsite, visit recreation.gov or call 1–877–444–6777.

NEAREST CITIES—Cuba, Nageezi, Farmington, and Albuquerque, NM

NEARBY PUBLIC PROPERTY—Bistí De-Na-Zin Wilderness, El Malpais National Monument, El Morro National Monument

SPECIAL CONSIDERATIONS—Bubonic plague and hantavirus exist in northern New Mexico, and rodents are the most common carriers. Keep yourself and your pets away from their burrows and nests as a reasonable precaution. Do not feed wildlife.

OVERVIEW

The first archeological evidence of human occupation in Chaco Canyon showed that hunter-gatherers resided here as far back as 900 BC, although occupation likely began much earlier. By AD 200, pithouses, partially subterranean residences of one or two rooms, began appearing throughout the canyon. By AD 500, larger pithouse villages arose. Two hundred years later, small house sites were visible from Casa Rinconada. Then, from 850 to 1250 Chaco became a major center of commerce and culture—unlike anything ever seen before or since . . . at least in this country.

Generations of astronomical observations and centuries of skillfully coordinated construction show Chacoan buildings aligned to capture the solar and lunar cycles. These ingenious people quarried sandstone blocks and hauled timber great distances to construct 15 major complexes that remained the largest buildings ever built in North America until the 19th century. Their roads connected to other Chacoan

The trail to Pueblo Alto travels along the rim for a bird's eye view of Pueblo Bonito, with views of Chaco Canyon in the distance.

establishments throughout the 7,500-square-mile San Juan Basin. Religion, art, architecture, and commerce flourished.

Around AD 1150, the building slowed, then stopped altogether. By around AD 1250, everyone was gone.

Deforestation and intense agriculture likely led to accelerated erosion, arroyo cutting, and lowering of the water table. Pestilence and natural catastrophes may have occurred, but there's no clear evidence of that. Certainly, the entire San Juan Basin was in the grip of a severe drought that research dates between AD 1130 and 1190. People can't live without water.

After so many centuries, perhaps the social fabric had steadily eroded and drought—with its associated debilitating hunger—exacerbated the exodus. In their 1981 book *Chaco Canyon—Archaeology and Archaeologists*, Robert and Florence Lister note that "continuous irrigation over many centuries, without any form of soil enrichment, caused the land to choke with alkali. Also, as timber resources were depleted and the forest withdrew, so did many kinds of plant and animal life basic to the economy of

THE WETHERILL BROTHERS: SEARCHING FOR THE ANCIENT ONES

Richard Wetherill, a rancher from the Mancos Valley in Colorado, was first credited for selecting the term "Ancient Anasazi," which roughly translated from Navajo means "enemy ancestors." It's a term no longer in use for this ancient culture, now referred to as Ancestral Puebloans. He also coined the term "Basketmaker," referring to people even older than the "Anasazi" who made intricate, tightly woven baskets to carry water instead of using clay pots.

Richard Wetherill and his brother-in-law Charlie Mason are credited with discovering the "Cliff Palace" in Mesa Verde while searching for lost cattle in the winter of 1888. Richard and his brother John discovered Keet-Seel in 1895. John and Navajo guide Clatsozen Benully discovered Betatakin in 1909, the year President Taft used the Antiquities Act to protect the area as Navajo National Monument. (See chapter 25, "Navajo National Monument.") That's the same year John Wetherill raced his horse beneath Rainbow Bridge to claim the first white man's discovery of one of the largest arches in the world. (See chapter 27, "Rainbow Bridge National Monument.")

For the next decade, the Wetherill brothers offered tours of ancient Native American sites. Some condemned them as vandals and looters as they uncovered many significant cultural sites across the Colorado Plateau. Deep in a box canyon of Bears Ears National Monument, for example, Richard uncovered one of the most important finds in the archeology of the Southwest—he dug up 98 skeletons from a previously unknown Basketmaker society that predated Ancestral Puebloans by hundreds of years.

Richard first visited Chaco in the autumn of 1895 as a guide for a roving Kansas family named Palmer and their 18-year-old daughter, Marietta. They explored Chaco for a month before winter set in. Chaco ruins surpassed anything Wetherill had ever seen. They were much larger and more complex than the cliff dwellings with which he was familiar.

the people. Labor forces that had been involved in raising and distributing food were no longer needed, the goods and products upon which the merchants depended were in short supply, and upkeep of the remaining irrigation and communication means were futile. Perhaps those who encouraged adoption of foreign ways became targets for the conservatives who found in their non-conformity to tradition a cause for the present scourge upon the land. Then social malaise and lack of confidence in those in authority, added to the insoluble problem of subsisting in such a parched area, forced the disintegration of the group."[11]

Richard and his new wife, Marietta, eventually ran a trading post at Chaco Canyon from 1898 until Richard was murdered in 1910. The Wetherills had filed a homestead claim on Chaco Canyon with the encouragement of native tribes, in hopes of protecting it until it could be declared a national park. They gave up their claim when President Theodore Roosevelt declared Chaco Canyon a national monument in 1907.

Differing accounts call Wetherill's death "murder in cold blood." A Navajo Indian debtor named Chiishchilí Biye' was convicted and sentenced to prison for the murder. Did he do it to keep from paying his debt, or was he manipulated by a local Indian agent who wanted to dam the canyon for water, fence both ends for grazing, and build an Indian school (forced "Americanizing")?

Marietta continued operating the trading post after Richard's murder, the canyon remained an unflooded national monument, and Marietta was as familiar as any Anglo with the Navajo way of life at the turn of the 20th century. She became close friends with one Navajo singer, who adopted her into his clan and gave her a close-up view of Navajo medicine and religion. In 1992 New Mexican writer Kathryn Gabriel published *Marietta Wetherill: Life with the Navajos in Chaco Canyon*,[14] which is "much more readable than a dry recitation of historical facts," according to the *Albuquerque Journal*. It discusses Marietta's life with the Navajo during those years. Marietta and Richard are buried along with several Navajo in the small cemetery behind a wooden fence about 100 yards west of Pueblo Bonito.

While the Wetherill discoveries were significant for understanding the lives of ancestral people, they launched a tradition of pot hunting by white settlers that, by the turn of the century, was out of control. That's why President Roosevelt signed the Antiquities Act in 1906.

Granted, the "cause for the present scourge upon the land" was drought and lack of resources, but that doesn't mean politics can't make it worse.

Chaco Canyon lies in the San Juan Basin, which includes much of northwestern New Mexico and a portion of southwestern Colorado. The San Juan River and its tributaries carry runoff from the mountains bordering north, east, and west of the basin to the Colorado River at what is now Lake Powell. Chaco Wash is one of the tributaries to the San Juan, a 150-mile-long intermittent stream known for its violent flash floods. It drains the southern portion of the San Juan Basin from the Chaco Plateau.

When these ancient people left their impressive masonry houses and most of their possessions in Chaco, some traveled a little west, to the northern slopes of Chacra Mesa, and the flanks of Mount Taylor to the southeast. Others continued to the Rio Grande Valley. More headed south to Laguna, Zuni, and beyond.

But where did they come from originally?

Southwestern archeologist Steven Lekson believes these Chacoans, along with the Cahokia people of the Mississippi Valley, had clear connections to Mesoamerica—middle America—an area comprising modern-day Costa Rica, Nicaragua, El Salvador, Belize, Honduras, Guatemala, and Mexico.[12]

Some archeologists concur that there were trade routes, sure, but Chacoans were unique and separate and they were the big dogs on the block.

Not so, insists Lekson. Cahokia existed at roughly the same time as Chaco—AD 900–1250. It was situated on the Mississippi River across from modern St. Louis and was much larger than Chaco. It looked very much like a Mesoamerican city built with stone masonry, although fewer Mesoamerican artifacts were found at Cahokia. By contrast, Chaco displayed stone masonry and had lots of Mesoamerican artifacts but did not look like a Mesoamerican town.

Lekson notes Cahokia was the largest native city north of Mexico, and far larger than most European cities of its time. "Chaco, a starter-kit kingdom on the edge of empire needed anything it could use to legitimate and bolster its fledgling nobility—always precarious because of the harsh Chacoan environment. With turquoise and Mesoamerican prestige goods, Chaco nobles could 'buy' legitimacy."

Chaco? A starter-kit kingdom? Not the center of all the action? Some archeologists bristle at Lekson's heretical words. Yet he firmly believes these Mesoamerican connections existed. Chaco did have access to turquoise deposits about 120 miles away in the Cerrillos Hills near present-day Santa Fe. Indeed, archeologists have found more than 200,000 turquoise pieces at Chaco. However, through "isotope analyses" scientists have found 22 different areas where Chaco residents acquired gems. (Just so you know, isotopes are atoms of the same element with different numbers of neutrons.) These gems were obtained through long-distance trade networks that stretched into Colorado, Nevada, and southeastern

The most popular hike in Chaco Canyon takes you to the Pueblo Alto complex, composed of six structures, only four of which remain visible.

California. The gems were often embedded in jewelry and figurines and were obviously important to Chacoan culture, akin to modern-day diamonds. Many artifacts from central America and Mexico were found at Chaco, including cacao (chocolate), metal artifacts, and scarlet macaw skulls and feathers, some found near Pueblo Bonito dated between AD 885 and 990.

Lekson also doesn't quite buy the religious importance placed on Great Houses. Rather, he sees class-stratified societies with nobles and commoners. "The best evidence," he writes, is "50,000 tons of rock and mud, stacked up thirty feet high over the area of a major league baseball field. That's Pueblo Bonito, Chetro Ketl, and Pueblo Alto"—plus the chocolate, jewelry and objects only rich people would possess.

A short self-guided tour through Pueblo Bonito displays an archetypical Great House. Anthropologist Brian Fagan once likened it to England's Stonehenge and Peru's Machu Picchu—high praise for a "starter-kit kingdom."[13] The back wall of Pueblo Bonito at one time stood 97 feet tall. In January 1941, a section of the canyon wall above it collapsed, destroying some of the structure's rear wall and a number of rooms. But walk around to the other side of Pueblo Bonito. Here, you'll discover a number of normal "unit pueblo houses," one just like the other. "It's not subtle; there's nothing difficult about this," Lekson writes. "The contrast is obvious and absolute: The architecture of a class society."

Pueblo Bonito is divided into two sections by a precise north-south wall through the central plaza. The site covers 3 acres and features nearly 800 rooms, 2 Great Kivas—one on each side of the central wall—a large central courtyard, and 30 smaller kivas. Parts of the structure were, at one time, 4 to 5 stories high.

Pictographs and petroglyphs are found throughout Chaco Canyon.

"Great Houses," Lekson insists, "are the stumbling block of pilgrimage models and indeed any ritual-centric model of Chaco. I've never heard a rational, convincing argument for why we should believe that Great Houses were 'ritual structures.' Great Houses are huge, obvious, unmistakable evidence of an elite class of nobles."

Chetro Ketl was completed by 1075, only to be remodeled around 1110–1115.

Just a bunch of rich guys' mansions. Huh. Lekson frames issues of scale, diffusion, states, cities, and cycles differently than the conventional view of Southwestern prehistory, which places a heavy emphasis on ritualistic and religious rites.

Lekson provides one more theory to ponder as you hike around these astounding structures.

SIGNATURE ACTIVITY: THE FIRST RAYS OF LIGHT

WHY GO?

Want to roll out of the tent or RV before dawn, wrap up in blankets in your PJs with 100 of the closest friends you've never met, then trundle up en masse to a 900-year-old ruin and peer through the doors? Then this is the place for you!

SPECS

ACTIVITY TYPE: See the sun rise through two doors of Casa Rinconada
TRAILHEAD/PUT-IN/ETC.: Chaco Visitor Center
DISTANCE/LENGTH: 6-mile drive to the site, then a 0.5-mile hike up the hill to Casa Rinconada
AVERAGE TIME REQUIRED: 1.5 hours
CONTACT/MANAGING AGENCY: National Park Service, Chaco Culture National Historical Park, 505–786–7014, nps.gov/chcu/index.htm
DIFFICULTY: Easy with an alarm clock!
SPECIAL CONSIDERATIONS: It's cold in the spring and fall at that time of morning. Bundle up!

SHORT DESCRIPTION: Follow rangers from the visitor center to the site in your own vehicle—before dawn—then climb out of your warm vehicle into the cold with everyone else and follow the rangers up the hill.

GPS COORDINATES: 36°03'15.02"N, 107° 57'33.46"W

OVERVIEW

The Chacoan people were intimately aware of the cycles of life and were close observers of the skies. This knowledge gave them the ability to time agricultural and ceremonial events that were essential to survival.

Experiencing Chaco during the equinox is mystical. A ranger-led tour to Casa Rinconada at dawn reveals a Chacoan culture with extremely advanced knowledge of the sun's movements. Sure, you've read about it, but until you've actually seen it, it's hard to imagine.

Chaco during the equinox is a mystical experience.

The spring equinox in the Northern Hemisphere happens around March 21, the day the sun moves north across the celestial equator. The autumnal equinox occurs around September 22, the day the sun moves south across the celestial equator. Day and night are equal on these dates. You may recall from your school years that days are longer around the summer solstice, June 21, and shorter around the winter solstice, December 21, just the opposite of the equinoxes.

So, why do you have to get out of a warm sleeping bag before dawn to experience this? Because if you're situated correctly at Casa Rinconada, you'll see the day's first light streak directly through two adjacent doorways. It only happens on an equinox. How did these people build so precisely, their masonry so straight and exact, as to accomplish this?

You need to check in at the visitor center the day prior to the equinoxes—March 21 and September 22—as the rangers need to know how many people to expect the next morning. They normally cap the group at about 100. That means you probably ought to stay in the Gallo Campground, not far from the visitor center. Otherwise, you have to get up really early in the morning and drive back to Chaco Canyon. Either way, get up early, dress warmly, and be ready for the Ancient Ones to amaze you!

CHAPTER 16
BISTÍ DE-NA-ZIN WILDERNESS AREA

SIZE—47,250 acres

YEAR ESTABLISHED—This was designated a wilderness area by President Ronald Reagan in 1984 as part of the San Juan Basin Wilderness Protection Act. The area was expanded in 1996 and again in 2019.

MANAGING AGENCY—Bureau of Land Management, Farmington Field Office

DOG-FRIENDLY?—Yes, they are allowed; but no, this high arid desert is no pal of dogs. It is nasty hot at certain times of year, there's no water or shade, and after a few miles of wandering, this rock takes a toll on dog paws.

FEES AND PERMITS—This is a fee-free area!

NEAREST CITIES—Huerfano and Farmington, NM

NEARBY PUBLIC PROPERTY—Wilderness boundaries enclose parcels of private Navajo land. Please respect private property. Other public property nearby includes Chaco Canyon, Aztec National Monument, Angel Peak Scenic Area, El Morro National Monument, and El Malpais National Monument

SPECIAL CONSIDERATIONS—This is a wilderness area. Don't expect trails, camping facilities, or anything else other than eerily remarkable scenery.

OVERVIEW

This is some of the weirdest, wildest rock I have ever seen, and I've seen A LOT of weird, wild rocks.

Bistí De-Na-Zin Wilderness in northwest New Mexico, located in the San Juan River basin about 35 miles south of Farmington, is bewildering and enchanting yet barren and harsh. Famed American artist Georgia O'Keeffe found its lines, curves, and colors sensuous and luminous, yet the searing desert heat is scalding hot. Look what it did to the rock!

That's part of the reason this place is so wild! *Bistí*, pronounced "Bis-TIE," with the accent on the "tie," is translated from the Navajo *Bistahi*, meaning "among the adobe formations." *De-Na-Zin*, from the Navajo *Déél Náázíní*, means "standing crane," as a number of petroglyphs of cranes have been found south of the wilderness along the Trail of the Ancients Byway, one of New Mexico's designated scenic byways.

Formerly known as the Fossil Forest prior to 1984, this wilderness had been split in two: Bistí Wilderness Study Area lay to the northwest, and De-Na-Zin Wilderness Study Area was to the southeast. Following congressional approval and President Ronald Reagan's signature, the two areas were combined as one wilderness area "in recognition of its paramount aesthetic, natural, scientific, educational and paleontological value."

Existing grazing permits were continued for lessees who apparently felt their cattle could live on dirt—with no water.

Some of the strangest rock formations have been marked as waypoints on a GPS system, but many others, like these, have not. You just have to wander and find your own hoodoos.

Go figure.

Existing coal leases were to be fully adjudicated once this became a wilderness area, yet that process continues more than three decades later. In 2017 Senate Bill 436, the San Juan County Settlement Implementation Act, which would have resolved many of the final issues, never made it to the president's desk. Sometimes government creeps ahead slowly, but in this case, swapping federal coal lease rights is tricky. What state receives the royalties if you move the lease from New Mexico to Wyoming? How about the rights of the Navajo and Ute Nations? Will they be ignored? Again?

Nonetheless, tribal leaders, extractive industry executives, and local and state governments have all agreed with the Department of the Interior's assessment that this wilderness offers some of the most unusual scenery found in the Four Corners Region. Natural sandstone weathering has created hoodoos—tall, thin spires of rock rising up out of the ground—pinnacles, caprock, and other unusual formations. In fact, this area recently received national attention following the discovery of two fossilized pentaceratops dinosaur skeletons.

In 1936, the Mother of American Modernism, Georgia O'Keeffe, drove 150 miles from her home at Ghost Ranch over horrific dirt roads to the Bistí badlands and found what she called "the black place." For the next 14 years, she returned again and again to camp, to sketch and to contemplate nature. This is where she found inspiration for her iconic oil paintings *The Black Place*, *The Black Place II*, and *The Black Place III*. Years later, her assistant, Maria Chabot, wrote to O'Keeffe's husband, famed New York photographer Alfred Stieglitz, about a 1944 camping trip to the Bistí badlands: "the black hills—black and gray and silver with arroyos of white sand curving around them—pink and white strata running through them. They flowed downward, one below the next. Incredible stillness!"

The area was expanded in 1996 to clean up some boundary issues, and again in 2019 with the John D. Dingell Jr. Conservation, Management, and Recreation Act, which also created the Ah-Shi-Sie-Pah Wilderness, located between Chaco Canyon and De-Na-Zin. It will be managed along with Bistí De Na Zin as one big badlands area.

For centuries, most people just thought this place was so weird, so wild, so remote, so unworldly, so harsh that maybe it should be left alone. Although it is located near Chaco Canyon and other prehistoric cultural sites, it appears the ancient Puebloans seldom made this area home. Some artifacts have been found here, yet they are scarce compared to other parts of the Four Corners region of New Mexico, Colorado, Utah, and Arizona. That, by itself, has helped keep this area relatively undiscovered.

The Bistí badlands resulted from the erosion of sandy layers, leaving bare a thick deposit of volcanic ash that exists in the Kirtland/Fruitland Sandstone found in this area. Petrified wood deposits are only one indication that this range was once a riverine delta on an ancient sea that covered much of west-central America 70 million years ago. Swamps along this ancient delta left behind large buildups of organic material. Over time, this became lignite (low-grade coal).

At some point, much of the coal in Bistí burned in an ancient fire that lasted thousands of years. The clay over the coal layer was metamorphosed by the heat into red "clinkers"—mounds of red rock chips that clink underfoot. The ash, lignite, and clinkers all create the gray, black, and red colors of the badlands to paint an unusual and surreal scene, with mushroom mounds and miniature mud towers. It is colorfully kaleidoscopic, yet monochromatic at the same time. It consists of miles and miles of unvegetated terrain, tiny gargoyles, gargantuan New Mexican skies, arroyos and volcanic ash, charcoal turrets, and sandstone castles.

Since it is one of the least-discovered and least-traveled national recreation areas in the United States, Bistí is pristine and wide open. Practically nothing grows on the Bistí side of the wilderness other than sparse patches of gramma grass and a barrel cactus or two, although botanists swear there are at least eight species of plants living here. Nonetheless, it's a vast playground for recreationists who are willing to strike out on their own, who don't need no stinkin' trail guides or cairns or directions whatsoever.

The De-Na-Zin side of the area has a little more vegetation. Pockets of piñon, juniper, yucca, and cactus can be found in arid sands and along shale hillsides. A remnant stand of ponderosa pine is located along De-Na-Zin Wash, lone remainders of a distant past when there was moisture in the area. Fossilized dinosaurs, plants, fish, mammals, and reptiles are littered across the landscape with bits of petrified wood.

During America's "Dinosaur Gold Rush," famed fossil collector Charles Hazelius Sternberg unearthed the five-horned skull of a five-ton herbivorous dinosaur called a pentaceratops in 1921. Much later, in 1997, volunteer researcher Paul Sealey discovered the meat-eating "Bistí Beast," now identified as a new tyrannosaur labeled *Bistahieversor sealeyi.*

With your head down in search of your own Bistí Beast, you could easily wander for miles across this colorful landscape, then look up and realize you have no idea where you are.

Nancy Harbert from Albuquerque, New Mexico, confronts a troop of what appear to be marching toads at Bistí.

Do you remember that map-and-compass course you took when you were in Scouts? Probably not. Besides, you lost that compass years ago and you left the map in the car. If you have a good GPS system and you know how to use it, that would help you find the map—and the car. Otherwise, you need a good sense of direction, because this place is so spacious, it's disorienting.

And it's got some of the weirdest, wildest rock you've ever seen!

SIGNATURE ACTIVITY: CRACKED EGGS

WHY GO?

You will find some of the weirdest, wildest rock formations you'll ever see, but there are no designated trails here. Sure, there's a "trailhead," but other than that, you must wander—or make a game of it while learning how to use that GPS you've been carrying for the past few years.

SPECS

ACTIVITY TYPE: Point-to-point orienteering
TRAILHEAD/PUT-IN/ETC.: South parking lot for Bistí
DISTANCE/LENGTH: 2 to 5 miles round-trip, or as far as you want to go
AVERAGE TIME REQUIRED: 3 hours
CONTACT/MANAGING AGENCY: Bureau of Land Management, Farmington Office, 6251 College Boulevard, Suite A, 505–564–7600
DIFFICULTY: Easy, unless you are trekking across here in the middle of the day in the middle of the summer. Then it's REALLY difficult. You could die!
SPECIAL CONSIDERATIONS: Take water, travel early in the morning or late in the evening, take water, wear a hat and sunglasses, take water, grease up with lots of sunscreen, and take a camera and water. Sunsets are FABULOUS! However, you may need a flashlight/headlamp to return to the parking area without falling into an arroyo and hurting yourself.

FIND THE TRAILHEAD/GETTING THERE

SHORT DESCRIPTION: Drive south from Farmington approximately 36 miles on NM Highway 371 and turn east (left) on County Road 7297. Take this gravel road for approximately two miles to a T-intersection and turn left (north). Proceed for about a mile to the Bistí parking area. There's another smaller parking area a quarter mile farther north.
GPS COORDINATES: 36°15′43″N, 108°15′10″W

OVERVIEW

OK, ready to learn something about GPS? Me too.

Ask your kid.

Then, call me.

From what they tell me, GPS is a network of about 30 satellites orbiting the Earth. Once your handheld GPS—a fancy radio receiver—receives radio signals from at least three satellites, it can pinpoint your location by trilateration. I did not make that word up. But I get the idea of three satellites triangulating on your position. It tells you where you are on the face of the Earth. It probably tells Facebook too. And if you have a bunch of "waypoints"—other GPS marks on the planet—you can program your handheld GPS to walk from where you are to that place. Of course, you may have to climb a mountain or ford a ravine—or walk around—but you can get there.

So, here's a little game you can all join in on. It's very simple and I hope it's new. Label hoodoos with names if you want to, any old names that you think will do!

You have to let yourself go here, because there are no trails. There's a trailhead, but that's about it. This is wilderness, in every sense of the word—uncultivated, uninhabited, inhospitable, and absolutely incredible. You've just got to see it! What's more, if you're successful playing this game out here, you get to survive! You can hardly beat that!

Here are a handful of GPS coordinates—or established waypoints. Previous adventurers have marked them. Some spots are named because of the unique rock formations found there. You can rename them anything you want. First, however, see if you can find one or two of them:

Cracked Eggs: 36°16'03"N, 108°13'25"W
Bistí Arch: 36°16'07"N, 108°13'34"W
Petrified Log: 36°16'05"N, 108°13'12"W
Petrified Cowboy: 36°15'57"N, 108°13'59"W
Chocolate Hoodoos: 36°15'32"N, 108°14'20" W

There are a bunch of apps you could download onto your phone with a GPS program. Some of them work even if you don't have cell coverage, since GPS uses satellites to "trilaterate." Sometimes you may lose satellite coverage too, but a GPS system will usually pick it up quickly in these wide-open spaces.

Other options: You could use an old-fashioned map and compass—if you know how to use them to begin with—or just go out and find your own hoodoo. Then find your way back to the parking area. It's not that scary. Really.

Wupatki Pueblo was a multilevel high-rise, with more than 100 rooms.

PART 5
FLAGSTAFF/SEDONA

THE VORTEX

They say not everyone who wanders is lost.

"We were in Sedona," exhorted my buddy Chris. "We went on a hike. It was just outside this fancy resort with all these cool people. It drove me nuts.

"I want to get away," he pled his case. "I want to hang out with rocks and trees. I don't want to be near people. I don't care about their vortexes-slash-vortices. I can find my own." He spread his long arms wide to the world, in a yoga-like star pose.

"It's the desert," he screamed quietly.

"Plus," he added, "there was this Mexican restaurant out there that was incredible."

I read Carlos Castaneda when I was younger. I thought I got the premise—about finding myself by "following the path with the heart."

Probably not.

Yet tens of thousands of people a year flock to Sedona, Arizona, from around the globe to "follow the path with the heart." They are in search of spiritual vortexes—or vortices—as Chris pointed out. These vortices are "transformational energy centers" located all around Sedona, "intersections of natural electromagnetic earth energy," according to Sedona Red Rock Tours, which hosts numerous spiritual vortex tours throughout the "lunar" year. One can only assume they host tours throughout the entire Gregorian calendar year as well.

Are you in vibrational alignment with your desires?

How often have you been asked that question?

Some say Sedona is an existential hospice for the terminally hip. Geoff Tischbein, who lived there for a couple of years in search of his own vortex—or its equivalent—never discovered one. "I had friends who were more connected to outer space than me, and they said they felt the vortexes."

Before you embark on any path ask the question: Does this path have a heart? If the answer is no, you will know it, and then you must choose another path. The trouble is nobody asks the question; and when a man finally realizes that he has taken a path without a heart, the path is ready to kill him. At that point very few men can stop to deliberate, and leave the path. A path without a heart is never enjoyable. You have to work hard even to take it. On the other hand, a path with heart is easy; it does not make you work at liking it.

—Carlos Castaneda, *The Teachings of Don Juan: A Yaqui Way of Knowledge*

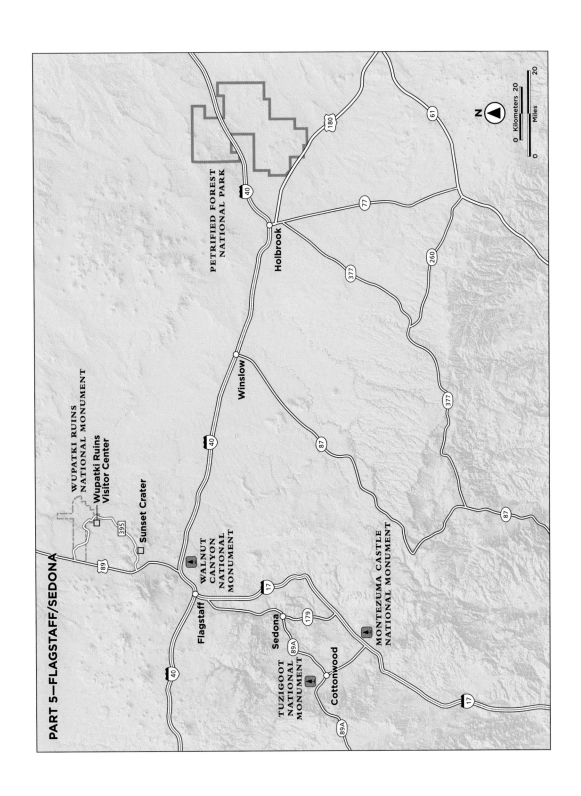

PART 5—FLAGSTAFF/SEDONA

If there's a place on earth where true vortexes exist, this has got to be one of those places. It's trippy even without drugs. Here on the very edge of the Colorado Plateau, where it has risen thousands of feet above the Basin and Plains province that abuts it, the scenery is stunning, spectacular, incredible.

Like Chris, I find my own vortex each time I wander through the desert Southwest. It's all around me. Sedona, however, is, like, the center of the universe of vortices, man. There are feminine vortexes and masculine vortexes. There are soul-searchers meditating along the trails to these vortexes, there are spandex-clad vortex hunters busting out yoga warrior poses, there are gurus disguised as guides, guides disguised as gurus, seekers in shorts, corporate scions in dungarees, and hippies in flip-flops. I even saw Speedo Man peddling through an intersection on a beat-up Schwinn 10-speed—dressed only in a Speedo and Converse tennis shoes—with a basket full of barrel cactus on his handlebars.

I sent out good vibes, hoping he didn't run over his vortex and spill the cactus in his lap, and felt like the great philosopher/comedian Steven Wright, who once said, "I was a peripheral visionary. I could see the future, but only way off to the side."

Sometimes my vision is way off to the side. Sometimes it's only seen through the rearview mirror. However, traveling across the Colorado Plateau, my path forward is easy. I am able to clearly see the magnificent opus that Mother Nature has produced.

And Sedona is right on the edge, off to the side.

CHAPTER 17
MONTEZUMA CASTLE NATIONAL MONUMENT

SIZE—1,015 acres

YEAR ESTABLISHED—In 1906, the year of the San Francisco earthquake, President Theodore Roosevelt designated this as one of the first four national monuments in the United States (Devils Tower in Wyoming was first, followed a month later by Montezuma Castle, Petrified Forest in Arizona, and El Morro in New Mexico). It was meant to protect prehistoric artifacts from being plundered by "collectors" and others unconcerned with history, culture, or environment.

MANAGING AGENCY—National Park Service, Camp Verde, AZ

DOG-FRIENDLY?—Dogs are welcome, but they must remain on a leash at all times.

FEES AND PERMITS—$10 per person, ages 16 and over, for a 7-day entrance pass to both Montezuma Castle and Tuzigoot National Monuments; Montezuma Castle/Tuzigoot Annual Pass is $35; National Parks and Federal Recreational Lands Pass ($80 annually for adults under the age of 62; $80 for a lifetime senior pass) also accepted.

NEAREST CITIES—Prescott and Sedona, AZ

NEARBY PUBLIC PROPERTY—Coconino National Forest, Tuzigoot, Walnut Canyon, Sunset Crater Volcano and Wupatki National Monuments, Petrified Forest National Park

SPECIAL CONSIDERATIONS—If you visit in the summer months, DO NOT leave your pets, kids, or grandparents in your parked vehicle! It's dangerously hot and could kill them. Seriously.

OVERVIEW

Just to be clear, this was never Montezuma's real castle.

Early "white settlers" to this area (see Sean P. Harvey's quote below) just assumed Aztecs must have built this prestigious high-rise for Montezuma, their great emperor.

Not.

Archeologists and scholars have since concluded that this ancient adobe structure in the Verde Valley of central Arizona was built by the peaceful, cliff-dwelling Sinagua people. *Sinagua* in Spanish means "without water." These pre-Columbian Native Americans were hunter-gatherers and farmers who grew corn, beans, and squash in this unusually dry desert.

To the native Hopi, this place is known as Sakaytaka and Wupat'pela—the "place where the step ladders are going up" and "long, high walls," respectively.

The Hopi, along with the Zuni, Yavapai, Hohokam, and other Puebloan groups, descended from the Sinagua people, who built this structure somewhere between AD 1100 and 1300. It sits about 90 feet up a 150-foot limestone cliff above Beaver Creek. They definitely needed ladders going up long, high walls.

Another assumption of early white settlers was that the "castle" was built high on the cliff for defensive reasons.

Not. Well, maybe not.

Archeologists now believe it was probably built high up the cliff face so people could escape the disasters of a flooded Beaver Creek below. The creek would swell to frightening depths each spring and carried tremendous debris following each summer thunderstorm. High up the cliff, Sinagua builders also took advantage of an enormous limestone overhang that provided shade during the hot summer months. Insulated alcoves that were cool in the summer kept the Sinagua warm in the winter. Building on the cliff also saved level land near streams and on the nearby mesas for farming, and these ingenious people took advantage of the alcove so that they did not have to build four walls and a roof.

Montezuma Castle is among the most important ancestral sites for the Hopi in the Verde Valley. Hopi consultants say that the Parrot, Bear, Water, Cloud, Bearstrap, Bluebird, and Spider clans all resided here.

Think of that in terms of a small neighborhood, where the Smith family and the Jones family lived mostly in harmony with the Haggertys, the Massaros, the Garcias, and the Jacksons. About 50 people lived here at one time. Five stories high, 20 rooms. It was a small apartment complex where that cute little Haggerty girl flirted with the Jones boy, and the eldest Smith boy was jealous. Look out. There's trouble a-brewin'.

The Jackson boy couldn't go far. He had a crush on that Haggerty girl too, but there were too many mothers watching; each family here occupied one room, leaving the rest for storage, work space, meetings, and ceremonies.

Could you live in the same room as your grandparents, parents, and all of your siblings, at least one of whom is hormonally enraged?

Maybe that's another reason these people vanished.

Just sayin'.

By 1300, Montezuma Castle was part of an intricate network of at least 40 Verde Valley villages. It's estimated that between 6,000 and 8,000 people may have lived in this vicinity 800 years ago.

Many of the other homes and structures from that period did not survive the harsh conditions here at the intersection of the Colorado Plateau and Basin and Range physiographic provinces. Yet Montezuma Castle survived because of its placement in a natural alcove that protects it from exposure to those elements.

Many of the artifacts found here are not from here, indicating that the Sinagua traded with other tribes of nomads wandering through the Verde Valley. For example, macaws were brought in from Mexico, and some decorated pottery found in the area originated from the north. Skilled artisans from here fashioned stone tools like axes, knives, and hammers, as well as bone awls and needles, for trade and for personal

Montezuma Castle

use. They wove attractive cotton garments and utilized shells, turquoise, and local red stone (argillite, sometimes called pipestone) for personal wear. They traded salt that was mined near here for shell jewelry from the coast. Sinaguan salt was prized for its taste as well as its preservative qualities. They also mined turquoise, argillite, copper, and azurite, all with stone tools.

Thus, these industrious farmers and hunter-gatherers also were skilled engineers, daring builders, adept miners, and astute traders, as well as master spinners and weavers.

Due to heavy looting in the late 19th and early 20th centuries, few original artifacts from Montezuma Castle survived. In fact, that's the reason this national monument was established—to prevent further destruction of its historic artifacts. The visitor center, however, includes a Sinagua Cultural Museum housing many remaining artifacts, such as manos and metates used for grinding corn, bone needles, and ornaments made from shells and gemstones, proof that they were fine artisans and prolific traders.

Montezuma Well is part of the Montezuma Castle Complex and is located about nine miles upstream from the castle. The well—like Montezuma Castle—was never visited by Montezuma, who lived from 1466 to 1520. There is evidence of human life here well

Race, as a concept denoting a fundamental division of humanity and usually encompassing cultural as well as physical traits, was crucial in early America. It provided the foundation for the colonization of Native land, the enslavement of American Indians and Africans, and a common identity among socially unequal and ethnically diverse Europeans. Longstanding ideas and prejudices merged with aims to control land and labor, a dynamic reinforced by ongoing observation and theorization of non-European peoples. Although before colonization, neither American Indians, nor Africans, nor Europeans considered themselves unified "races," Europeans endowed racial distinctions with legal force and philosophical and scientific legitimacy, while Natives appropriated categories of "red" and "Indian," and slaves and freed people embraced those of "African" and "colored," to imagine more expansive identities and mobilize more successful resistance to Euro-American societies. The origin, scope, and significance of "racial" difference were questions of considerable transatlantic debate in the age of Enlightenment and they acquired particular political importance in the newly independent United States.

—Sean P. Harvey, "Early National History," *Oxford Research Encyclopedias*, April 2016[15]

Dwellings beneath Montezuma Castle

before that, from between 700 and 900. Archeologists and historians believe that's when ancestors of the Hohokam culture moved here from southern and central Arizona.

Called Yuvukva ("sunken spring") by the Hopi, Ah-hah gkith-gygy-vah ("broken water") by the Yavapai, and Tú sii ch' iL ("water breaks open") by the Western Apache, this well is a holy place of emergence in some tribal histories. Its continuous current of water enabled agricultural communities to flourish here for several centuries. The well is a surprising oasis in the middle of the desert. It's a limestone sink formed eons ago and still fed by continuously flowing springs. A nearby pithouse dates to AD 1050.

Each day, about 1.6 million gallons (6 million liters) of water flow through two main vents at the well's bottom. Divers report that fine sand boils up in swirling, cascading mounds at 55 feet deep. They estimate the actual vents are another 65 feet farther down. The amount of water flowing here is fairly regular, and the temperature is a nearly constant 74°F (23°C). No fish exist here because of the high levels of dissolved carbon dioxide. There are, however, thousands of freshwater leeches swimming around.

This well is the world's only home for five species, including a miniature shrimp-looking amphipod, a leech, a tiny snail, a water scorpion, and a type of one-celled plant called a diatom.

Scientists believe the water bubbling into Montezuma Well each day fell as rain and snow from atop the Mogollon Rim and the edge of the Colorado Plateau about

10,000 years ago. A similar aquifer exists at Tuzigoot, located about 36 miles north-west of here (see chapter 21, "Tuzigoot National Monument").

Interested learners may visit Montezuma Well, Montezuma Castle, and Tuzigoot in a half day of easy hiking and interpretive display reading. It's fascinating what you can learn just by reading. It's even more fun to be there and read about it at the same time. It helps with retention—at least for me!

SIGNATURE ACTIVITY: INTERPRETIVE SIGN SPEED-READING

WHY GO?

Miles from nowhere on the edge of the plateau, there's lots to read and nowhere else to go—other than the casino in Camp Verde, and you'll certainly get in trouble there.

SPECS

ACTIVITY TYPE: Interpretive sign speed-reading
TRAILHEAD/PUT-IN/ETC.: Back door of the visitor center
DISTANCE/LENGTH: 0.3-mile loop
AVERAGE TIME REQUIRED: Depends on how fast you read!
CONTACT/MANAGING AGENCY: Montezuma Castle National Monument, National Park Service, 928–567–3322
DIFFICULTY: Tricky
SPECIAL CONSIDERATIONS: It's all in English, with a smattering of Latin, Hopi, and Yavapai, so this may be tricky.

FIND THE TRAILHEAD/GETTING THERE

SHORT DESCRIPTION: Walk out the back door of the visitor center.
GPS COORDINATES: 34°36′36″N, 111°50′24″W

OVERVIEW

This is a totally wheelchair-accessible trip, and Grandma and the young grandkids can participate, especially if the kids are pushing Grandma in a wheelchair. This is an exciting, ⅓-mile-long speed-reading trip since, as Grandma would say, there are more signs than you can shake a cane at. That's why Grandma is so important here. She can read faster than you.

You'll discover that the velvet mesquite (*Prosopis veluntina*) is actually in the pea family and was a very important resource for the Verde Valley people. Seeds and pods were ground into meal and baked into cakes, providing a staple protein. Mesquite sap was used as candy, resin, and adhesive.

Grandma, give the kids a little candy now and watch 'em go!

With cliff dwellings built directly into the rock, Montezuma Well provided freshwater for drinking as well as for crops.

Parts of the mesquite tree were also used to treat eye and skin ailments as well as the common cold. There may be a few road rashes on Grandma's legs if the kids dump her over in the wheelchair.

The roofs of Montezuma Castle are still supported by sycamore beams today, 700 years after construction. The large white-barked Arizona sycamore (*Platanus wrightii*) is one of Arizona's largest trees. You'd know that if you read the sign instead of racing by to beat Grandma. Cheaters never prosper!

Because of extensive looting at Montezuma Castle, much of what we know about life here—what people ate, what they made, whom they traded with, and when they lived—comes from the excavation of a site just below and adjacent to the castle itself. At the base of the cliff, archeologists found a pueblo with about 45 rooms on multiple levels. Look closely, Grandma. Here, use little Johnny's 516 mini-monocular adventure scope that you just bought for him in the gift store.

Signs tell of plants and animals and how they were important to survival between AD 1150 and 1400. You'll discover that Beaver Creek, which flows through here, has always been a major focus of life in the Verde Valley.

Water in the desert. Huh. Who'da thunk?

So, why race through here? Well, you don't really have to. However, if you want to visit Montezuma Well and Tuzigoot, you'd better get a move on. There's a restroom at the visitor center.

CHAPTER 18
SUNSET CRATER VOLCANO NATIONAL MONUMENT

SIZE—3,040 acres

YEAR ESTABLISHED—May 26, 1930, by President Herbert Hoover, following intense public outcry over a Hollywood plan to detonate large quantities of explosives on the side of the crater to create an avalanche for Zane Grey's motion picture *Avalanche*.

MANAGING AGENCY—National Park Service, Flagstaff Area National Monuments

DOG-FRIENDLY?—Pets must be kept on a leash at all times and are not allowed in the visitor center or on any of the trails.

FEES AND PERMITS—$25 per passenger vehicle; $20 per motorcycle; $15 per cyclist or pedestrian; annual pass, senior pass, access pass, and active duty military pass also accepted

NEAREST CITY—Flagstaff, AZ

NEARBY PUBLIC PROPERTY—Wupatki National Monument, Walnut Canyon National Monument, Coconino National Forest, Tuzigoot National Monument, Montezuma Castle National Monument

SPECIAL CONSIDERATIONS—Be prepared for variable and extreme weather conditions, including windy afternoons, summer temperatures above 100°F (38°C), afternoon storms from July through September, and occasional snow in the winter and early spring. Never leave your pet in a vehicle. Desert temperatures can quickly cause heat stroke and death!

OVERVIEW

Thank you, President Hoover, for saving this place from Zane Grey and the Hollywood hordes in 1930. I would not know as much about volcanoes as I do today if it hadn't been for your foresight. Geologists, volcanologists, other scientists, and all those interested in the wonders of the world also thank you.

Sunset Crater Volcano is the youngest volcano on the Colorado Plateau and the youngest in a group of volcanoes known as the San Francisco Volcanic Field near Flagstaff, Arizona. Born in a series of eruptions between AD 1040 and 1100, Sunset Crater Volcano, according to archeologists, "profoundly affected the lives of local people and forever changed the landscape and ecology of the area."

Ya think?

Ask the people on the big island of Hawaii about the Kilauea Volcano in 2018, or the people in Guatemala about volcanic explosions from Volcán de Fuego that same year. Ask them if those eruptions "profoundly affected the lives of local people."

They are still profoundly affected, and yes, the landscape and ecology have changed forever.

Sunset Crater

Dozens of fissures erupted on Hawaii's Kilauea Volcano, sending lava flows to the ocean and destroying more than 700 structures, although because Kilauea is a "shield" volcano and the lava flow was slow-moving, there were no human casualties. In Guatemala, more than 500 people died or were missing and presumed dead two years following the explosion of Volcán de Fuego, which scientists call a "stratovolcano." The pyroclastic flow spewing from this volcano reached temperatures of 1,300° (700°) and speeds of 430 miles per hour (700 kilometers per hour). It caused instantaneous devastation.

Now, say you lived 1,000 years ago and knew nothing about volcanoes, or about the shifting of tectonic plates, or about the other powerful forces that shaped and continue to shape the earth—forces that created more than 600 hills and mountains in the San Francisco Volcanic Field alone.

Would you then say the gods were angry?

People living at the Wupatki Pueblo only 12 miles from this now 1,000-foot-high volcano must have been pretty freaked out when molten rock sprayed high into the air from a crack in the ground, solidified, then fell to earth as large bombs or smaller cinders.

These people were displaced by the eruption and moved to a lower elevation. Others, however, were drawn to this area by the eruption, most likely for religious reasons, but maybe just to gawk, just like people in Hawaii a couple years ago.

Nonetheless, it took three generations—100 years—for people to begin moving back to the Wupatki Pueblo site. By that time, the dust would have settled. That dust, a mixture of volcanic cinder and ash called tephra, spread across 800 square miles. The tephra layer is more than 60 feet deep on the slopes of Sunset Crater and gradually thins to only a few inches near Wupatki. This actually improved agriculture by holding and retaining the little moisture this area received, even back then.

No matter how much moisture that ash could hold, however, farming on this part of the Colorado Plateau was marginal at best. That's why early archeologists called the people who lived here *Sinagua*, "without water." They scratched out a living with very little of this precious commodity available on a year-round basis, or even from season to season.

A Hollywood film company named the Famous Players-Lasky Corporation wanted to detonate large quantities of explosives on the side of Sunset Crater in 1928. They were attempting to create an avalanche for Zane Grey's motion picture, *Avalanche*. Gratefully, common sense prevailed as public outcry over this plan in part led to the proclamation of Sunset Crater Volcano National Monument by President Herbert Hoover in 1930.

Archeologists are quite sure they've nailed the creation of Sunset Crater between the fall of 1064 and the spring of 1065. They accomplished this by carbon-dating the timbers used in construction at Wupatki Pueblo. Eruptions, however, may have continued on and off for about 150 years. It is now considered an extinct volcano, with no further eruptions expected.

This particular volcano—unlike either the shield volcano of Kilauea or the stratovolcano of de Fuego, was a basalt cinder cone volcano, like most of the 600 volcanoes in the San Francisco Volcanic Field. Basalt has the lowest viscosity of all common magmas. (In contrast, magma from de Fuego had very high viscosity and thus moved 430 miles per hour!)

The basalt magma at Sunset Crater was formed during the early explosive stages of this volcano's life. A mixture of molten rock and highly compressed gasses, this magma rose upward from its underground source, and as it ascended, the pressure dropped and the gasses were released. When that happened, the gas in the magma caused an explosion out of the central vent.

WHAT CRATER?

Sunset Crater is an extinct volcano that erupted in 1064–1065; its lava continued to flow until 1100. Meteor Crater, located off I-40 (Old Route 66), about 35 miles east of Flagstaff, is an impact crater—a collision between an asteroid traveling 26,000 miles per hour and planet Earth approximately 50,000 years ago.
  Ouch!

In flight, these lava "blobs" cooled and fell back to the ground as the dark volcanic rock you see, containing cavities created by trapped gas bubbles. The small pieces became "cinder," while the larger ones were literally "bombs." As the fragments accumulated, they built up a cone-shaped hill.

There was still a lot of gas left in this baby. Magma with lower gas content produced lava flows that crept out of the side or base of the cone like toothpaste squeezed from a tube.

That's what created the Kana-a Lava Flow the year Sunset Crater was created in 1064–1065. Yet 75 percent of the magma flowing from this volcano formed the Bonito Lava Flow, which probably flowed until 1100.

A one-mile Lava Flow Trail at the base of the volcano allows visitors to see how habitat changes have affected some species and created new niches for others over the last 900 years. Aspen grow along the sides of the lava flow, while stunted ponderosa pine, scarlet gilia, and pink penstemon grow in the cinders.

The crater is now closed to climbing to protect its fragile resources. It was climbed so much earlier in the 20th century that it was sliding and collapsing.

The best place to actually view the entire volcano and its lava flows is from O'Leary Peak, just to the west of Sunset Crater Volcano in the Coconino National Forest. (See "Signature Activity: Climb a Peak to View a Crater.") At 8,916 feet, O'Leary offers an excellent 10-mile round-trip hike onto another ancient volcano that, unlike Sunset Crater, de Fuego, or Kilauea, was a lava dome volcano. Lava domes are formed by relatively small, bulbous masses of lava too viscous to flow any great distance.

On the other hand, the San Francisco Peaks just north of Flagstaff (southwest of Sunset Crater) are remnants of a volcano once called San Francisco Mountain. It has erupted several times in the past three million years.

The six highest individual peaks in Arizona are contained in this range, including 12,633-foot Humphreys Peak. This was formed as a stratovolcano, similar to Volcán de Fuego in Guatemala. It's the only one of its kind in this volcanic field, and while its last eruption was about 220,000 years ago, it's still not considered "extinct."

Now that you know as much about volcanoes as I do, go visit one—and thank President Hoover for protecting it!

SIGNATURE ACTIVITY: CLIMB A PEAK TO VIEW A CRATER

WHY GO?

If you want to see inside Sunset Crater Volcano without hiring a private plane and pilot, climb O'Leary Peak. It's five miles up and five miles back, so do it early in the day, but this hike offers spectacular views of the San Francisco Volcanic Fields any time of year.

SPECS

ACTIVITY TYPE: It's a hike. It's a climb. But it's not technical. It follows an old jeep road all the way to the top!
TRAILHEAD/PUT-IN/ETC.: O'Leary Group Campground
DISTANCE/LENGTH: 10 miles up and back; elevation: 6,846 feet to 8,916 feet
AVERAGE TIME REQUIRED: About 4 hours
CONTACT/MANAGING AGENCY: National Forest Service, Coconino National Forest, Flagstaff District, 928–526–0866, fs.usda.gov/coconino
DIFFICULTY: Moderate (strenuous, if you're not ready for a little altitude)
SPECIAL CONSIDERATIONS: Take two quarts of water with you and hike early in the day. Most of this hike is in the open, so it gets hot!

GETTING THERE

SHORT DESCRIPTION: From Flagstaff, go north on U.S. Route 89 for 15 miles to Forest Road (FR) 545 (the road to Sunset Crater Volcano National Monument). Turn right onto FR 545 and continue 1.7 miles to FR 545A. Turn left onto FR 545A and continue 0.3 mile to the trailhead, located at the O'Leary Group Campground.
GPS COORDINATES: 35°22′18.8″N, 111°32′28.1″W

OVERVIEW

I took a long hike with my daughter to O'Leary Peak. Sure, she led me on a 10-mile death march, but what the heck—I spent the entire day with her. How special.

That we hiked up a small volcanic peak named for an Irishman to view the center of Sunset Crater Volcano was pretty special too.

We arrived at the trailhead early—for us—at about 6:45 a.m. We knew we needed to beat the day's heat, and we both carried extra water.

Apache plume flowers beneath the cinder-strewn sides of Sunset Crater.

Average daytime temperatures in early June had been about 85°F, 45°F at night. A good portion of this trail, actually an old graded jeep road that leads to a fire tower on top of O'Leary Peak, is exposed to the sun. It's hot, and it's a 10.7 percent grade up the last mile of this trek (5 miles up, 5 miles back, remember?)

A horned lizard blends into the rock along the trail to O'Leary Peak.

It was tough on this old man, as six runners and four other hikers passed us on the way up. Daughter Bridgette could have stayed with them but chose to stay with her dear old dad. What a sweetheart!

This is really the only place where you can get a good look at the inside of the cone on Sunset Crater. It also provides stunning views of the 600 hills and mountains in the San Francisco Volcanic Fields that stretch for miles to the horizon.

The first mile of trail is mostly level before it begins a slight ascent. Within another 15 minutes or so, it veers northwest and really begins to climb.

The road is still used by the fire ranger in the lookout tower on top of this peak. All others walk. It gives you time to check out the cinder fields dotted with piñon pine among the ponderosa. The oldest of these piñon are about 250 years old, which shows that things are slowly changing in this environment.

Biologists have documented 166 plant species here, including cliffrose, Apache plume, rabbitbrush, and an interesting variety of pink penstemon. Mule deer, Abert's squirrels, and Steller's jays are common, and don't be surprised to see horned lizards. Also known as horny toads, this common name is a metaphor for its flattened, rounded body, blunt snout, and spines or horns on its back and sides.

Even if you can't hike with your daughter, it's still a fine trip!

CHAPTER 19
WUPATKI NATIONAL MONUMENT

SIZE—35,000 acres
YEAR ESTABLISHED—December 9, 1924, by President Calvin Coolidge, following extensive looting of priceless archeological resources
MANAGING AGENCY—National Park Service, Flagstaff Area National Monuments
DOG-FRIENDLY?—Pets must be kept on a leash at all times; they are not allowed in buildings or on park trails.
FEES AND PERMITS—$25 per passenger vehicle; $20 per motorcycle; $15 per cyclist or pedestrian; annual pass, senior pass, access pass, and active duty military passes also accepted
NEAREST CITY—Flagstaff, AZ
NEARBY PUBLIC PROPERTY—Sunset Crater National Monument, Walnut Canyon National Monument, Coconino National Forest, Tuzigoot National Monument, Montezuma Castle National Monument
SPECIAL CONSIDERATIONS—Be prepared for variable and extreme weather conditions, including windy afternoons, summer temperatures above 100°F (38°C), afternoon storms from July through September, and occasional snow in the winter and early spring. Never leave your pet in a vehicle. Desert temperatures can quickly cause heat stroke and death!

OVERVIEW

The National Park Service website for Wupatki National Monument reads: "Please be advised there is continuing trail work on the Wupatki Pueblo trail behind the visitor center. Partial closures of the trail are in effect and may restrict access to the blowhole."

What? Restricted access to the blowhole?

What's a tourist to do?

Oh, and by the way, what's a blowhole doing in the middle of the desert anyway? Aren't they found on whales?

A blowhole is a unique geological phenomenon (see "Yaapontsa" sidebar), and there are a number of them around here. But that's not the only peculiar thing about Wupatki.

Archeological evidence suggests this was a prosperous, multicultured community whose people lived and worked together peacefully for hundreds of years.

That seems odd in this day and age.

One reason they got along was obvious: They had to work together just to survive in this harsh and unforgiving climate with very little rain, intense summer heat, frigid winters, and intense winds any time of year.

Wupatki, which means "tall house" in the Hopi language, was first inhabited around AD 500. The largest of the ancient ruins found here, the Wupatki Pueblo, was an

The San Francisco Mountains near Flagstaff, Arizona, dominate the southwestern horizon above Wupatki National Monument.

incredible architectural achievement as a multilevel high-rise with 100 rooms. It was built around and over a large sandstone outcrop in the middle of a shallow and narrow canyon.

This structure displays a change in thinking, an adaptation to living. Not only was it above the canyon rims so preferred by many ancient Puebloans, this cultural mix of people constructed a ventilation system throughout the pueblo that allowed them to build fires within their homes—quite ingenious for the time and the area.

This pueblo had kivas, community rooms, single-family and multifamily dwellings, storage rooms, a "dance plaza" or community gathering space for social events, a ball field, and a blowhole.

Those ancestral people who lived here considered the blowhole a "breathing cave." Sacred ionized air rushed through it, and a vibrant community grew around it.

This was a trading post of sorts, on the crossroads of an ancient human migration route with many different people arriving from drought-stressed areas across the Colorado Plateau.

At least 125 different types of pottery have been found at Wupatki, suggesting a rich culture that lived and traded here. The Hohokam people, who lived to the south, brought shells, salt, and cotton, which may have come from as far as Mexico's Toltec and Aztec regions. Ancestral Puebloans traded copper and turquoise. Sinagua, Cohonia, and Kayenta traditions are all displayed here, living together in a melting pot of cultures.

Naturally, as with the people who inhabited the big island of Hawaii or Guatemala City in 2018, smoke plumes and tremors must have warned these folks before Sunset Crater erupted sometime between 1040 and 1100.

Archeological records indicate lava flowed from the sides and base of the cinder-cone volcano, while debris exploded from the cinder-cone hill and rained down on their homes. The erupting cinders forced these farmers to vacate the rocky lands.

Did they view this as an omen from their gods? Probably. In fact, some Hopi believe it was a sign that their migration and search for the center of the universe should continue.

Yet archeological records also show that a few generations later, at Wupatki and nearby Walnut Canyon, families returned to grow crops for another 100 years in the shadow of Sunset Crater. The cinder and ash had created a thin layer that absorbed precious moisture, helped prevent evaporation, and improved agriculture—mainly corn (maize) and squash.

By 1180, archeologists believe thousands of people were farming on the Wupatki landscape. As one gazes across this barren topography today, that idea is unfathomable.

Descendants of the Ancient Ones continued to live nearby, including Hopi, Zuni, and Navajo people. Early archeologists here named them Sinagua—"without water"—reflecting the people's ability to farm and live virtually without it.

The importance of this site is underlined by the fact that it had the only ball court in the Sunset Crater region. The court measured 78 feet wide and 100 feet long, and it had a 6-foot-high wall. Perhaps one of the last ones built in this era, it was the only known masonry court in the Southwest.

At least one game ball has been recovered in the region, from a Hohokam site near Toltec, Arizona, about 200 miles south of Wupatki. The ball was dated to AD 900–1200 and is now in the Arizona State Museum in Phoenix.

These balls—larger than today's professional baseballs—were made from carefully chosen rocks covered in pine pitch and other materials. Similar to an ancient Aztec

A blowhole is an opening in the ground through which air will suck in or blow out. It's like a combo shop-vac/leaf blower. The blowhole at Wupatki blows air out or sucks air in depending on barometric pressure aboveground. When the air is warm and light above, the cold air from below blows out with such force that it literally makes the hair on your head blow straight up—if you're not follicly bereaved. But when the air gets heavy and moist, it reverses itself and sucks the air down.

Today, Hopi descendants of the original builders at Wupatki refer to the blowhole as the breath of Yaapontsa, the wind spirit, who lives in an earth crack in the black rock at the base of Sunset Crater. There are several blowholes in this area. The easiest one to find is located near the ceremonial ball court east of the Wupatki Pueblo.

Research on blowholes in northern Arizona indicates that the openings connect with an extensive underground fracture system. Fractures open to the surface are locally known as "earth cracks," underground passages formed by earthquake activity in the Kaibab limestone bedrock.

Before a masonry box was placed over this blowhole in 1965, spelunkers descended 18 feet down a very small opening to an underground fracture too constricted to explore. Measuring the amount of air blowing in and out of the blowhole, they estimated the underground air space to be 7 billion cubic feet—equivalent to a tunnel 165 feet by 165 feet square and 50 miles long!

What symbolic function did the blowhole serve for the Ancient Ones who built the Wupatki complex? Odds are it was thought of as much more than just a cooldown station after a big game in the adjacent ceremonial ball field.

Was the earth breathing, or was this truly an opening to the underworld?

ball game, the objective was to move the ball toward a goal by using a curved stick or kicking it.

In Aztec times in what is now Mexico, the losers of the game would be sacrificed to the gods. In ancient Mayan times further south, in present-day Guatemala, only royal families played the game, and it was the victors who were sacrificed, since only the best and finest royal blood should be offered to the gods.

No one is sure what occurred at this site. Though often portrayed as extremely brutal, the game must have performed a sacred task or an important social function.

Was it revered more than modern American football? Hard to say.

Early 19th-century explorers marveled at the well-preserved pueblos in this area: Wupatki, but also Wukoki, Citadel, Nalakihu, and Lomaki Pueblos, all now situated within this national monument.

People like John Wesley Powell were intrigued with the ball fields and awestruck by the beguiling volcanic landscape. Navajo families brought sheep to the land. Later, white men introduced cattle, tapped groundwater supplies, and suppressed fire. This led to other environmental changes. Juniper trees encroached upon grasslands, while some seeps and springs stopped flowing. The pronghorn (though not a true antelope, it resembles one) has nearly disappeared from this landscape, even though its outline is sketched on ancient rock art throughout the region.

By the time Flagstaff was founded in 1881, people sought out these unique environs and began looting archeological sites and taking rocks as souvenirs. By this time, the West had been "won." America's philosophy of Manifest Destiny ruled the day (see chapter 33, "Pipe Spring National Monument").

> Loop drives are extremely popular with the petroleum industry—they bring the motorist right back to the same gas station from which he started.
>
> —Edward Abbey, *Desert Solitaire*

Now, however, Native Americans who were once feared and scorned as uncivilized heathens were part of an intriguing and desired past.

An abstract by Tyson Pendery found in the archives of the University of Northern Arizona stated, "Developments in transportation technology, including railroads in the 1880s, and automobile and road development in the 1920s allowed greater economic prosperity. Mobility and the growth of the middle class lifted economic barriers to visiting and experiencing these indigenous peoples."[16]

According to Pendery, three primary trends in American life perpetuated the use and development of preserves like Wupatki as tourist destinations at the expense of preservation archeology: "First, as native peoples gained cultural importance and increasingly became appropriated by Americans, U.S. citizens sought to experience Indian culture. Second, technological developments and nation-wide prosperity increasingly allowed more to visit places like Wupatlu. Finally, early preservation politics codified a tradition of bringing visitors to both scenic and historic places as a means to support preservation values."

Whether one agrees with it or not, those same forces remain in place. In fact, one could easily argue that this book and its author continue to codify those preservation politics by allowing visitors to see these places through his eyes and on these pages "as a means to support preservation values."

SIGNATURE ACTIVITY: DRIVE, THEN STROLL, THEN DRIVE A LITTLE MORE!

WHY GO?

A 35-mile driving/walking tour of both Wupatki and Sunset Crater Volcano National Monuments takes about four hours—if you do it right! It will introduce you to an incredible landscape and the people who inhabited it, even as a volcano was erupting, 900 years ago.

SPECS

ACTIVITY TYPE: Driving tour—but it's only really worth it if you get out of the vehicle to walk in the path of the Ancient Ones.
TRAILHEAD/PUT-IN/ETC.: Start either at the visitor center, Sunset Crater Volcano, or Wupatki.
DISTANCE/LENGTH: 35 miles
AVERAGE TIME REQUIRED: 1 to 2 hours for the drive only; 3 to 4 hours includes visits to the sites to feel them and touch them and smell them and enjoy them.
CONTACT/MANAGING AGENCY: Flagstaff Area National Monuments, 6400 North Highway 89, Flagstaff, AZ 86004, 928–526–1157, nps.gov/waca/learn/management/flag_parks.htm
DIFFICULTY: Easy
SPECIAL CONSIDERATIONS: It's hot out here. Don't leave your pet in the vehicle even for 5 minutes—seriously!

GETTING THERE

SHORT DESCRIPTION: Sunset Crater Volcano Visitor Center is located two miles east of the park entrance off U.S. Highway 89, 15 miles north of Flagstaff, AZ. Wupatki Visitor Center is 15 miles farther north of the Sunset Crater turnoff on U.S. Highway 89, or 30 miles north of Flagstaff.
GPS COORDINATES: Sunset Crater Volcano National Monument, 35°21′51.1″N, 111°30′14.4″W; Wupatki National Monument, 35°31′12.6″N, 111°22′15.8″W

OVERVIEW

A lazy driving tour leads visitors through both of these national monuments, from open grasslands in the Wupatki Basin, through a piñon-juniper woodland, and into a high-elevation ponderosa pine forest.

The drive may take only an hour or two. However, if you stop to walk the trails and visit the marked sites, your three or four hours will invigorate you and excite your mind.

For example, only a short distance from the Sunset Crater Volcano Visitor Center, you'll find the Lava Flow Trail, a one-mile loop trail that winds through the Bonito

This multicultural society constructed a ventilation system throughout the pueblo that allowed them to build fires within their homes.

Lava Flow. Here, at an elevation of about 7,000 feet, you'll discover quaking aspen trees growing along the edge of the black lava flow.

Moisture is greater where it channels off the lava flow onto ground covered in cinder, which aids in retaining moisture. Cinder is slowly formed into soil, and the succession of plants over the past 900 years has changed. It will continue to change as wind, rain, and new plant life will cause even the hardest rocks to erode through weathering.

Soil also has been carried in on the wind and collected in small pockets protected by the lava flow. While the margin of success for flowers, shrubs, and trees here is small, life continues to thrive in this fragile landscape.

Another short turnoff from the main loop road extends to the Wukoki Pueblo. In 1896, archeologist Jesse Walter Fewkes wrote: "This ruin . . . is one of the most impressive masses of aboriginal masonry . . . it is visible for many miles, and from a distance resembles an old castle as it looms . . . above the plain."

Of course, the main attraction—other than the volcano itself—is the Wupatki Pueblo, a 100-room architectural wonder found just behind the Wupatki Visitor Center. It's a must! (If you want to see the volcano, check out "Signature Activity: Climb a Peak to View a Crater" in chapter 18!)

And don't forget to stick your head above the blowhole at Wupatki! It will certainly blow your hair—if not your mind!

CHAPTER 20
WALNUT CANYON NATIONAL MONUMENT

SIZE—3,600 acres

YEAR ESTABLISHED—November 30, 1915, by President Woodrow Wilson, following a huge public outcry over looting and vandalism of the cliff dwellings, especially after pothunters began dynamiting the walls of ancient dwellings to let in more light. Father Cyprian Vabre, a Catholic priest from Flagstaff, led the charge, preaching that this vandalism amounted to desecration.

MANAGING AGENCY—National Park Service, Flagstaff Area National Monuments

DOG-FRIENDLY?—Pets are not allowed in the visitor center or on the trails.

FEES AND PERMITS—$15 per individual, good for 7 days. Free entrance for children under 16; $45 for an annual Flagstaff Area National Monuments Pass (which allows entrance into Walnut Canyon, Wupatki, and Sunset Crater Volcano National Monuments); annual pass, senior pass, access pass, and active duty military passes also accepted.

NEAREST CITY— Flagstaff, AZ

NEARBY PUBLIC PROPERTY—Sunset Crater National Monument, Wupatki National Monument, Coconino National Forest, Tuzigoot National Monument, Montezuma Castle National Monument

SPECIAL CONSIDERATIONS—Not only is it hot in the summer, but it's at an elevation of 7,000 feet. Drink LOTS of water and take water with you on the trails. Be careful when attempting strenuous activity such as climbing stairs. There are a couple hundred here.

OVERVIEW

Beds of Kaibab Limestone that now form Walnut Canyon's rim once rested on the floor of an ancient sea. A hike along the Rim Trail here will take visitors past fossil shells and sponges embedded in this limestone at 7,000 feet in elevation.

For 60 million years, Walnut Creek cut through this rock, gouging out the softer layers to form overhanging ledges and eventually carving out a canyon 20 miles long and 400 feet deep. This, in turn, exposed evidence from 225 million years ago of blowing winds over a coastal dune that left permanent patterns in cross-bedded layers of Coconino Sandstone.

The earliest documented passage of humans here occurred more than 3,000 years ago. Hand-size figurines made from willow branches were found hidden in the canyon. Similar figurines that may represent bighorn sheep were found in caves at the Grand Canyon.

Were they crafted as part of an early hunting ritual? Perhaps.

Early farmers had settled east of the San Francisco Peaks by AD 600. They lived in pithouses and farmed open parks in the forest. It appears Walnut Canyon, just south

Dwellings may be spied beneath overhangs throughout this canyon

of the San Francisco Peaks, was only lightly used until 1100. Between 1125 and 1250, however, it bustled with life. Then, these people—later called Sinagua—gradually drifted away as more and more families discovered the advantages of larger, newer settlements on Anderson Mesa, a short distance to the southeast.

Dr. Harold S. Colton, who conducted the first official survey of Walnut Canyon's prehistoric sites in 1920, labeled them "Sinagua." The name came from an old Spanish designation for the region—Sierra Sin Agua, "waterless mountains."

By the time Dr. Colton undertook his survey, five years after Walnut Canyon was designated a national monument, many ruins had been gutted and their scientific value diminished. Colton, who later founded the Museum of Northern Arizona, pioneered numerous studies of human and natural history in the region.

The museum, located in Flagstaff, continues to serve as a fountain of knowledge and information on Ancestral Puebloans and the Colorado Plateau. This small yet extremely important museum is loaded with artifacts and is certainly worth a visit since you've come this far!

Following Dr. Colton's work, and thanks to the CCC (Civilian Conservation Corps) during the Great Depression in the 1930s, there are 240 man-made steps along Island Trail. They lead visitors around a natural island full of partially restored ruins in the middle of Walnut Canyon. (See "Signature Activity: Island Trail Hike.")

The trail offers a close-up view of this ancient culture. It's steep—thus all the steps. Yet with residences and storage rooms on both south-facing and north-facing sides of the canyon, you can see how a bustling community could take advantage of sun, shade, and native vegetation throughout the year.

What you see are not necessarily original structures due to looting and destruction. As with the trail, much of the rehabilitation was the work of the Mount Elden CCC Camp located in Flagstaff.

Flowering prickly pear cactus is found along the Island Trail as it passes through the upper Sonoran desert, with yucca and prickly pear, to mixed conifer forests and back again.

Created by President Franklin D. Roosevelt, the CCC provided impoverished young males between 18 and 23 years of age with the opportunity to improve their education and to earn a living. This, of course, was during the Great Depression. The work of the CCC across the nation also helped realize Roosevelt's goal of conserving the human and natural resources of the nation.

At Walnut Canyon, CCC crews used construction materials quarried on-site, blending the new with the old as a way of preserving the natural character of the landscape. That natural character, along the Island Trail in Walnut Canyon, is fascinatingly urban, with doorway after doorway of abodes side by side underneath hundred-foot-long limestone overhangs, like rowhouses or condos.

What a ruckus, living with a couple hundred of your closest friends and relatives. Can you imagine talking to your girlfriend across the canyon?

"Hey, Numa'vaya, are you going to the kiva on Friday night for the harvest celebration?"

"Shhh. My little sister is listening."

"And I'm telling Mom."

"MOOMMMM! MOM . . . MOM . . . mom," echoes down the canyon walls.

No one knows for sure exactly how these people lived, especially since most of what survived the centuries was so vandalized in the 1880s. Nonetheless, through what was left, and through the oral history of the Hopi, the probable descendants of the Sinagua, much can be inferred.

FIRE

Of all the natural processes, fire has the greatest potential for severe damage as well as lasting benefit. Fire management has become a primary National Park Service tool in the past two decades, following large, devastating fires that resulted in loss of human life and property and having a severe impact on regional ecosystems.

Fire was suppressed in the United States for a century until we realized some fire is normal and essential in the proper management of any natural landscape. However, with such huge fire loads, some forest fires can be devastating.

In the late spring and early summer of 2018, most of the Coconino National Forest surrounding Walnut Canyon, Wupatki, and Sunset Crater Volcano National Monuments was closed to all activity due to high fire danger. That same summer saw dozens of major fires on the Colorado Plateau, triggered either by dry lightning strikes or by stupid human acts.

Now small, controlled burns are part of the Park Service's arsenal to battle these deadly blazes.

There are at least 80 dwellings and structures sheltered by overhanging cliffs scattered throughout this canyon. This includes about 300 separate rooms, most of which were probably used for storage. At its peak between 1125 and 1250, several hundred people lived here.

Most sites face the warm sunlight, yet straight across the canyon from one site, you may see another in the shade. One could have been occupied in the winter, the other used as a summer home.

Most of the cliff sites are found within 150 feet of the bottom of the canyon on two main ledges scoured from softer layers of limestone. These masonry-walled rooms were lined end on end by prehistoric masons who would shape limestone blocks and place them in a clay mortar to create a foundation underneath the overhang. They would then construct the front walls and partitions and plaster the walls inside and out.

Small T-shaped entryways helped to control the flow of air. When the wide section of a door was covered, fresh air flowed in the bottom opening, and smoke escaped through the vent hole above the door. Thick deposits of black soot streak interior walls of rooms used for cooking and heating. Some soot, found in storage rooms, suggests the Sinagua may have periodically fumigated the rooms to rid them of pack rats and other unwelcome critters.

Many reasons are given for clan migration in Hopi traditional history, including drought, famine, cold weather,... disease, warfare,... and natural disasters. However, from a Hopi perspective, the primary reason for migration is the fulfillment of a spiritual covenant.... The religious intentionality of Hopi migration receives scant attention in most archeological reconstructions of the past.

—Ferguson and Lomaʹomvaya, "Hopi History, Culture, and Landscape," in *Sunset Crater Archaeology: The History of a Volcanic Landscape*, Center for Desert Archaeology, Tucson, 2005[†]

Piñon pine nuts, yucca fruits, and Arizona walnut (for which the canyon is named) were valuable food sources for these local people. They also hunted deer and bighorn

Gnarly pinón pine twists in the wind alongside Island Trail in Walnut Canyon.

sheep and raised turkeys. A major part of this indigenous people's diet was maize—corn—although they also grew beans and squash. For that, the farmers needed the rims of the canyon. They were probably more open than they are today, having been cleared for fields, firewood, and construction timbers. And, oh yes, we've suppressed fires for hundreds of years, so current fuel sources have grown to dangerous proportions. (See "Fire" sidebar.)

Travel from the rim to the canyon bottom was still strenuous as these native people followed natural breaks in cliff walls along game trails used by deer, bighorns, and other animals. And scarcity of water dictated everything, especially since Walnut Creek did not always flow. Large urns displayed in the Museum of Northern Arizona played a huge role, as they could collect up to 35 gallons of water, to be kept in the back of cool, rock-lined storage rooms for later use. Hundreds of these large pieces of pottery, perhaps thousands, must have been needed to collect water dripping off the overhangs following infrequent rain- or snowstorms.

The 13th century on the Colorado Plateau was a time of climatic change. It forced many people to migrate into larger villages near more dependable water sources. That doesn't appear to be the case here. Nonetheless, they left. Not all at once.

They slowly trickled away. Perhaps a growing population put greater demands on the resources at hand. Surrounding forests may have been cleared for fields or firewood. Local game could have been hunted out. The corn itself could have depleted the soil's nutrients fairly quickly.

Or, as the Hopi believe, their migration simply continued.

It's hard to say, but for a while at least, this place was jammin'.

SIGNATURE ACTIVITY: ISLAND TRAIL HIKE

WHY GO?

This intimate trail provides visitors with a close-up look at 25 partially restored cliff dwellings, with interpretive signs discussing the various plants clinging to life in the cliff faces before you. You'll get a taste of how life really felt for the people of the canyon 800 years ago.

SPECS

ACTIVITY TYPE: Hike

TRAILHEAD/PUT-IN/ETC.: Directly behind the visitor center

DISTANCE/LENGTH: 1 mile

AVERAGE TIME REQUIRED: 1 hour if you stop and read all the informational signs

CONTACT/MANAGING AGENCY: Flagstaff Area National Monuments

DIFFICULTY: Challenging, especially if you're not acclimated to 7,000 feet. The trail drops 200 feet on 240 rock steps and returns the same way.

SPECIAL CONSIDERATIONS: Carry—and drink—lots of water. It's hot and steep, and you're at 7,000 feet.

GETTING THERE

SHORT DESCRIPTION: To reach Walnut Canyon from Flagstaff, travel east on Interstate 40 (I-40) toward Albuquerque. Take exit 204 and head south. The Walnut Canyon Visitor Center is located at the end of this three-mile road. The trail is directly behind the visitor center, where you pay your entrance fee.

GPS COORDINATES: 35°10'16.97"N, 111°30'33.46"W

OVERVIEW

Ready? Do you have water? An energy bar? A camera? A hat? Sunscreen? Water?

The first step is down. So is the next one.

After a few more, you can take a break and read an interpretive sign. Then you can go down a few more—like 235 more—before you come to a natural saddle. Here, the trail tracks from the side of the canyon to the island itself, a small promontory created by the meander of Walnut Creek.

Protected areas on both the south- and north-facing sides of the island provide shade and shelter.

Don't worry about the way down, unless you have bad knees. There's a handrail most of the way. It's the climb back up that makes most people huff and puff.

However, thanks to the CCC and continued maintenance by the Park Service, it's a smooth trail. Once across the saddle, it circles the island, following a ledge where Native American masons built a series of cliff homes, all in rows under the overhangs of great limestone ledges.

You'll find individual rooms large enough to lie down in with a few personal belongings and maybe the dog. Other rooms were used for heating and cooking, while others stored corn, beans, and squash. Some of these rooms stored water in assorted sizes of pottery, some large enough to hold up to 35 gallons. (Once you hike out of here, hike over to the Museum of Northern Arizona and view some of the vessels found here.)

The interpretive signage along the trail discusses both life in the canyon and its various plant and wildlife species. Huge prickly pear cactus blooms bright yellow in the late spring. Arizona walnut trees—for which the canyon is named—turn brilliant colors, from yellow to orange to bright red, in the fall. Mule deer and turkeys still meander through the canyon, while turkey vultures catch drafts above its rim and canyon wrens catch gnats below.

The Sinagua supplemented their diet with numerous wild plants, such as walnuts from the namesake tree and Fremont's mahonia, or barberry, a tart berry with antimicrobial qualities. Many of these plants still thrive in the canyon.

While these plants may not be in season when you visit, if you took the extra water and an energy bar with you, they could give you a little boost to help you out of the canyon!

CHAPTER 21
TUZIGOOT NATIONAL MONUMENT

SIZE—382 acres
YEAR ESTABLISHED—July 25, 1939, by President Franklin Roosevelt to protect antiquities and put men to work during the Great Depression
MANAGING AGENCY—National Park Service
DOG-FRIENDLY?—Due to extreme temperatures, dogs on-leash are welcome on the trails at Tuzigoot. Do NOT leave pets in your vehicle, even with the window down!
FEES AND PERMITS—$10 per person 16 and older. Admission covers both Tuzigoot and Montezuma Castle monuments for 7 days. Children 15 and younger are always free. There is no entrance fee to visit Montezuma Well. All other interagency passes, such as the America the Beautiful Pass, are accepted.
NEAREST CITIES—Jerome, Clarkdale, Cottonwood, and Sedona, AZ
NEARBY PUBLIC PROPERTY—Coconino National Forest, Prescott National Forest, Montezuma Castle National Monument, V Bar V Heritage Site, Palatki Heritage Site, Honanki Heritage Site, Slide Rock State Park, Red Rock State Park, Fort Verde State Historic Park, Jerome State Historic Park, Verde Canyon Railroad
SPECIAL CONSIDERATIONS—(With apologies to the late John Hartford)

Don't leave your CDs in the sun;
They warp and they won't be good for anyone!
Don't leave your CDs in the sun,
They get all wavy and they just won't run.
They just wont play, just won't play, just won't play, just won't play, just won't play,
just won't play . . .

OVERVIEW

The abandoned ruins of Tuzigoot Pueblo rise about 120 feet above the Verde River Valley of central Arizona—high enough to scan the landscape for miles. More than 100 rooms are nestled within this intricate rock complex, built around AD 1100 along the spine of a natural limestone ridge.

The ruins overlook the lush Tavasci Marsh and the nearby Verde River. Completely abandoned by AD 1425, its remains were unnaturally protected by a copper mining company in the 1900s. Looters couldn't get to it since it was situated on private property. Also, since it sits 120 feet above the valley, its foundations remained protected from nearby toxic waste ponds of the aforementioned copper mine.

University of Arizona archeologists Louis Caywood and Edward Spicer worked with the Work Projects Administration (WPA) during the Great Depression in the 1930s

More than 100 rooms are nestled into this intricate rock complex, built around AD 1100.

to excavate the ruins. By then, the copper mine had graciously sold the site to Yavapai County for a dollar. The excavation work was then done under federal WPA programs. The copper company built tailing ponds in the valley, pumping tons of copper smelting waste products from mines in Jerome and the smelter in Clarkdale. They also leased land to ranchers such as the Tavasci family, for whom the marsh is named.

Smelting operations have long since ceased in Clarkdale, and so has the pumping. Its present owner, Freeport-McMoRan Copper and Gold Company, Inc., "participates in a cooperative effort to clean up and restore this valuable wetland habitat," according to University of Arizona researchers.

Tavasci Marsh is located in limestone beds on the northernmost edge of an ancient oxbow isolated from the Verde River nearly 10,000 years ago. The marsh is primarily fed by a natural spring emerging from a "sand boil." These unique outlets occur where springwater discharges into the base of a pool under enough pressure to cause the sand grains to "boil."

This marsh was extremely important to the Sinagua people who dwelled here 900 years ago. It was key to survival in a harsh environment. Clean water, fuel, and ample food harvested from native plants and animals made for a good life—for a few hundred years, anyway.

To the east and south of the ruins lies a small man-made lake—Peck's Lake—created by the copper company as part of a planned golf course that never materialized. This tiny impoundment, along with Tavasci Marsh and its natural spring, provides habitat for more than 245 different species of migrating birds. Only an estimated 5 percent of Arizona's watercourses remain in a natural state. Thus, preservation of the site is especially important in 2020 and beyond. Freeport-McMoRan Copper and Gold, Inc., owns both bodies of water, and a cooperative agreement allows the National Park Service to manage Tavasci Marsh as a wildlife sanctuary.

The Sinagua people cleared and farmed this rich bottomland extensively. They grew corn, beans, squash, and cotton. After their departure, the area probably reverted back to a natural state with native grasses, which gave way to open water surrounded by cattails, sedges, and other water-loving plants. From the late 1800s to around 1990, the area was again cleared, grazed, and farmed extensively—at least the portions not occupied by waste ponds from the copper mine.

Today, vegetation in this basin varies considerably. Once farming activities ceased here about 30 years ago, native and exotic invasive plants spread like wildfire and began changing the marsh.

The view from the top of the ruins to the west shows the alteration of the distant Black Hills from mining and the processing of rich metal ores. Individual communities such as Jerome on the slope of the mountains, Clarkdale with its cement plant and old smelter buildings, and Cottonwood stretch down the valley. A black slag pile still may be seen by the river, as can the flat expanse across from the ruins, where tailings from the smelter operations were deposited. The Park Service covered this area in 2007 with a few feet of topsoil and seeded with native vegetation. The hope is that it will eventually resemble the land adjacent to it in the north, which is covered mostly with mesquite and creosote bush.

While many modern travelers may sneer at mesquite and creosote, the native Sinaguans had many uses for these plants. Roots from the creosote bush, *Larrea tridentata*,

Tuzigoot Pueblo rises 120 feet above the Verde Valley below.

for example, aggressively soak up water, and a resin coating on the leaves reduces moisture loss and gives the plant a distinctive smell that intensifies after rain. Creosote was a Sinagua pharmaceutical wonder, treating infections, toothaches, colds, body odor (yes, BO!), nausea, and sprains.

Sinaguans used mesquite for food, medicine, beverages, glue, firewood, construction material, and furniture making. Both pods and seeds from the mesquite were ground into meal. The native people sprinkled ground mesquite meal with a little water to form small, round cakes. Slices of dried cake then were fried, used to thicken stews, or eaten raw. The meal also was used as flour to make flatbread. Mesquite meal, by the way, is gluten free.

If allowed to ferment, a mixture of water and mesquite flour produces a fizzy alcoholic drink. A liquid made from boiling the inner bark of the tree was used as a laxative. Apparently, modern man just has to loosen up a bit when it comes to mesquite and creosote.

Although early ethnographers labeled this group "Sinagua," meaning "no water," this southern group of Sinagua people actually had plenty of water—at least for the number of people who lived here in the 1200s. However, by the time Tuzigoot was abandoned in 1425, something was certainly amiss. Perhaps there were too many people, or they exhausted their wood supply, or a drought dried up the Verde River and local springs. Perhaps they exhausted the soil and depleted the wild game that sustained them.

Whatever the reasons, they're long gone now, and only the foundation of this unique living complex remains, thanks to an unnatural protector—a copper mine.

SIGNATURE ACTIVITY: BIRDING!

WHY GO?

From a historical and cultural standpoint, there are many good reasons to visit Tuzigoot. However, bird enthusiasts from around the globe travel here to catch a glimpse of some of the 245 species of birds that utilize this area throughout the year.

SPECS

ACTIVITY TYPE: Birding
TRAILHEAD/PUT-IN/ETC.: Visitor center at Tuzigoot National Monument
DISTANCE/LENGTH: From 0.6 mile to 3 miles round-trip
AVERAGE TIME REQUIRED: Most of the morning
CONTACT/MANAGING AGENCY: National Park Service, Tuzigoot National Monument
DIFFICULTY: Easy; wheelchair-accessible for a portion of the trip
SPECIAL CONSIDERATIONS: The early bird gets the worm. It's hard to find birds later in the day.

GETTING THERE

SHORT DESCRIPTION: The nature trails at Tuzigoot all begin at the visitor center, and a wheelchair-accessible trail leads to the Tavasci Marsh overlook; the trail leading down to the marsh cuts off the wheelchair-accessible trail within a hundred yards of the visitor center and follows an old dirt service road for 0.7 mile to the bottom. Another 0.6-mile hike takes visitors to the back (southwest) side of the marsh and a birding platform.
GPS COORDINATES: 34°46'22.1"N, 112°01'45.5"W

OVERVIEW

Because 245 species of birds have been found here at one time of the year or another, the Audubon Society has dubbed Tavasci Marsh an "Important Bird Area." It's been identified using an internationally agreed-upon set of criteria as globally important for the conservation of bird populations.

Species such as the black-throated sparrow, Bewick's wren, and the brown-headed cowbird are among the most common species found here. Yet approximately 75 percent of the breeding species are neotropical migrants. In other words, they breed in Canada and the United States during our summer season and spend the winter in Mexico, Central America, South America, or the Caribbean islands.

As a result of this migration, there is a tremendous change in bird community composition at Tavasci Marsh at any given time. For example, the black-chinned hummingbird is common in both riparian and desert zones here, yet it is found only

Two hundred forty-five species of birds have been identified at Tuzigoot, including this white-crowned sparrow.

in the summer. By contrast, Anna's hummingbirds are quite uncommon, yet they are year-round residents, and the broad-tailed hummingbird is common yet migratory, escaping to South America for the winter.

No matter what time of year you visit, you'll find birds here. Year-round residents such as Anna's hummingbirds may be hard to find, but others like ravens and mourning doves are abundant. Summer residents like Lucy's warbler and northern rough-winged swallows are at the park roughly from June to August, while winter residents like the northern flicker appear from approximately November to February. Migratory birds may be seen from March to May and again from September to October.

CHAPTER 22
PETRIFIED FOREST NATIONAL PARK

SIZE—218,533 acres (50,000 acres of designated wilderness)

YEAR ESTABLISHED—President Theodore Roosevelt created Petrified Forest National Monument on December 8, 1906, because "the mineralized remains of Mesozoic forests . . . are of the greatest scientific interest and value and it appears that the public good would be promoted by reserving these deposits of fossilized wood as a National monument with as much land as may be necessary for the proper protection thereof."

MANAGING AGENCY—National Park Service, Petrified Forest National Park, Arizona

DOG-FRIENDLY?—Pets are allowed on a leash 6 feet or less in length.

FEES AND PERMITS—$25 auto/7-day pass to Petrified Forest National Park; $15 bicycle and walkers/per person; $20 motorcycle; $45 Petrified Forest National Park Annual Pass

NEAREST CITIES—Holbrook and Winslow, AZ

NEARBY PUBLIC LAND—Hubbell Trading Post, Homolovi Ruins State Park, Meteor Crater, Coconino National Forest, Apache-Sitgreaves National Forest

SPECIAL CONSIDERATIONS—Pet owners, sign up for the park's Bark Ranger program. Treats are given to four-footed participants! When you visit the park, remember to B.A.R.K.: Bag your pet's poop. Always keep your pet on a leash. Respect wildlife. Know where you can go.

OVERVIEW

The late Triassic period was the "dawn of the dinosaurs," when smaller dinosaurs competed with various crocodile-like reptiles for survival. It pitted the predator, a 15-foot-long postosuchus, against two-tusked herbivorous dicynodonts, the prey. That was about 237 million years to 201.3 million years ago, give or take 200,000 years. That's how precise fossil dating has become.

Petrified Forest National Park is one of the best places in the world to see this fossil record. It's a land where giant dinosaurs roamed and giant forests toppled. Yet, gazing into a smoke-filled haze as a 30-mile-an-hour "breeze" scrapes across this sparsely vegetated landscape called the Painted Desert, it's hard to imagine this was once a gigantic, prehistoric rain forest.

We visited this national park in the spring of 2018 when too much of the Colorado Plateau was on fire—man-made and lightning-induced.

Not far from Winslow, Arizona, off the I-40 corridor, the Petrified Forest tells the story of ancient ecosystems. Fossils provide evidence of animals and plants that lived millions of years ago. Petrified wood found in the park and surrounding region is the fossilized remains of an immense, ancient forest.

Deposits of clay and sandstone, sculpted by volcanic eruptions, earthquakes, floods, sunlight, wind, and rain, reflect an altering display of colorful radiance in the Painted Desert.

The petrified wood here consists of almost solid quartz—a giant, sparkling crystal with a rainbow of colors produced by impurities in the quartz from iron, carbon, and manganese. According to the Park Service, here's how it got that way: A couple hundred million years ago, there was this huge, gigantic tree living on the edge of the stream. It finally died of old age. It's foliage, bark, and smaller branches fell off. Then the stream flow cut away the bank under its roots. The tree was so huge, it eventually toppled into the stream (there weren't any houses or barns to fall on back then, nor was there insurance). The dead log was eventually transported downstream, where sooner or later it snagged on the bank and was buried under sand and mud in the stream channel. Now, think of how much water, mud, and sand this stream must have been carrying to bury a log bigger than a gigantic redwood or sequoia. That would be a lot of water over a long period of time.

Eventually the log was buried more deeply. We're talking millions of years here. It was cut off from oxygen and microbes, so it ceased to rot. Silica in the groundwater began infiltrating the log, and through a chemical reaction, it replaced the organic material with quartz crystals.

The log was "petrified."

Millions more years pass, and subsequent erosion of the surrounding rock re-exposed the petrified log. Continued erosion undercut the log, causing it to crack and break into segments. Some of the segments rolled downslope. Some of them were sliced in half, as though a chain saw had carved through them.

That was Mother Nature's saw cut! The Park Service explains that the quartz within the petrified wood was hard and brittle. It fractured easily when subjected to stress—just like me, I guess. During the gradual uplift of the Colorado Plateau beginning 60 million years ago, this stress caused the petrified trees to break like glass rods. The crystal nature of quartz created clean fractures.

Voilà! Straight cuts.

It's impossible not to notice the numerous curio shops and "Indian Artifact Museums" along I-40 in this part of the world. Stop and shop for Navajo rugs, knives, cold beer, and clean restrooms. They're at every exit off I-40 from Gallup, New Mexico, to Flagstaff, Arizona, it seems.

Most of them are completely surrounded by petrified wood. It's free, according to the billboards. While some of this petrified wood probably came from Park Service land, much of it was collected on private or Navajo Nation land surrounding the park.

In addition to petrified wood, this park also protects more than 600 archeological sites inside its boundaries. John Muir explored this area in 1905–1906. In 1916, the

> Too many people just eat to consume calories. Try dining for a change.
>
> —Renowned Chef John Walters

1932 Studebaker stuck in the mud

Indian art centers, artifact museums, and curio shops may be found off most I-40 exits from Gallup, New Mexico to Flagstaff, Arizona.

Organic Act approved by Congress and signed by President Woodrow Wilson created the National Park Service, which took over management of the national monument. The purpose of the Park Service was to "conserve the scenery and the natural and historic objects and the wildlife therein and to provide for the enjoyment of the same in such manner and by such means as will leave them unimpaired for the enjoyment of future generations."

In 1958, President Dwight D. Eisenhower first approved legislation to expand this area from the national monument that was designated by Teddy Roosevelt in 1906, but it wasn't designated a national park until December 9, 1962, by President John F. Kennedy.

On December 2, 2004, President George W. Bush signed a bill authorizing expansion of the park, more than doubling its size from 93,533 acres to 218,533 acres.

There's a lovely 28-mile park road that slowly wanders through the Painted Desert and Petrified Forest with numerous stops along the way. You'll enjoy spectacular views of the Painted Desert from several overlooks and view Ancestral Puebloan homes and petroglyphs at others. There are six hikes of various lengths, and with 50,000 acres of designated wilderness, hiking off trail is a great option.

As you look across the Painted Desert, however, ask yourself, "Am I sure I want to hike across this desert?" It's hot. It's dry. The wind is probably blowing. There is no vegetation taller than your tennis shoe growing here. There are rattlesnakes. There are no people. There is no cell service.

Another option is to get back in the car and check out the 1932 Studebaker that's been stuck in the mud for decades where famed Route 66 once cut through the park. Check out Newspaper Rock, covered with more than 650 petroglyphs, some as old as 2,000 years.

There's a visitor center at either end of this road. Both are well worth your time. Then, hop into the car again and hightail it to La Posada Hotel in Winslow. Don't forget to check out the statues standing on the corner, right next to the flatbed Ford.

SIGNATURE ACTIVITY: FINE DINING IN THE DESERT

WHY GO?
It's the best restaurant in the entire Four Corners area, and the hotel is really cool! Great art, great ambience.

SPECS
ACTIVITY TYPE: Fine dining
TRAILHEAD/PUT-IN/ETC.: Turquoise Room in La Posada Hotel, Winslow, AZ
DISTANCE/LENGTH: A couple hundred feet from door to table
AVERAGE TIME REQUIRED: A leisurely couple of hours
CONTACT/MANAGING AGENCY: La Posada Hotel
DIFFICULTY: As easy as pie (or soufflé)
SPECIAL CONSIDERATIONS: Allow an extra half hour if you order the chocolate soufflé for dessert! It's fabulous! They serve breakfast and lunch too.

GETTING THERE
SHORT DESCRIPTION: Located on the Amtrak Railroad line at the intersection of Route 66 (now called 2nd Street) and AZ Highway 87 in Winslow. The train stops at the hotel daily on the Los Angeles–Chicago line. By car, take I-40 East to exit 255 and turn left (south); or take exit 252 off I-40 West and turn right (south). From Phoenix, go north on I-17, then northeast on AZ 87 for 185 miles (about three hours).
GPS COORDINATES: 35°01′17.00″N, 110°41′41.05″W

OVERVIEW
Without a doubt, the Turquoise Room in La Posada Hotel in Winslow, Arizona, is the finest restaurant in the entire Four Corners region. This unique restaurant inside a splendidly restored hotel provides an enticing presentation of Southwestern fare. It is THE place to stop in this part of the world—despite the fact that it's also about the only place to stop.

La Posada Hotel, built in 1930, was one of the last of the great Fred Harvey–Santa Fe Railroad hotels. Mary Jane Colter, considered one of the greatest Southwestern architects, designed it. It's on the National and State Registers of Historic Places.

In Winslow.

Buried for millions of years, this log was cut off from oxygen and microbes, so it ceased to rot. Silica in groundwater infiltrated the log and through a chemical reaction, it crystalized and became "petrified."

If you were born after, say, 1980, you may not know anything about Winslow other than that Glenn Frey and Jackson Browne made it famous with the hit song "Take It Easy."

Since Interstate 40 was built, most people just buzz by Winslow. In its day, though, it was a hoppin' spot on Route 66 where it paralleled the Santa Fe Railroad line.

Fred Harvey was an entrepreneur who, in the 1880s and 1890s, was credited with creating the first restaurant chain in the United States. He built a string of restaurants along the Santa Fe Railroad line catering to the wealthy as well as the up-and-coming American middle class. Harvey was a strong promoter of tourism and was known as "the Civilizer of the West." He died in 1901, but the Fred Harvey Company was kept alive by his sons and grandsons until 1965, when they still maintained 47 Harvey House restaurants, 15 hotels, and 30 dining cars operating on the Santa Fe Railway line between Cleveland and Los Angeles.

Colter, one of very few female architects of her day, was the designer and architect of many of Harvey's landmark buildings, such as Hopi House, Lookout Studio, and Hermits Rest inside Grand Canyon National Park.

The restaurant, now run by Chef John Sharpe, serves the most mouthwatering chocolate soufflé you've ever tasted! Before you can get to dessert, though, you'll have to try the grilled chicken breast with tomatillo sauce and tamale; or perhaps elk medallions so tender you can cut them with a spoon; or the "killer" vegetable platter featuring a corn tamale filled with squash, corn, and chilies (vegan); a corn masa empanada filled with quinoa, currants, and pine nuts; and a grilled mild chile stuffed with three cheeses and topped with papaya salsa.

You may be lucky enough to arrive on a night when fresh grilled halibut is served with a forest bounty broth of fragrant yellow foot and chanterelle mushrooms, fiddlehead fern tips, blistered tomatoes, and organic sugar snap peas and fava beans from McClendon's, a local farm.

Naturally, each dish is paired with the perfect wine—a lemony yet full-bodied Eric Chevalier La Noe Muscadet for the halibut, a Sonoma County Chardonnay from Chateau St. Jean for the vegetable platter, and an exuberant Kim Crawford Spitfire Sauvignon Blanc from Marlborough for the grilled chicken breast.

Bring your appetite.

And your wallet.

Be sure to spend time browsing through the hotel. Not only is it restored with grace and charm, its hostess, Tina Mion, is an excellent artist. Her work is featured throughout. You'll enjoy every bit of it!

PART 6

NAVAJO NATION

Protected Navajo rock art remains
unscarred from vandalism and graffiti.
This area is sacred to native inhabitants.

OVERVIEW

The Navajo Nation was starving from decades of fighting with Spanish and American soldiers—not to mention battles with other native tribes—when it was forced to march 400 miles from its ancestral home in the dead of winter in 1863, the same year President Abraham Lincoln's Emancipation Proclamation took effect.

That year, Colonel Christopher "Kit" Carson, following orders from Department of New Mexico commander Brigadier General James H. Carleton, oversaw the start of the Navajo Nation's grueling "Long Walk." It began from Canyon de Chelly in what is now northeast Arizona, and led to the barren Bosque Redondo Reservation near Fort Sumner, New Mexico, 400 miles east. Hundreds of the approximately 5,000 Navajo who had surrendered to Colonel Carson perished in the arduous trek.

Colonel Carson and his volunteer militia had forced the Navajo—most of whom lived and farmed in Canyon de Chelly—into pockets and corners of the canyon by capturing their livestock, destroying their homes (hogans), and ravaging their crops, starving the Navajo into surrender. While the Navajo were on their "Long Walk," more American soldiers entered Canyon de Chelly to capture renegade Navajo warriors and to chop down the trees—the precious peach trees—that the Navajo valued so highly both for eating and for trading.

After four years at Fort Sumner, the Navajo signed a treaty with the United States, agreeing to fight no more and to return to a shrunken reservation closer to their ancestral home. They were given many promises. They were to receive good land, water, and schools. What remained of the decimated Navajo Nation moved to its reservation in Monument Valley in 1868. This arid, high-desert plateau, however, provided scant water, and the U.S. government provided no schools.

Little has changed in more than 150 years. While there are now two relatively new high schools, many of the inhabited hogans within the reservation still do not have running water or electricity. Some prefer it that way. Some don't.

There are approximately 350,000 people living on the Navajo Nation. The median age is 28 years. The unemployment rate is 48.5 percent. This is one of the poorest spots in North America, yet its people remain proud. Many of them are now employed in the tourism industry. They escort photographers, geologists, cultural historians, and anyone else who's interested on breathtaking tours of this barren yet incredibly magnificent area.

It's one of the most majestic and photographed places on earth—where fragile pinnacles of rock are surrounded by miles of mesas and buttes; where sandstone masterpieces towering from 400 to 1,000 feet high cast luxurious shadows across the windswept desert floor; where surreal pastel colors of evening sunsets mesmerize one's soul and the brilliant yellow sheen cast upon the red rock walls at sunrise satisfies our desire to be one with the universe—at least for one fleeting moment.

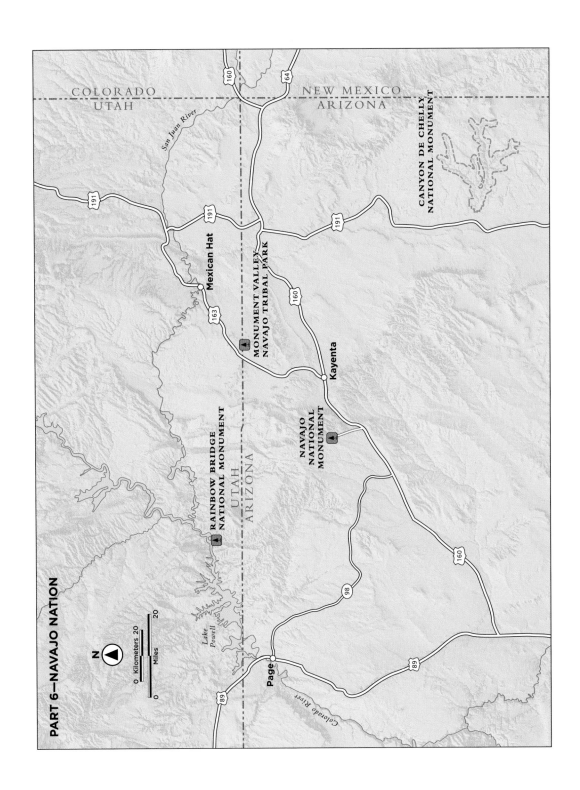

PART 6—NAVAJO NATION

CHAPTER 23
SAN JUAN RIVER

SIZE—102 miles total from Montezuma Creek, UT, to Clay Hills on the boundary of Glen Canyon National Recreation Area and Lake Powell. The major floatable section on a normal year, however, is the 87-mile stretch from Sand Island put-in near Bluff to the Clay Hills.

YEAR ESTABLISHED—Millions of years ago; however, we've damned it up quite a bit in the last century, so it's not the same.

MANAGING AGENCY—Bureau of Land Management, Monticello Field Office, 435-587-1544

DOG-FRIENDLY?—No pets are allowed.

FEES AND PERMITS—You cannot float this river without a permit. Permits are issued only through a preseason lottery and advance reservations to applicants 18 years of age or older. For permit information, go to recreation.gov. The Navajo Nation requires additional permits to camp, hike, or visit archeological sites on river left (the south side of the river). River right (the north side) is permitted by BLM.

NEAREST CITIES—Bluff and Mexican Hat, UT

NEARBY PUBLIC PROPERTY—Valley of the Gods, Bears Ears National Monument, Natural Bridges National Monument, Glen Canyon National Recreation Area

SPECIAL CONSIDERATIONS—Commercial outfitters operate on this river, so you don't have to put together your own trip if you don't have lots of friends with rafts. A list of outfitters is available at blm.gov/sites/blm.gov/files/uploads/San JuanRiverCommercialOutfitters.pdf.

OVERVIEW

The San Juan River originates high in the Rocky Mountains on the west side of the Continental Divide in southwestern Colorado. The river first flows from the San Juan Mountains south to Pagosa Springs, then enters the extreme northwestern corner of New Mexico via Navajo Reservoir, one of the major water storage projects of the Colorado River Basin.

Below Navajo lies a world-class tailwater trout fishery. The course of the river then turns westward for 140 miles through the deserts of northern New Mexico before heading north again to reenter Colorado just east of the cartographic landmark known as Four Corners. (The original 1878 cartographic landmark for the spot where the states of Colorado, New Mexico, Utah, and Arizona meet is actually off by 2.5 miles, but what the heck, it's close!)

The San Juan then resumes its westerly direction, slicing through the red rock canyonlands of southern Utah, ultimately flowing to Lake Powell on the main arm of the Colorado River.

The San Juan River House was occupied by Ancestral Puebloans sometime between AD 900 and 1200.

This river, one of the main tributaries of the Colorado River system, carries more than water. Along its 383-mile route, it picks up 25 million tons of silt and sediment each year.

It's that silt and sediment that helped carve this magnificent drainage through the heart of the Colorado Plateau.

The best way to see this river is to float it.

There are three major access points on the river: Sand Island to Mexican Hat is about 27 miles, typically a two- to three-day float; Mexican Hat to Clay Hills is approximately 57 miles, another four- to five-day trip. The entire trip from Sand Island to Clay Hills is about 84 miles and typically takes six to seven days. Clay Hills is the only viable takeout below Mexican Hat. There is a dangerous waterfall downstream of Clay Hills.

SIGNATURE ACTIVITY: FLOAT YOUR BOAT!

WHY GO?

Relieve stress. Revel in nature. Learn how to smile again. Bond with your friends. Make new friends. Soak up a little vitamin D. Get a little exercise. Have a little thrill. Get the adrenaline pumping. Step out of your comfort zone. Visit places no one else can reach. Refresh your mind, body, and spirit.

SPECS
ACTIVITY TYPE: River rafting down the San Juan River
TRAILHEAD/PUT-IN/ETC.: Sand Island Campground and Boat Ramp
DISTANCE/LENGTH: 27 miles, from Sand Island Campground to Mexican Hat

AVERAGE TIME REQUIRED: 2 to 3 days; we took 6 leisurely days!
CONTACT/MANAGING AGENCY: Bureau of Land Management, 435–587–1544, blm.gov/office/monticello-field-office
DIFFICULTY: On high-water years, watch out! Normally, it's an easy float.
SPECIAL CONSIDERATIONS: Be prepared. Rafting is an inherently dangerous activity!

FIND THE TRAILHEAD/GETTING THERE

SHORT DESCRIPTION: From West Main Street in Bluff, UT, travel southwest on U.S. 191 for four miles to the BLM's Sand Island Campground and Petroglyphs. Turn left and head toward the river.
GPS COORDINATES: 37°15′47″N, 109°36′44″W

OVERVIEW

May 2, 2018: Day 1 on the San Juan River

It's wet after raining last night . . . what a weird weather phenomenon here in the desert. This was the first rain of the year here.

It's still damp and chilly as we slowly load the boats. We sip coffee from insulated mugs. We're in no big hurry. We've had to cut our original 84-mile trip to 27 miles because there just isn't enough water for our larger rafts to get through.

When we applied for permits in January (all of us applied and only one of us drew), we didn't know the water would be THIS low! The annual runoff should be peaking, but there is no runoff this year. There wasn't much snow in the southern Rockies. That's what feeds this river.

Twelve of us stand in a semicircle on the banks of the San Juan to receive our instructions from the BLM River Ranger—always wear life vests; if you fall out of the boat, swim with your feet downstream; don't get stuck between the raft and the rock; use the groover (portable, environmentally sound toilet), don't be like the bear and (defecate) in the woods; only camp in designated group sites on river right. River left is Navajo Reservation land, and you can't go there without a permit.

We have the permit.

He tells us the river is running at about 900 cfs when we get on. Normally, at this time of year, it's running between 2,000 and 3,000 cfs.

Cfs is cubic feet per second. That's how water is measured. One cubic foot of water equals 325,851 gallons, enough to fill a football field with one foot of water.

Claret cup cactus in bloom

That's a lot of water, but not if you consider that 39.5 million Californians consume about 85 gallons per person per day (see lao.ca.gov/Publications/Report/3611).

We're still going to float for the full six days. No sense wasting vacation time.

Six days for 27 miles, less than five miles a day. Wow. Stressful.

Not.

Day 2

It was chilly and wet when we got onto the river yesterday. I left my camera well packed. Today the sun is out and so is the Nikon. We took a long hike to the Butler Wash panel of petroglyphs and a small ruin in Butler Wash that a couple of us visited four months earlier.

The scenery is much different today. The cottonwood trees have fully leafed. The non-native, water-guzzling, and invasive Russian olive trees and tamarisk have as well. The river runs chocolate brown from a second rainstorm last night and the birds are happily singing, grateful for this little bit of moisture in their desert home.

Swallows swoop up and down the river, and spotted towhees tweet their distinctive call: two short introductory notes followed by a trill—*chirp chirp trilllllll.*

We heard wild turkeys gobble along the banks and then saw one glide across the river yesterday. We've seen deer prints, rabbit droppings, and a big old black bear print in the sand. Bear scat filled with seeds from Russian olives dried in the sun along the trail.

Paddling upstream with nothing better to do . . .

A couple guys in our group are now playing guitar on the beach, while others prepare for dinner. Another bunch is playing a sophisticated game of tossing plastic washers into a round hole.

We've taken some great hikes, played some good horseshoes, drunk good beer (and cheap beer), and celebrated two birthdays with party favors, a cake, and a piñata full of small whiskey shooters. You can carry a lot of stuff on a raft.

Yet the river is low and is expected to drop even more by the time we take out. Obviously, one of the topics of conversation is drought. We're experiencing it now in the desert Southwest. Is this what drove the ancient Puebloans away?

We could probably make this short trip in two or three days, but we're not going to waste time heading home when we're already out here! There are 12 of us from Grand Junction, Fruita, Glenwood Springs, Carbondale, and Denver, Colorado. There are three women named Lori, Lori, and Laurie. That makes it easy to find stuff.

Just yell, "Hey, Lori . . ."

Someone will answer.

Among our group are ski patrollers from Snowmass, a doctor of family medicine from Carbondale, and a semiretired engineer and water court referee. There are three biologists, one retired from the Colorado Division of Wildlife and two who are current Colorado Parks and Wildlife biologists, and Ordy the Orkin man from Grand Junction.

Bob, our plastic great blue heron decoy, guards the groover. If someone is sitting on it, Bob is laid down with his beak to the sand. When that person is done with that particular chore, they stand Bob back up and he continues to guard the unoccupied groover. ("Bob is much classier than a pink flamingo!" exclaims Lori, or Laurie, or was it Lori?)

Day 3

I'm sitting on the ledge of an overhang about 50 feet above the river and I'm totally mesmerized by the billions of stars shining so brilliantly tonight. I'm thinking about my niece, Shannon, as she lies in her hospital bed, dying.

I saw her last week, just prior to this trip. My son had me record a message to her that he could play next to her ear as she lay in the hospital with her siblings and her parents and her cousins at her side. Her husband was there and both her boys. My message was this: "I am visiting the ruins of the ancient Puebloans and I am channeling their spirits and you are one with them."

Life goes on. The river flows to the ocean. The spirits of our ancestors live in our souls.

Day 4, maybe

This is a lifestyle with which I could easily become accustomed.

No phone. No internet. No TV.

I don't know how the Colorado Rockies baseball team is doing. I don't know what the weather forecast is. I don't know what Stormy Daniels's acquaintance is up to.

I don't hear the noise.

Yet there is a noisiness to all this quiet. The river flows to the Pacific as a quiet whisper and a gentle roar. The wind whistles through the tamarisk, Russian olive, rabbitbrush, and native willows along the river. Spotted towhees and canyon wrens and ravens and wild turkeys sing their water song in this arid desert. Territorial geese honk loudly at any intruder—another goose, a raft, a raven.

We hear ewes—female bighorn sheep—bay as we float by, guarding their young, which we cannot see high on the cliffs overlooking the San Juan River in this remote section of southeast Utah.

We float through an incredible canyon gorge, multilayered and multicolored from millions of years of being covered, then exposed by ancient seas as our planet took shape, followed by millions of years of upward thrust from the shifting of tectonic plates, and of course the immense effects of erosion from wind and water.

It is magnificent and serene and beautiful and hot.

I am crouched in the nook of a couple of very large granite boulders. Rock bed. Eons of sandstone erode above me. Slowly. Slowly.

I have found a small piece of shade that won't last. I know I will have to move in another 5 or 10 minutes. Nonetheless, it is a welcome respite from the intense desert heat that invades this canyon country.

As I gaze up at the brilliantly clear azure sky, I see a layer of white rock, then a rustic layer of red, then a jagged layer of brown, then another layer of white and red and white and tan and brown and gray—all the way down to the river's edge. I'm amazed at the many levels of ancient sea that rolled through here over hundreds of millions of years.

We see desert bighorn sheep by the dozens graze along the banks of the river as we float leisurely by. We watch as great blue herons fly over, barely glancing at Bob. Wild turkeys gobble before they burst out of hiding like Huey helicopters, then set their wings and silently glide across the river in front of us.

Now, as I observe a crystal-clear night sky through the mosquito netting on my tent (I don't need the rain fly), the brilliance of Ursa Major—the Big Dipper—is significant. In the Southwest, one dazzling star outshines the rest. That must be Jupiter. Another planet works toward the horizon to the west. Venus.

Desert bighorn ram on the banks of the San Juan River

I listen to the serenade of the river as the crickets keep time. The bugs flying toward my headlamp don't get through the netting tonight, but I know they will be voracious later in the year. This place becomes unlivable with gnats and mosquitoes at certain times. Tonight, however, their activity is minimal this early in the year, with the evening temperature at about 50°F.

It is a most pleasant time to be in the desert, and I feel pretty confident, lying here on my back on my Therm-a-Rest sleeping pad, that I am in a much more peaceful place than most people on earth tonight.

I am grateful for that.

I saw sparkling lights just to the west of the Big Dipper in a constellation that I cannot name. I believe those lights are my niece, Shannon, and I wish her the best in union with our ancestors and their ancestors as she becomes part of the spirit of the universe and of my heart forever.

Day 5

We have to take out tomorrow. Boo hoo.

We'd better have some fun today. Who hasn't tried the paddleboard? Anyone up for a hike into that canyon we passed this morning? Hey Lori/Laurie, what's for lunch? How about one more game of horseshoes? JT is sound asleep again. Let's prop up the empty beer cans and party stuff around him and take pictures!

Day 6

We awoke to a glorious sunrise, and no one was in a big hurry to leave. We would miss each other's company. We would miss the raucous honking of the territorial geese waking us up each day. We would miss the gentle flow of the river and hum of the canyon.

When we took out today, it was a cluster. There were two large groups of school-age kids just getting onto the river, floating that lower stretch to Chalk Cliffs. We still think the water is too low for our larger rafts. However, they have a lot of kids to drag rafts across the rocks if flows recede any further. We didn't have that workforce floating with us.

One group leader spent more than an hour at river's edge delivering his 10-minute safety speech. He lost all the kids after the first 5 minutes, but that did not deter his oratory.

Ah, back to civilization.

On the highway heading toward Bluff, my cell phone dinged with numerous unanswered messages and phone calls.

Only the one from my brother mattered. Shannon passed away at 9:15 p.m. on Saturday, May 5.

She was only 44 years old.

Cancer is indiscriminate. We are brokenhearted.

As I gaze out the window while the sparse and arid desert of the Colorado Plateau blurs by, I realize—the desert knows.

This desert has seen life and death and rebirth.

Life rolls on.

I'm home now. I just talked to cousin Kevin and he said, "I'm glad you're back and I'm glad you went to the desert. It puts something in your soul that you normally can't get."

CHAPTER 24
CANYON DE CHELLY NATIONAL MONUMENT

SIZE—84,000 acres within the Navajo Reservation

YEAR ESTABLISHED—1931, by President Herbert Hoover, in order to preserve important archeological resources from erosion and vandalism, with the stipulation that "the grazing and other rights of the Indians are in no way interfered with."

MANAGING AGENCY—National Park Service in conjunction with the Navajo Nation Parks and Recreation

DOG-FRIENDLY?—Pets are allowed on-leash at the overlooks and in the campground. Pets are not permitted in the welcome center, on the White House Trail, or on canyon tours.

FEES AND PERMITS—Travel along the paved roads on the North and South Rims of Canyon de Chelly is free. You can also hike into White House Ruin on a public trail. The Navajo Parks and Recreation Department (NPRD) issues backcountry permits and manages the Cottonwood Campground. The NPRD office is located at the entrance to the campground and collects fees for backcountry permits and camping. Call 928–674–2106 for more information.

NEAREST CITY—Chinle, AZ

NEARBY PUBLIC PROPERTY—Hubbell Trading Post National Historic Site, Petrified Forest National Park, Monument Valley Navajo Tribal Park, Navajo National Monument, Yucca House National Monument, Cibola National Forest, Zuni Mountains, El Morro National Monument, Chaco Culture National Historical Park

SPECIAL CONSIDERATIONS—Managed by the NPS in conjunction with Navajo Nation Parks and Recreation, this national monument is situated in the middle of Navajo Nation. There are a number of families who live here. Please respect their privacy. You must hire a native Navajo guide to escort you on tours along the canyon floor by hiking, horseback, or vehicle. A list of guide services, costs, and tour lengths is available at https://navajonationparks.org/guided-tour-operators/canyon-de-chelly-tour-operators/.

OVERVIEW

Humans have occupied the labyrinth known as Canyon de Chelly (pronounced "d'SHAY")—including both Canyon de Chelly and Canyon del Muerto—since the Archaic period dating to 2500 BC. Physical evidence from petroglyphs, pictographs, pottery, weavings, corncobs, and peach pits shows that people have continuously lived here longer than anywhere else on the Colorado Plateau.

At about the same time Egypt's Great Pyramid of Giza was completed and before the great Toltec culture emerged in the Tula Valley (southwest of the present state of Hidalgo, Mexico), the earliest people here were seasonal campers. They huddled under rock shelters and ate deer, pronghorn, and rabbit and foraged on more than 40 varieties of plants. Eventually, with proximity to consistent water sources, they began farming.

About 2,500 years ago, people known as Basketmakers because of their extraordinary weaving skills improved farming techniques here. They grew consistent supplies of beans, squash, and corn, which had been introduced from further south on the continent.

Canyon de Chelly provided rich, fertile soil for these agricultural endeavors. Those soils had been deposited over millions of years by the same flooding streams that carved these astonishingly beautiful cliffs.

Sometime around 1,250 years ago, the dispersed hamlets of the Basketmaker era gave way to a more communal way of living. These ancient Puebloans may have gathered together for defense, to be closer to their farms, or simply because their rock shelters had become too crowded. Here in the canyon, they constructed intricate multistoried villages, compounds, and religious kivas with decorated walls.

They created T-shaped doorways, possibly to haul heavy loads, but certainly as part of impressive ventilation systems. "The Anasazi, accustomed to sprawling communities and open skies, now lived in towers and packed cliff dwellings, breathing one another's breath, inhaling the smoke of winter fires from down the hall, listening to other people's sexual activities," wrote nature and travel writer Craig Childs in his classic 2008 book, *House of Rain: Tracking a Vanished Civilization across the American Southwest.*[18] While continuing to farm for corn, squash, and beans, they also raised turkeys and grew cotton, which led to new weaving techniques.

Then, suddenly, about 700 years ago, Puebloan life ended. Archeologists still debate the causes of this dispersal of a once great civilization. It seems likely that drought, disease, conflict, and religious migration all played a role. The soil's fertility certainly declined due to overuse. However, many of the ancient Puebloans' descendants were Hopi, who believe this movement was part of a migratory cycle and belonged in the natural order of things.

According to traditional Hopi beliefs, ancestral villages were purposely settled and left, but their ancestral spirits still reside in the areas they left behind. The Hopi believe that when the people stay too long in a certain area or fail to lead moral and responsible lives, then social and environmental disasters will remind them of their destiny. Astronomical events like solar eclipses or meteor showers, or events such as the explosion of Sunset Crater Volcano west of here, also were signals to continue migrations toward the center of the universe, according to Hopi tradition. Archeological evidence supports the theory that the Hopi were seasonal farmers here for centuries, continuing to carry on pilgrimages with occasional stays in the canyons.

By the 1700s, the Navajo occupied these canyons. They called themselves "Diné," or "the people," and also may have descended from ancient Puebloans—although the

While people have lived in Canyon de Chelly for more than 5,000 years, Ancestral Puebloans built White House around AD 1060.

term "Anasazi" means "ancient enemy." They brought domesticated sheep and goats with them, along with centuries of migration and adaptation. They were superb horsemen, having obtained the animals in the 1500s from the Spanish. They were exceptional weavers. Their blankets were highly valued, as were the weavers themselves.

And here in this area, they could really grow peaches!

Canyon de Chelly was known far and wide for its peach orchards as well as its cornfields. The Diné learned peach cultivation from the Hopi, who still lived on the mesas above and around Canyon de Chelly. The Hopi, in turn, had garnered this knowledge from the Spanish centuries earlier.

> We cannot change others, nor can we change the past. But we can change ourselves.
>
> —Richard Rohr, Center for Action and Contemplation, Albuquerque, NM

The Diné located their peach orchards on alluvial terraces receiving runoff from cliffs and small tributary drainages. They ate fresh peaches, dried them, and used them as a "ceremonial purgative." They boiled them, stewed them, and, in general, incorporated them as an integral part of the local diet. They traded peaches for other necessities of life with diverse tribes and travelers, and even used peach pits in polishing stone griddles.

But sometimes the Diné did not trade. Sometimes they took what they felt was theirs. They had been fighting with other native tribes for centuries, and other native tribes had been fighting with them. They also fought the Spanish, the Mexicans, and the Americans. They were very adept raiders, and their warriors were fierce and capable.

Through war and disease, the Spaniards had nearly decimated the Paiutes, a tribe further to the west. They also wreaked havoc on the Hopi, the Zuni, the Pueblo, the Hohokam, and the Utes until all were weakened and crushed by American Manifest Destiny in the mid- to late 1800s. (See chapter 33, "Pipe Spring National Monument.")

The Diné people's brush with extinction occurred during the "Long Walk" of 1864. American soldiers destroyed Navajo hogans where they lived. They trampled and burned fields, killed livestock—and chopped down the peach orchards. (See overview of part 6, "Navajo Nation.")

When the Navajo returned home four years later, they still faced starvation. Food distribution centers were established to help them recover. Practices taken from Spanish and Mexican traders provided the blueprint for trading posts that grew up around the newly formed Navajo Reservation. One of the most famous—and still existing—is Hubbell Trading Post, located about 40 miles south of here. It's worth a visit if you're in the area. They have a cooler full of ice-cream sandwiches.

Today, the Diné continue to live both in the canyon and on the canyon rims. According to native guide Reginald "Regg" Etsitty, his people have survived because they have adapted. "We've always had to adapt, to take what other cultures give us and blend them with what we know." Traditional beliefs are reflected in everyday life. "We still collect plants for ceremonial and medicinal uses," he said, yet his people also "adapt to changes in our physical world."

The Navajo Reservation in the Four Corners area is 17,544,500 acres, larger than Wisconsin, the 23rd-largest state in the United States.

Regg said there are more than 130 trails that drop into Canyon de Chelly. Only the White House Ruin Trail can be accessed without a guide. Most are very steep and rugged. The White House Ruin was not a Navajo ruin, but rather was constructed by ancient Puebloans. It was named for the white streak of paint in the back of the ruin.

Besides the White House, Regg said there are more than 2,700 archeological sites in the area, including 700 standing ruins. Most of the ruins are located in Canyon del Muerto, while most of the incredible standing rock structures, and some of the best farmland, are located in Canyon de Chelly. Together, they form "Chinle," the Navajo word for "flowing out," where the water flowing within the two canyons meets and flows out onto the plain.

The Navajo lived—and some still live—in hogans. Hogans also serve as locations for certain ceremonies. These six- to nine-sided structures were built from materials readily available—wood, earth, and stones. The doorway always faces east to allow occupants to greet the day.

Many hogans still do not have electricity or running water. As you drive across the tops of the mesas above Canyons de Chelly and del Muerto, you may see trucks hauling firewood or water from community wells. You will not see towns or cities in the traditional sense. Navajo families live in family groups spread throughout the nation. Small clusters of hogans and trailers may signify more than one generation of a family.

Since Archaic times, nearly 5,000 years ago, people have lived within these canyon walls and on the canyon rims. It's a high-altitude desert with scant water, and the Navajo who remain here have proven their adaptability.

SIGNATURE ACTIVITY: CANYON DE CHELLY TRIFECTA—DRIVE, HIKE, LISTEN TO A NATIVE

WHY GO?
Meet Native Americans with a different perspective who will discuss their fascinating history and show you some amazing antiquities. There are 2,700 archeological sites here, including 700 standing ruins.

Listen to Diné legends. Spider Rock is an 800-foot-tall sandstone spire, the top of which is said to be the home of Spider Woman.

What more do you want?

SPECS

ACTIVITY TYPE: Driving, hiking, and private jeep tour of the canyon bottom with a native guide! It's the trifecta!

TRAILHEAD/PUT-IN/ETC.: Both driving tours begin at the national monument visitor center, three miles from downtown Chinle on Route 7; the trailhead for the hike to White House Ruin begins six miles from the visitor center on the South Rim Drive; the meeting place for the guide tour can be pretty much anywhere—in Chinle, at the Cottonwood Campground, or at the national monument visitor center.

DISTANCE/LENGTH: North Rim Drive is 34 miles round-trip, overlooking Canyon del Muerto; South Rim Drive is 37 miles round-trip, overlooking Canyon de Chelly; the hike to White House Ruin is 2.5 miles round-trip; the private jeep tours run from 15 to 60 miles, depending on what you book.

AVERAGE TIME REQUIRED: Allow 1.5 to 3 hours each for the driving trips, including stops at overlooks; the hike takes about 3 hours, with time to gawk, catch your breath, and shop for Navajo jewelry at the tables under the trees near the ruin; the jeep tours take from 3 hours to all day.

CONTACT/MANAGING AGENCY: Canyon de Chelly National Monument, 928–674–5500, nps.gov/cach/index.htm; for private tours, a list of guides is available at canyondechellytours.com

DIFFICULTY: The driving is easy; the hiking is moderate to strenuous if you're not ready for altitude (5,876 feet above sea level here), or a 600-foot drop to the canyon floor and the hike back out; the jeep tour is easy if you're in the front seat. It's a little wilder if you're in the back. These guides have to gun it in a few sections to get through the deep sand.

SPECIAL CONSIDERATIONS: Take food, water, cameras, and imaginations with you!

FIND THE TRAILHEAD/GETTING THERE

SHORT DESCRIPTION: The visitor center is 3 miles from Highway 191 in Chinle, AZ, on Route 7. From Flagstaff, AZ, take I-40 East then Highway 191 North; From Gallup, NM, take Highway 264 West then Highway 191 North; from Kayenta, AZ, take Route 59 Southeast then Highway 191 South.

GPS COORDINATES: 36°09′11.40″N, 109°32′20.45″W

OVERVIEW

Reginald "Regg" Etsitty has lived most of his 41 years in Canyon de Chelly. He's seen floods and drought and tamarisk and Russian olive.

He's listened to the stories of his elders and now passes them on to his children.

He knows all of the 20 or so permanent year-round residents of this canyon and has touched the lives of thousands across the Navajo reservation that straddles Arizona, Utah, and New Mexico.

His first language was Navajo, and in the 1980s, when he was in kindergarten, he was thrashed in school for speaking his native tongue.

"I still remember," he says. Nonetheless, he'd like to find each of the teachers and elders he's known over the years to thank them for all they shared with him.

He's grateful, and like all Navajo, he's adaptable.

He is college-educated and was a recruiter for the trade school on the reservation—the res, as he called it. He was and is an IT professional, not only fixing computers but running websites, filming YouTube videos, designing and printing T-shirts and flyers. He's a father, a brother, a guide, and a hard worker.

He was our guide for a tour through Canyon de Chelly and did a marvelous job of not only describing the antiqui-

Spider Rock is an 800-foot-tall sandstone spire, the top of which is said to be the home of Spider Woman.

ties discovered here—the ruins and archeological sites and artifacts of ancient civilizations—but also the geology, geography, history, and culture of the area.

He told us the story of the Spider Woman. She lives on top of Spider Rock, an incredible, 800-foot-tall sandstone monolith that marks the mouth of Monument and de Chelly Canyons. "She taught the Diné to create beauty in their own lives and to spread the 'Beauty Way,'" teaching a balance of mind, body, and spirit. "But," he said, "our grandmother would tell us that disobedient children would be taken by Spider Woman, who wove them up tight in her web. She would boil and eat the bad little kids, and that is why there are white streaks on the top of Spider Rock. That's where the bones of the bad children would bleach on the rocks to this day," he said.

The Navajo culture is rich in oral history. Grab a guide, take a tour, listen to the stories and the legends, and discover a different way of life.

CHAPTER 25
NAVAJO NATIONAL MONUMENT

SIZE—360 acres

YEAR ESTABLISHED—President William Howard Taft declared this a national monument in 1909 because of "a number of prehistoric cliff dwellings and pueblo ruins . . . which are new to science and wholly unexplored, and because of their isolation and size are of the very greatest ethnological, scientific, and educational interest."

MANAGING AGENCY—National Park Service, Navajo National Monument

DOG-FRIENDLY?—Leashed pets are allowed in campgrounds and parking lots.

FEES AND PERMITS—This is a fee-free monument!

NEAREST CITIES—Kayenta, Shonto, and Tuba City, AZ

NEARBY PUBLIC PROPERTY—Nothin'. There's really nothing close, but since you're in the vicinity: Canyon de Chelly (on Navajo Reservation Land), Monument Valley Tribal Park (also on Navajo Reservation land), Rainbow Bridge National Monument, Glen Canyon National Recreation Area and Lake Powell, San Juan River, Bears Ears National Monument, Natural Bridges National Monument

SPECIAL CONSIDERATIONS—GPS systems have been leading visitors to travel on Indian Route 221 to and from Shonto, which is an unpaved dirt road! It is not advisable to drive on this road due to impassable road conditions, especially for large RVs and cars. Save your vehicle and your wallet. Ignore the GPS and take the highway.

OVERVIEW

Three of the largest surviving ancient Puebloan cliff dwellings ever discovered lie here in northeastern Arizona between Page and Monument Valley, in the midst of the Navajo Nation. Betatakin and Keet Seel (Kits'iil) are 160-acre islands of federal land enveloped by Navajo Nation boundaries. Inscription House is hidden in a shallow alcove on 40 acres of federal land not far away. All three are considered unique, culturally important, and, as President Taft said in 1909, "[of the] very greatest ethnological, scientific, and educational interest."

The Inscription House site has been closed to the public since 1968 because visitation damage to the extremely fragile structure cannot be mitigated. However, the Park Service offers guided tours of Keet Seel and Betatakin, the second- and third-largest ancient Puebloan dwellings ever discovered, behind only the Cliff Palace at Mesa Verde.

Betatakin is Navajo for "ledge house." To the Hopi, it is known as Talastima, or "place of the blue corn tassels." With 135 total rooms, it housed about 75 to 100 people. Tree-ring dating—the science of dendrochronology (see chapter 12, "Aztec Ruins National Monument")—shows that this site was occupied between AD 1250

With more than 150 rooms, Keet Seel (Kits'iil) was not discovered until 1895 by Colorado ranchers Richard and John Wetherill. GEOFF TISCHBEIN

and 1286. The people who lived here grew corn, as well as beans and squash, and fashioned intricate ceramics and textiles.

Sometime after 1286, Betatakin inhabitants simply left their Tsegi Canyon home and headed south. Was it drought that drove them away? Bad blood? Did they exhaust the soil with overuse, or did valuable farmland become eroded? Did poor politics and bad leaders govern them? No one really knows. They just split, leaving behind pretty much everything, including signs that they had traded far and wide. Scarlet macaw feathers from central Mexico were found here, along with seashells from the Gulf of California. Unfortunately, most of the valuable antiquities had been looted from these sites by the time they came under federal protection. However, many fine pieces of pottery and other artifacts from these sites may be found in the national monument visitor center.

Like Betatakin populations, the people who once built and lived at Keet Seel also moved south after 1286. Keet Seel was even larger than Betatakin, with more than

THE FOUR SACRED MOUNTAINS

In Diné Bahane'—the Navajo Creation Story—the creator placed the Diné on land between four mountains, representing the four cardinal directions. The Four Sacred Mountains in Diné bizaad (the Navajo language) are:

- Blanca Peak, also known as Navajo Mountain/Sisnaajiní—the sacred mountain of the east, "the dawn," or "white shell mountain." Associated with the color white.
- Mount Taylor/Tsoodził—the sacred mountain of the south, "turquoise mountain," or "blue bead." Associated with the color blue.
- San Francisco Peak/Dook'o'oosłííd—the sacred mountain of the west, "the summit which never melts," or "abalone shell mountain." Associated with the color yellow.
- Hesperus Mountain/Dibé Nitsaa—the sacred mountain of the north, "big sheep." Associated with the color black.

The mountains represent the major parts of traditional Navajo religious beliefs, enabling the people "to live in harmony with their Creator and with nature."

150 rooms, including living quarters, kivas, and storage areas. It's possible as many as 150 people could have once lived here.

Some anthropologists suggest the Navajo migrated to this area around AD 1400 to 1525. Navajo oral tradition, however, holds that Navajo originally arrived here around AD 700 or 800, making them descendants of ancient Puebloans. When Spaniards arrived around 1540, the Navajo were well entrenched here and across the Colorado Plateau.

By the mid-1800s, America's philosophy of Manifest Destiny changed all that. Native populations were devastated by hunger and diseases they had no natural immunity to as Anglos marched west. The Navajo Nation also was subjected to overwhelming conditions on their "Long Walk" in the winter of 1863. They were not allowed to return to these ancestral homes for another four years. By then, the Navajo were demoralized, shattered, and decimated. (See overview of part 6, "Navajo Nation.")

These sites were not discovered until Richard and John Wetherill, a couple of Colorado ranchers, found Keet Seel in 1895. The brothers had a keen interest in all things "Anasazi." Although they uncovered Keet Seel in 1895, it wasn't until 1909, when John Wetherill and Navajo guide Clatsozen Benully discovered Betatakin, that the area was dedicated as a Navajo national monument. (See sidebar on the Wetherill brothers, chapter 15.)

Today, the Navajo Nation and National Park Service work together to protect and enhance this significant cultural resource for future generations for educational and scientific purposes. Work continues on Inscription House, and only experienced rangers lead tours of Keet Seel and Betatakin. You can't visit these on your own. However, a paved one-mile, self-guided round-trip walk leads from the Navajo National Monument Visitor Center to an overview of Betatakin. The trail winds through a pygmy forest of dwarfed, gnarled piñon and juniper trees leaning at odd angles, sprouting peculiar limb growths and bearing tangles of exposed roots. Along the way, you may see mountain chickadees and scrub jays, or watch as turkey vultures catch drafts above the canyon rim. The trail leads to an observation deck with a scope for viewing the ruins more closely.

Betatakin Pueblo at Navajo National Monument wasn't discovered until 1909 by Colorado rancher John Wetherill and Navajo guide Clatsozen Benully. It's been protected ever since.

Daily ranger-led tours begin at this center during times of the year when there's no snow on the trail. These tours take visitors into the canyon bottom and directly to the restored ruins themselves. It's a tough hike, but not as tough as the one into Keet Seel. That hike is 17 miles round-trip, with a 1,000-foot drop from the canyon rim to the canyon floor, and of course the corresponding 1,000-foot climb out! (See "Signature Activity: Backpack to Keet Seel.")

SIGNATURE ACTIVITY: BACKPACK TO KEET SEEL

WHY GO?
You're hiking to one of the largest and most culturally significant ancestral sites on the Colorado Plateau! A trip here offers rich insight into the customs, culture, life, and historical contributions of people who lived 900 years ago.

SPECS
ACTIVITY TYPE: Backpacking
TRAILHEAD/PUT-IN/ETC.: Keet Seel Trailhead is located about 0.25 mile from the visitor center.
DISTANCE/LENGTH: 17 miles round-trip

Hikers to Keet Seel WILL get their feet wet! GEOFF TISCHBEIN

AVERAGE TIME REQUIRED: Hikers have the option of hiking in 1 day or staying overnight in a designated campground. Most choose the overnight option.
CONTACT/MANAGING AGENCY: Navajo National Monument, 928–672–2700
DIFFICULTY: Rugged and strenuous. Not for the faint of heart.
SPECIAL CONSIDERATIONS: This hike is only open roughly from Memorial Day to Labor Day (excluding Tuesdays and Wednesdays). The ONLY way to get the required free permit is to begin calling the national monument in February. Reservations are limited to 20 people per day and are available on a first-come, first-served basis.

GETTING THERE

SHORT DESCRIPTION: Elevation: 7,772 feet. From Tuba City, AZ, take U.S. Highway 160 East for about 50 miles. Turn left onto AZ 564 and continue 9 miles to the park visitor center. From Kayenta, AZ, head west on U.S. Highway 160 for about 19 miles. Turn right onto AZ 564 and continue north for about 9 miles until you reach the visitor center.
GPS COORDINATES: 36°40'56"N, 110°32'36"W

OVERVIEW

The diminutive Navajo National Monument is a great stop to or from Page, Arizona, Monument Valley, and the Grand Canyon. But if you really want to get a feel for this country and its cultural history, take a backpacking trip into Keet Seel.

The trail is only open from around Memorial Day to Labor Day. You must obtain a permit, which is distributed on a first-come, first-served basis beginning in February. You also must attend a mandatory meeting at the visitor center the day prior to your hike. If you miss the meeting, you don't get the permit.

From the canyon rim, the trail drops sharply 1,000 feet to the canyon floor on rocky switchbacks and sand dunes, then it crosses Keet Seel Creek 30 or 40 times. Your feet WILL get wet. Once you arrive, however, you'll be treated to one of the most culturally significant ancient Puebloan cliff dwellings remaining on the Colorado Plateau. At its height, this cliff dwelling had more than 150 rooms—it stood as an ancient sandstone apartment complex.

Keet Seel (Kits'iil) means "broken pottery" in Navajo. You'll still find plenty of that lying around—mostly because this place now is super-protected. A ranger is stationed at the site from Memorial Day to Labor Day, providing daily tours of the ruins and keeping a close eye on "antiquities" and things.

Since this is 17 miles round-trip, most hikers prefer to stay overnight at the designated campground, located near the ruin in a pleasant grove of Gambel oak, providing at least a little shade. You must bring all your own water on this trip, as the creek water is not safe to drink. That means your backpack will be heavy. You may want to lighten your load a bit by stashing a water bottle or two along the trail so you've got a little for the way out, but mark your stash so you don't leave your own "artifacts" behind. And don't forget your sunscreen, sunglasses, and a good hat. This can be a very harsh environment, but the hike will give you a feel for what it was like to make a living in this canyon more than 730 years ago.

CHAPTER 26
MONUMENT VALLEY NAVAJO TRIBAL PARK

SIZE—91,696 acres (extending into Arizona and Utah)

YEAR ESTABLISHED—Established in 1958 by the Navajo Nation's Tribal Council, making it accessible to the public as an expression of goodwill: "Navajo people treat visitors as honored guests. They are offered shelter, warmth and nourishment so they can continue on with their journey. The same hospitality we offer to you, and we hope that you have a safe and pleasant visit to our land."

MANAGING AGENCY—Navajo Nation Parks and Recreation, navajonationparks.org

DOG-FRIENDLY?—Pets are allowed ONLY if they are kept on a leash at all times. The backcountry is open range for livestock.

FEES AND PERMITS—$20 per day per vehicle (1 to 4 people); $6 per additional person; $10 per motorcycle; $12 for 24-hour backcountry permit (hiking and camping

NEAREST CITIES—Mexican Hat, Bluff, and Blanding, UT; Kayenta and Page, AZ

NEARBY PUBLIC PROPERTY—Valley of the Gods, Bears Ears National Monument, Glen Canyon National Recreation Area, Navajo National Monument, Natural Bridges National Monument

SPECIAL CONSIDERATIONS—National Park and Golden Eagle passes are not accepted. This is Navajo Nation, not U.S. territory. You can motor along "Valley Drive" through the park by yourself. It's a dirt road that takes about 1.5 to 2 hours to complete. Buses and RVs are not allowed. However, if you really want to see the Navajo Nation, you need to hire a native guide. You can catch one of them in the parking lot of the Monument Valley Trading Post any day of the year the park is open.

OVERVIEW

"So, what's with all the hands," asked my buddy JT to Larry, pointing to a sandstone wall with a couple dozen white handprints left from ancient Puebloans about 1,200 years ago.

"Lots of people," the native Navajo guide said.

We were deep inside the Navajo Nation's Tribal Park in Monument Valley (also known by the Navajo name Tse'Bii'Ndzisgaii [pronounced tseeh-bee-ni-zees-kay]). This was a section of the park that the general public was not allowed into without a native guide.

Larry was a man of few words, but his meaning was clear and his knowledge of the tribal park and its history was impressive.

A lot of his ancestors lived here at one time.

"Today," he told us on our daylong guided tour of Monument Valley, "we have 350,000 Navajo on the reservation. It is spread across the Four Corners [where

Colorado, New Mexico, Arizona, and Utah meet]. We have our own president and vice president who are elected every four years," he proudly stated. "We have 110 chapters within the Nation."

These chapters, he explained, meet in local chapter houses and decide most matters that concern their own chapter. They can also express their concerns about the Navajo Nation to a council delegate. There are 24 delegates to the Navajo National Tribal Council. They represent all 110 chapters. (If you'd like to know more about Navajo governance, check out David Wilkins, *The Navajo Political Experience* [Rowman & Littlefield, 1999].[19])

There are lots of issues to discuss at the chapter meetings, just like any city council or county commission meeting in the United States. Water lines, sewer issues, electricity needs, roads, bridges, drunk drivers, trash, poverty, jobs, water, and water issues all are discussed.

Monument Valley sunset

There are bigger issues as well. Larry believes then Navajo president Russell Begaye and the Navajo Nation in general are finally dealing with some of them. "Seventy percent of the people living on Navajo Nation lands don't speak Navajo, and 80 percent don't write it," he said. Hopefully that's changing. "Now, we have our own high schools, and they teach English along with our own language, as well as weaving and cultural history. Now, the kids are staying." (Jonathan Nez, current Navajo president, continues with Russell Begaye's policies.)

But poverty runs rampant in the Navajo Nation. Asked what the one thing he thought his people needed, Larry simply revolved his thumb against the index and second finger of his right hand.

Money.

"There are a few more jobs in tourism and natural resources now," he said, "but if the coal mine closes, we'll lose a lot of jobs there, too." Navajo and Hopi will both lose jobs. The Navajo Nation draws revenue from multiple sources (coal operations in New Mexico, casino gambling, and access to major highways to tap into tourism). The 15,000-member Hopi tribe has little else but subsistence farming. (Note: The Navajo coal-fired generation station was closed in November 2019, forcing closure of the Kayenta coal mine. The closures reduced the Hopi budget by $12 million, or 80 percent of the total budget.[20])

> The scalloped canyon walls rippled in the heat like drapery folds.
> —American novelist, playwright, and screenwriter Cormac McCarthy

Monument Valley panorama

"When I was small," Larry continued as he wrestled his late-model Suburban over the sandy trails of Monument Valley, "they didn't teach us how to write or speak the Navajo language. Back in the 1960s, we had to go to boarding school. There were no high schools on the reservation. Our schools only went to sixth grade. They would bus us to Riverside, California, intermountain Utah, or Oklahoma. We'd leave in August and not come home until May.

"The Bureau of Indian Affairs used to want the Navajo to become like the white people," he said, "with the same language, same farming techniques, same way of doing things.

"Same with the LDS church," he said. "It was big around here, and if you went to one of their schools, you learned their ways, not the Navajo way."

As we continued through this kaleidoscopic landscape, Larry stopped to show us ruins and explained the importance of different ceremonies still practiced by the Navajo. He showed us pictographs and petroglyphs and discussed their meaning. At one point, he took us to an active hogan village where we met a woman named Katherine.

Decked out in a vibrant teal-colored skirt, shyly hiding her blue jeans, with a purple crushed-velvet top and beautiful Navajo turquoise necklace, she showed us how the

Navajo still make yarn from the wool of sheep and how they weave it into the exquisite rugs that were as highly valued 800 years ago as they are today.

Katherine displayed her rugs and other Navajo wares in a large, round, comfortable hogan—a female hogan—just as her grandmother, Susie Yazzie, had done for decades prior to that. Revered as a tribal matriarch, Susie died in 2013 at age 92, although no one is certain of her exact age since no records were kept.

In this hogan, the ways of the old ones continued with Susie, and now with Katherine, who demonstrates her art on a large loom made of juniper. She shows us a traditional Navajo cradleboard and talks about how it swaddled Navajo babies and made them "strong-willed." She discussed the importance of moccasins, what they were made of and how they were sewn. She talked about different native plants and how they were used not only for medicinal purposes but to create the different, vibrant colors used to dye the wool and produce the subtle, intricate colors of the weave design.

"The browns and grays, cream-colored and black," she said. "That is the more traditional, but most people now want the colorful weavings, with lots of red."

Larry then showed us a male hogan, which was tepee-shaped. The female hogans are for family, he explained, while male hogans are used mostly for ceremonies.

Photogenic? You bet. Not only have still photographers from around the world traveled to take photos of Monument Valley, so has the movie industry. Ask John Wayne and his Hollywood director John Ford, who began making films here as early as 1939 with the hit movie *Stagecoach*.

While Ford shot 10 Westerns here, a number of them featuring John Wayne, Westerns weren't the only movies filmed here. So were *Easy Rider*; *2001: A Space Odyssey*; *The Eiger Sanction*; *Forrest Gump*; *Back to the Future Part III*; *National Lampoon's Vacation*; and many more.

"When they build the hogans," he said, "the door always faces east, for sunlight and praying." The female hogan is shaped with nine cedar-log legs all the way around, since women are pregnant for nine months.

The hogans are well insulated with layers and layers of mud. Inside, the polished cedar supports are exposed. There is a chimney, "and by the way the sunlight streaks through the chimney, they can tell the time of day," he explained.

Many of the Navajo Nation's elderly continue to live in hogans, while most of the younger people live in trailer homes throughout the tribal park and across the Navajo Nation in general. They still use coal to heat. The coal came from the nearby Peabody Coal Company mine near Kayenta, about 20 miles northeast of the tribal park, until it closed in November 2019. There are virtually no trees here, so timber used for construction of hogans and for firewood comes from Bears Ears, 60 miles to the north.

Bears Ears is considered sacred to these people, and many of the medicinal plants, as well as their timber, come from this area. Also, many of their ancestors are buried beneath Bears Ears.

In the scorching summertime heat that reaches 110°F, the hogan is much cooler—it's insulated with mud, and the residents dampen the floors to keep things cooler. In the winter, they keep warmth in and cold out.

Historically, and even today, these adaptive people use yucca for sewing needles and buffalo grass as a tea to ward off bad dreams. Numerous other native plants known by the medicine men (or women) are used for cancer, gout, and upset stomachs. Native baskets made of sumac were lined with pine pitch (pine tar) to create water jugs. Skins from harvested animals were used for such things as moccasins, shirts, and drums.

These were very resourceful people—with very long memories.

There is a Hopi village in the middle of the Navajo reservation, on the top of the mesa not far from Monument Valley. The village is controversial, as the Hopi want to build a fence around their area, yet Navajo live there too.

"The Hopi are trying to buy them off by building the Navajo new homes away from the Hopi land," said Larry. "But it was originally Navajo land. The Hopi moved in around the late 1800s and just stayed."

Just as the Navajo have been intensely marginalized by American society over the past two centuries, so too have the Navajo marginalized the Hopi and Paiute. But then, they've been fighting each other for centuries—much longer than either the Spanish who arrived in the 1500s or the Americans in the 1800s.

Katherine spins wool for an intricate blanket.

SIGNATURE ACTIVITY: HIRE A GUIDE, TAKE A RIDE!

WHY GO?

You can see a lot of Monument Valley on the self-guided 1.5- to 2-hour drive along the 17-mile Valley Drive. However, if you really want to get into it, hire a guide. He or she will show you petroglyphs, pictographs, ancient storage bins, and occupied hogans—and explain Navajo culture along the way.

SPECS

ACTIVITY TYPE: Guided driving tour
TRAILHEAD/PUT-IN/ETC.: In the parking lot of the visitor center at Monument Valley Tribal Park
DISTANCE/LENGTH: Tours range from 20 to 60 miles.
AVERAGE TIME REQUIRED: 1.5 hours to all day
CONTACT/MANAGING AGENCY: The tribal park contact is Navajo Parks and Recreation Department, 435-727-5870, navajonationparks.org. Note: All guide services are private. The park can provide you with a list. We went with Navajo Guided Trails Service, 435-444-9674, navajoguidedtours.com. It was started by Larry's mother when the park first opened in 1958. It's still operated by Larry's sister and niece. You can just show up in the parking lot, look for the covered wooden shacks that say "Guides," and hire someone working that day. Navajo Parks and Recreation Department has dictated that the guide services work on a rotating schedule with a competitive price scheme, apparently because competition for clients in the parking lot used to get pretty ugly!
DIFFICULTY: As easy as riding in someone else's vehicle

SPECIAL CONSIDERATIONS: Make sure you like the vehicle before you get in. It could be a long drive on rough roads. You could also ride a horse, since there are guided horse tours available. Note, however, that depending upon the time of year you visit, you may never want to ride a horse again as long as you live! Remember, John Wayne had an air-conditioned trailer!

GETTING THERE

SHORT DESCRIPTION: Take U.S. Highway 163 25 miles southwest from Mexican Hat, UT, or 22 miles northeast from Kayenta, AZ, to the Navajo Tribal Park Visitor Center parking lot. Look for the covered wooden booths housing the guides. They're easy to find.
GPS COORDINATES: 36°59'22.24"N, 110°07'52.43"W

OVERVIEW

He'll describe how the East and West Mitten Buttes look like hands, yet they signify spiritual beings watching over the valley. He'll put you in the perfect spot at the perfect time of day to really see Elephant Butte, and you can imagine a gigantic elephant facing west. He'll allow you to climb up to that incredible ancient ruin built underneath a natural arch to get a closer look. The spirits of his ancestors, however, will not permit him to enter that sacred place.

That's why you hire a guide here: It's to really experience a magical and spiritual place up close and personal.

And it may not be him. It may be her. And she knows what she's talking about. She's trained, she's educated, and she's native. This is her land. These are her people.

Nature took its time to sculpt this incredible landscape, she'll tell you. Before human existence, about 570 million years ago, the entire basin was underneath the Gulf of Mexico. Then, as the sea receded and the young Rocky Mountains rose, minerals were buried by shoreline sands and sediments washed down from the deltas.

Then, she will tell you, the lowland basin became a plateau as the uplift of the Colorado Plateau started to develop about 65 million years ago. It followed the collision of the Pacific and North American tectonic plates off the coast of California, sending shock waves eastward.

Endless erosion by water, wind, and ice then chiseled rock formations into the unique shapes you see in Monument Valley, and they were named and revered by the native people who first settled this stark, remarkable land.

Do your homework, certainly, but if you really want to experience all of it—hire a guide, take a ride!

CHAPTER 27
RAINBOW BRIDGE NATIONAL MONUMENT

SIZE—160 acres

YEAR ESTABLISHED—1910, by President William H. Taft, because it was "an extraordinary natural bridge, having an arch which is in form and appearance much like a rainbow." And, by the way, it's of "great scientific interest as an example of eccentric stream erosion."

MANAGING AGENCY—National Park Service, Glen Canyon National Recreation Area, Page, AZ

DOG-FRIENDLY?—Pets are not allowed on the docks at Rainbow Bridge or on the trail to the bridge.

FEES AND PERMITS—This is a fee-free area!

NEAREST CITIES—Page, AZ; Bullfrog, UT

NEARBY PUBLIC PROPERTY—Bears Ears National Monument, Natural Bridges National Monument, Grand Staircase–Escalante National Monument, Canyonlands National Park

SPECIAL CONSIDERATIONS—There are two ways to get here. One involves a 17-mile, 2-day backpack trip through Navajo Nation property; the other involves a LONG, expensive boat ride from Wahweap or Bullfrog Marinas on Lake Powell, then a short 1-mile hike to the bridge. You choose!

OVERVIEW

We humanoids love Mother Nature's rainbows. Always have. It's a sign of good things—sunshine, fresh air, a clean start after the rainstorm. In chapter 9 of the book of Genesis, a rainbow was used as a sign of God's covenant with Noah, promising no more global floods. In Norse mythology, the world of men and the realm of gods were connected by a rainbow bridge. The Irish leprechaun's secret hiding place for his pot of gold was at the end of the rainbow. Rainbow flags were used in the 16th-century German Peasants' War and for 21st-century gay pride and LGBTQ social movements.

Rainbows unite us. We love 'em. That is reason enough to check out Rainbow Bridge National Monument, on an elegant finger of the Colorado River's Lake Powell in southeast Utah on the Arizona border. Rainbow Bridge is one of the largest natural arches in the world, standing 290 feet tall from its base to the top of the arch. It spans 275 feet across the creek channel that helped carve this natural wonder. The top of the arch measures 42 feet thick and 33 feet wide. The National Park Service notes that it's nearly as tall as the Statute of Liberty, and you can "practically tuck the US Capitol Building Dome underneath the bridge."

One of the forces of nature that helps protect it today will eventually help it erode and collapse—drought! Drought in the American Southwest for the past decade or more has drawn Lake Powell down nearly 130 feet. This massive lake in the middle of the desert no longer backs water beneath Rainbow Bridge. Now, a one-mile hike keeps some tourists at bay—about 85,000 people visited the arch last year. The high and dry Kayenta Sandstone abutments of Rainbow Bridge also remain safe from the lapping waters of the lake, although they probably never were threatened. Yet time—along with wind-whipped sand and the freeze and thaw of what little moisture there is in the desert seeping into sandstone—will eventually erode even these stout bases and the Navajo Sandstone arch itself.

The last time Lake Powell backed water beneath Rainbow Bridge was in 1999 when the lake elevation rose to 3,696 feet above sea level. That pushed 42 feet of standing water into the Bridge Creek channel beneath the bridge. When Lake Powell is full, which is 3,700 feet of elevation, 46 feet of water pools under the bridge, and no, you can't jump in or swim here! At one time there was actually a register on top of the arch for people who climbed up. Thankfully, the Park Service put a stop to that in the mid-1950s for environmental reasons and because this is a sacred place to the Navajo. Directly behind this wondrous arch and to the southeast rises the 10,388-foot Navajo Mountain, one of the four sacred mountains of the Navajo, along with Mount Taylor (near Chaco Canyon in New Mexico), Mount Hesperus (near Cortez and Durango, Colorado), and San Francisco Peaks (near Flagstaff, Arizona).

Of course, Lake Powell hasn't been full in years. In fact, in mid-April 2019, the lake level stood at 3,568 feet, 132 feet below capacity. That's a point of great concern. People and agriculture need water, and that's a lot of water! Also, Lake Powell wasn't designed just to store water for the upper Colorado River basin states of Wyoming, Colorado, New Mexico, and Utah. It also was designed to generate hydroelectric power for the energy needs of an ever-growing western American population. (Water for the lower-basin states of Arizona, Nevada, California, and small sections of New Mexico and Utah are stored in Lake Mead, which also was half full—or half empty—in 2019.)

The hydropower plant on Glen Canyon Dam and Lake Powell was designed to run efficiently when the lake level is as low as 3,570 feet. It stood two feet below that prior to the 2019 runoff. Significant snowfall in the Rocky Mountains in the winter of 2018–2019 raised the lake's level to 3,614 feet. That still left Lake Powell 86 feet below full pool and its shoreline nearly a mile from Rainbow Bridge.

While scientists now believe the lake would not cause any permanent damage or drastic undercutting of Rainbow Bridge, this was a major bone of contention prior to commissioning Glen Canyon Dam. Public Law 485, through which the 84th Congress authorized the Colorado River Storage Project (approved on April 11, 1956), stated specifically that adequate protective measures had to be taken to protect Rainbow Bridge and that "no dam or reservoir constructed under the authorization of this act shall be within any National Park or Monument."

Love it or hate it, Lake Powell offers incredible scenery and immense blue skies along the border of Utah and Arizona.

An acre-foot of water can cover an area the size of a football field with one foot of water. That one-foot-deep pool equals 325,851 gallons of water, or 1,233.48184 cubic meters.

That's a lot of water.

Now, multiply that by the size of Lake Powell. Check this out.

With the lake level at 3,600 feet above sea level:

Reservoir capacity is 14,753,000 acre-feet.

Reservoir area is 101,770 acres.

Shoreline is 1,500 miles long.

With the lake level at 3,700 feet above sea level:

Reservoir capacity is 27,000,000 acre-feet.

Reservoir area is 161,390 acres.

Shoreline is 1,900 miles.

A few years later, Congress decreed that Lake Powell would not impair Rainbow Bridge and instructed the Bureau of Reclamation to move forward with its plan to flood Bridge Canyon, invading the boundaries of Rainbow Bridge National Monument. Naturally, lawsuits followed, but the bottom line was this: People and politicians in the West wanted water, electricity, and jobs building big projects.

Construction of Glen Canyon Dam and Lake Powell affected the entire southwest portion of the United States, both positively and negatively. This was, after all, the great compromise after scrapping plans for a dam in Echo Canyon on the Yampa River in Dinosaur National Monument. (See "Echo Canyon Controversy!" sidebar in chapter 1.) Through it all, Rainbow Bridge has remained standing as splendidly as it did when ancient Puebloans lived in Bridge Canyon between AD 1050 and 1300. Artifacts from that era have been found near the site, as have pictographs and petroglyphs.

Navajo stories from the 1400s tell of a male and female coming together under the rainbow bridge and being frozen in time—in perfect union. This is a site of religious significance to the Navajo, a site of ritual offerings and sacred ceremonies. Most likely, that's one reason it was left undiscovered as Anglo-Americans settled the West. Navajo guides hid this and other sacred areas because they did not want their religious sites disrupted. It wasn't until the summer of 1909 that two different Anglo-American groups arrived at Rainbow Bridge simultaneously, one of which was led by Mancos, Colorado, rancher John Wetherill (see chapter 15 sidebar). A year later, *National*

Geographic magazine featured Rainbow Bridge, and in September of 1925, the famous magazine published its first color picture of the bright and vibrant arch—er, bridge.

So, which is it? An arch or a bridge? Actually, it's both, since a natural bridge is a type of natural arch. Generally, a natural bridge is distinguished from other types of arches because a current of water, such as a stream, was a clear agent in the formation of an opening. Some arches or windows have eroded from the action of wind and from freeze-thaw cycles that erode sandstone beneath a more dense rock above. (See chapter 30, "Natural Bridges Natural Monument.")

Numerous other sandstone walls within the confines of Lake Powell will someday become arches, perhaps as magnificent as Rainbow Bridge. But probably not until long after I cross that bridge in search of my old dog Boone, who crossed his own rainbow bridge years ago.

SIGNATURE ACTIVITY: REACHING FOR RAINBOWS

WHY GO?
William Howard Taft designated this a national monument because it was shaped like a rainbow. Teddy Roosevelt and the great Western novelist Zane Grey visited here in 1912 and were pretty blown away. You will be too.

Rainbow Bridge stands 290 feet tall with a span of 275 feet. The top of the arch measures 42 feet thick and 33 feet wide.

ACTIVITY TYPE: Drive, boat, hike

TRAILHEAD/PUT-IN/ETC.: Bullfrog Marina or Wahweap Marina on Lake Powell

DISTANCE/LENGTH: 45 miles from Bullfrog; 50 miles from Wahweap

AVERAGE TIME REQUIRED: All day!

CONTACT/MANAGING AGENCY: National Park Service, Glen Canyon National Recreation Area, 691 Scenic View Drive, Page, AZ 86040, 928-608-6200, nps.gov/rabr/index.htm

DIFFICULTY: Easy, although the hike may get hot in the middle of the day in the summer.

SPECIAL CONSIDERATIONS: Even though this is a relatively short hike, take water, wear a hat, and use sunscreen.

FIND THE TRAILHEAD/GETTING THERE

SHORT DESCRIPTION: Take a boat ride 45 miles south from Bullfrog Marina or 50 miles north from Wahweap Marina on Lake Powell. Head for River Mile Marker 49, cut the engine, and travel south into Forbidding Canyon. Follow the navigational signs to Bridge Canyon from there.

GPS COORDINATES: 37°05'10"N, 110°58'17"W

OVERVIEW

Trains, planes, and automobiles? Nope. Autos, boats, and hiking shoes. That's what it takes to reach Rainbow Bridge National Monument. First, you need to drive to Lake Powell's Wahweap or Bullfrog Marinas, and that's a long drive from anywhere. Then, you have to borrow, beg, or pay for a boat ride of about 50 miles from either marina to Forbidding Canyon at River Mile Marker 49 on the lake. From there, a short boat ride up Forbidding Canyon to Bridge Canyon leads to a floating dock. It's time to don the hiking shoes and take a mile-long hike up Bridge Canyon to view Rainbow Bridge. (There are restroom facilities here!)

It's worth the trip! This is supposedly the largest sandstone arch in the world, it is shaped like a rainbow, and it's about as colorful as one. Dissolved iron and magnesium from within the Navajo Sandstone leached to the surface as rust and black-colored streaks of tarnish called "desert patina." The red Navajo Sandstone itself is set off perfectly by a bright azure sky with Navajo Mountain, known as White Mountain to the Navajo, in the background. Springtime finds white alyssum, desert primrose, and delicate pinkish-white sego lilies—Utah's state flower—blooming along the trail as snow lingers toward the top of the 10,388-foot Navajo Mountain. Summertime can be hot, and winters cold, but the rainbow remains intact through all seasons and all weather.

There is another way to view this arch. That is at the end of a 17-mile hike around Navajo Mountain on Navajo Reservation property. You need a permit from the Navajo Nation for this trip, and it's an excellent backpack trip if you're in good shape

Anglers look for calm waters and rocky benches at Lake Powell.

and carry lots and lots of water with you. Contact Navajo Nation Parks at https://navajonationparks.org/permits/backcountry-hiking-camping/ or call 928–698–2808.

If you don't have a buddy with a boat, a tour boat leaves from Wahweap Marina most days and delivers visitors to the Rainbow Bridge floating dock to begin the one-mile-long hike. The trip takes all day and in 2019 cost $125 per adult and $80 per child.

Even if you're traveling in a hot-rod bass boat, it'll take most of the day from either marina. Also, gas prices are very expensive since this location is so remote. Fuel costs were around $2.75 per gallon in the western United States in October 2019, yet gas prices at Lake Powell hovered around the $5.40-per-gallon mark. Be prepared with a full wallet!

PART 7
BEARS EARS

Night sky photography at Natural Bridges National Monument is made possible by wide-open spaces far away from unnatural light.

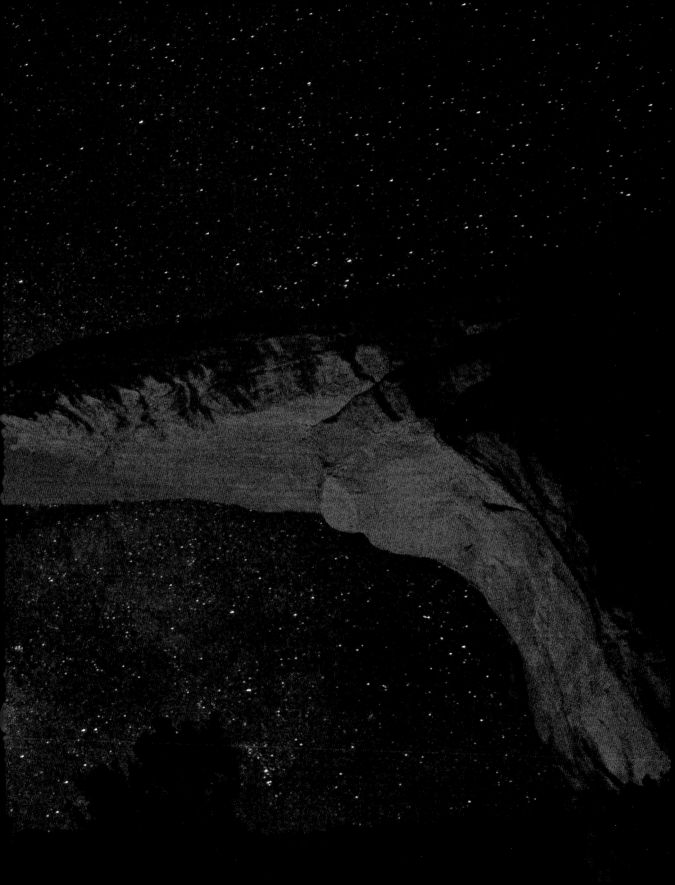

OVERVIEW

There still are a few bears roaming this country, but they're not as scary or as threatening as the politics of the region. Archeological evidence suggests that ancient people coexisted here with Pleistocene mammals such as mammoths, bison, and possibly giant short-faced bears 13,000 years ago. That's more than 8,000 years before the great pyramids of Egypt were built. Black bears forage through this area now, along with desert bighorn sheep, elk, mule deer, and turkey. There aren't many bears, and they were never the problem.

Religion. Now, that's a different omnivore altogether. Five Native American tribes describe this area as sacred to their religions and cultures. This is their church. This is their burial ground. Their forefathers lived and worshipped here for thousands of years. The Church of Jesus Christ of Latter-Day Saints (LDS), known as Mormons, also believe this is their sacred land. They migrated here after their leader, Joseph Smith, and his brother Hyrum were killed by a mob in Carthage, Illinois, in 1844. Brigham Young led many of Joseph Smith's followers here to escape religious persecution in 1848.

There are many other socioeconomic issues that rage like a momma bear protecting her cubs, but that's really the biggie—religion.

As you'll read in these chapters, there are issues of oil, gas, and uranium interests wishing to extract as much natural resource "as necessary." There are off-road-vehicle users wishing to ride where they please. There are hikers stomping on archeological sites, rafters crapping in the woods, dogs chasing wildlife, drunks shooting holes in pictographs, looters stealing antiquities, and Utah politicians attacking a tourism industry that keeps the state alive. And all the while, "industrial tourism," a term coined by Edward Abbey 50 years ago, could crush it.

Yet you'll also read about magical flights over Valley of the Gods; incredible archeological finds in Grand Gulch, Comb Ridge, and Cedar Mesa; spectacular starry nights beneath the incredible arches of Natural Bridges National Monument—and you'll be able to scratch the Bears Ears themselves, with a ride directly between them.

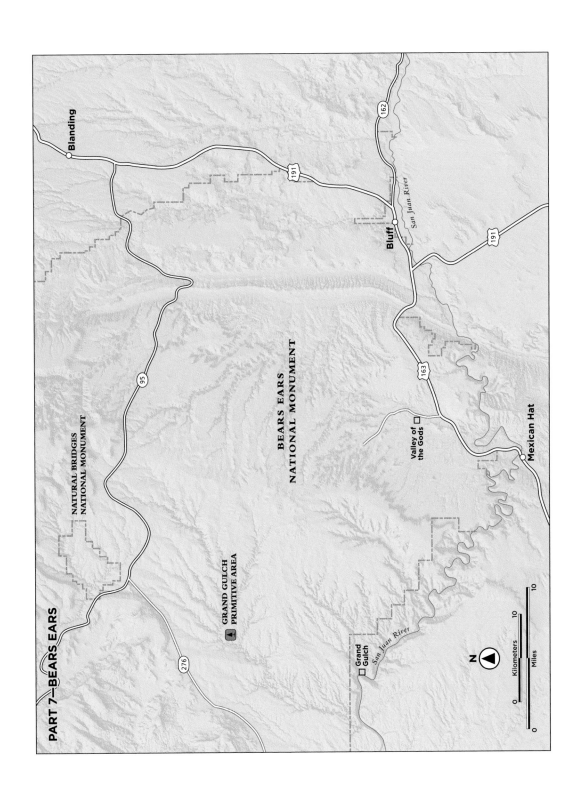

PART 7—BEARS EARS

NATURAL BRIDGES
NATIONAL MONUMENT

GRAND GULCH
PRIMITIVE AREA

BEARS EARS
NATIONAL MONUMENT

Blanding

Bluff

San Juan River

Valley of
the Gods

Mexican Hat

Grand
Gulch

San Juan River

276

95

191

191

163

162

N

Kilometers

Miles

CHAPTER 28
BEARS EARS NATIONAL MONUMENT

SIZE—It was 1,351,849 acres; it is now 201,876 acres—pending court action.

YEAR ESTABLISHED—Following decades of negotiation with the five Native American Nations who first roamed here, Bears Ears was designated a national monument by President Barack Obama on December 28, 2016. It was downsized by 67 percent in December 2017 by President Donald Trump.

MANAGING AGENCY—Comanaged by the Bureau of Land Management, the Manti–La Sal National Forest, and the coalition of five Native American tribes: the Navajo Nation, Hopi, Ute Mountain Ute, Ute Indian Tribe of the Uintah and Ouray Reservation, and the Pueblo of Zuni

DOG-FRIENDLY?—Dogs are not allowed in any archeological site. They are allowed on a 6-foot leash elsewhere.

FEES AND PERMITS—This is a fee-free area. Free permits are necessary in some areas.

NEAREST CITIES—Bluff, Monticello, and Blanding, UT

NEARBY PUBLIC PROPERTY—Valley of the Gods, Cedar Mesa/Grand Gulch, Comb Ridge, Natural Bridges National Monument, Manti–La Sal National Forest, Glen Canyon National Recreation Area, Canyonlands National Park, Dark Canyon Wilderness

SPECIAL CONSIDERATIONS—The road traveling between the Ears gets lots of snow. It's impassible in the winter and very muddy in the spring and fall. Note that a tow truck is expensive out here.

OVERVIEW

"Bears Ears is the first national monument ever created at the request of a coalition of five Native American Tribes," according to text on a map recently printed by Friends of Cedar Mesa, a nonprofit 501(c3) corporation. Friends of Cedar Mesa works to ensure that the public lands in San Juan County, with all their cultural and natural values, are respected and protected.

In the face of an 85 percent reduction of the national monument by President Trump in December 2017, the work of Friends of Cedar Mesa seems daunting. While legal challenges to the monument reduction continue, Friends of Cedar Mesa established a new visitor center in Bluff to celebrate this unique outdoor museum. And while national politics rage over the subject, local politics have been askew for a long time. Janet Ross, who built and directed the Canyon Country Discovery Center in Monticello before retiring, views the fight for Bears Ears as "standing up to the white Republican former majority."

This is an extremely divided rural county where, prior to the last election cycle, the white Mormon majority of San Juan County had dominated since Utah statehood in

Views to the south and east display the red rock country of Comb Wash.

1896. In the 1980s and again in 2012, federal judges lashed out at the county, noting that rural Native Americans were being struck from voter registration rolls illegally. Sparsely populated San Juan County, with wondrous natural resources in its backyard, never had street addresses. "To find someone, you go to the third juniper tree and turn right," Ross explained. "So Native Americans were sent away from the polling places since they had no street address."

The Rural Utah Project changed that. Every citizen was given a real address—a GPS address. Now they could not be turned away from the polls. In 2018, Rural Utah Project's massive get-out-the-vote campaign shook the foundations of county government when two Native Americans, Kenneth Maryboy and Willie Grayeyes, were elected to the three-person county commission. Turns out, San Juan County is about 52 percent Native American, and they wonder what the next census will bring.

In the meantime, the economy is not fueled by extractive industries, but rather tourism. "Bluff is the next Moab," says Andrew Gulliford, author and professor of history and environmental studies at Fort Lewis College in nearby Durango, Colorado. "Bluff

WHAT'S VALUABLE?

What is the value of an archeological site? Is it intrinsic? Is it utilitarian? Is it monetary? Is it spiritual? Is it educational?

Archeological sites across the Colorado Plateau, and around the world, have different values for different people.

In 2001, the Taliban placed no value on two incredibly giant Buddhas carved from a cliff in central Afghanistan 1,400 years ago. They were considered two of the world's greatest artistic treasures. The Taliban believed these incredible archeological and historical sites were "idolatrous" and pulled them down, destroying them. Their mullahs were outraged after the United Nations Educational, Scientific, and Cultural Organization offered money to protect the giant standing Buddhas at Bamiyan.

"When your children are dying in front of you, then you don't care about a piece of art," said a Taliban envoy.

Politics, money, and survival in a harsh environment—it's a tough mix.

The same is true for much of the country surrounding Bears Ears.

"Look how much country there is just between here and the Bears Ears," said a local resident in Blanding, Utah, one hot summer day. "And they want to block it all up?" she asked. "I want to four-wheel-drive out there and see what there is to see." She was in favor of downsizing these national monuments, which she mistakenly believed restricted motorized travel. In fact, all the roads now in existence would remain in the national monument dedicated by President Barack Obama in 2016. None of them would have been blocked.

On the other hand, said one Navajo who eavesdropped on the conversation, "This is my connection to my past and the history of my ancestors. Their spirits still live here. Would you like it if I took my four-wheeler and raced through your cemetery?"

Federal and state land management agencies try to protect these special places and educate people about them. Sometimes it works. Sometimes it doesn't. Sometimes there's too much space to effectively manage with a puny staff and few resources. Sometimes there are too many people.

And sometimes current political decisions override both national law and common sense. For example, maps that show the downsizing of both Grand Staircase and Bears Ears are identical to maps that show mining claims for oil, gas, and uranium.

Most claims will never be mined because this is rugged, nasty, rocky, remote country. There are no towns, no services, no power lines, and no paved roads, as well as no rain and no reason. Alternative management plans allow for mineral extraction in this area, just in case we need it in 40 to 50 years. It would take that long before it would be economically feasible to extract fossil fuels from such a rugged environment.

A *Wall Street Journal* article in September 2018 stated that the peak of mineral extraction could come as soon as 2023. We are transitioning out of a world of extractive industries and into one where renewable energy propels the future. The *Wall Street Journal* article posed this question to the energy industry: "What are you doing for your shareholders to keep up?"[21]

The Bureau of Land Management prohibits the use of motorized vehicles in many culturally sensitive areas and has always prohibited the theft of ancient Puebloan artifacts. A major sting operation led by the BLM and FBI in 2009 centered around Blanding, Utah, on the edge of Bears Ears National Monument. It ended with 23 arrests. Federal prosecutors said they busted "a major ring of archeological grave robbers who looted pristine sites on the Colorado Plateau, desecrated ancient American Indian burial sites and stole priceless artifacts, selling them to dealers and collectors who were associated with the network."

Some locals still fume. They felt that the bust, led by heavily armed federal agents against family members and neighbors, was unjust and unfair. A well-respected local resident eventually committed suicide over the incident, which provoked more hatred and mistrust of government employees. In 2014, irate motorized outdoor enthusiasts, led by former San Juan County commissioner and current Utah state senator Phil Lyman, led an illegal motorized ride through Recapture Canyon. Lyman believed that the BLM unlawfully closed the dirt two-track Recapture Canyon road in 2007, and his simple act of civil disobedience set off a firestorm when Ryan Bundy—yes, the son of Cliven—joined the ride and drove much farther along a primitive trail than Lyman was willing to travel.

Prohibited use of motorized vehicles in some areas across the arid Southwest has protected sensitive desert habitat from extensive erosional, noise, and dust issues. In the case of Recapture Canyon, the BLM had closed the controversial road due to potential damage to archeological sites.

"I have the right to drive my machine anywhere I want," shouted one protester at the illegal event. Her issue had nothing to do with habitat degradation or archeological protection.

The State of Utah and retired senator Orrin Hatch tried to pass a Public Lands Initiative (PLI) as an alternative to the national monument designation. Native American tribes balked at that idea for two reasons: It put federal lands in control of white county commissioners, and there was no room for Native Americans at the table when it came to managing those lands.

Anyone who has ever stepped onto this fragile environment knows how easily it can be destroyed. Meanwhile, five local Native American tribes all believe this is sacred ground and are disturbed that once again their issues have been ignored.

accepts the type of tourism that is coming. They're embracing it. Monticello is on the edge. Blanding just doesn't get it."

There are millions of visitors now driving down U.S. Highway 191, heading to the Grand Canyon. "They're driving right through your town," Gulliford said of Blanding. "You show disdain for tourists and you WANT a scarred piece of earth with an old oil derrick on it?" he asked rhetorically.

Gulliford finds similarities between fights over Bears Ears and Grand Staircase–Escalante and fights that took place in Alaska in the 1980s. The Alaska National Interest Lands Conservation Act (ANILCA) was passed by Congress and signed by President Jimmy Carter on December 2, 1980. The act protected 157 million acres of land, including 11 national monuments.

"There was a lot of local grumbling, but now they embrace it. All they ever wanted to do was hunt and fish. Well, the tourism season is summer. So now, they just open their towns to the tourists during the summer, then hunt and fish in the fall. They love it."

Even downsized—and despite lawsuits and hard feelings and prejudices on all sides—most of the area remains under federal control, as it has been since the Treaty of Guadalupe Hidalgo in 1848. (See chapter 37, "Grand Staircase–Escalante National Monument.")

The current boundaries of Bears Ears include two separate units—the Shash JÁA Unit and the Indian Creek Unit. The Shash JÁA Unit includes Comb Ridge northward to Bears Ears Buttes. The Indian Creek Unit includes historic Newspaper Rock along State Route 211 on the way to Needles Overlook and Canyonlands National Park. Between the two units lies a portion of the Manti–La Sal National Forest.

Indian Creek offers world-class rock climbing, with more than a thousand routes in the corridor. There is some private property in the area that is relatively well marked. Respect private property. A vault toilet and campground are available at Bridger Jack Mesa within the current national monument boundaries. Outside the boundary to the north, yet still within the Indian Creek Wilderness Study Area, there are four other campgrounds: Superbowl Campground, Creek Pasture Campground, Hamburger Rock Campground, and Indian Creek Falls Campground.

On the upper end of the Shash JÁA Unit rests Bears Ears, twin flat-topped buttes at 8,929 feet and 9,058 feet above sea level. These sacred buttes are at the heart of this landscape. A seasonal dirt road is found just east of Natural Bridges off Highway 95 and traverses between the ears. You will find no facilities here—only the spirits of the Ancient Ones. Butler Wash Ruins and Mule Canyon Kiva Rest Area are also found in the upper end of Shash JÁA. They lie adjacent to U.S. Highway 95, which runs from Blanding to Natural Bridges and eventually to Lake Powell. Further south along Comb Ridge is the Lower Fish Creek trailhead and an excellent hike for those wishing to explore this unique monocline—a steplike crease in the earth's crust. It exposes

Numerous ruins, petroglyphs, and pictographs are found in Comb Wash.

Permian age Organ Rock from 280 million years ago and Navajo Sandstone from the Jurassic period, about 185 million years ago.

The southern end of Comb Ridge is the San Juan River. Numerous ruins, pictographs, and petroglyphs are found along the river, and the best way to see them is to float your boat. (See chapter 23, "San Juan River.")

Despite battle lines being drawn in the red-rust sand of Bears Ears over boundaries, most of this land remains under federal control as public land. What's not under federal control probably belongs to Native Americans, who once controlled it all.

As Janet Ross so emphatically stated, "The Native Americans need a voice, and they need a meaningful voice!"

What can you do? Visit. Listen to all sides. Then, listen to the wind as it whistles through the spectacular canyons lying at the base of the revered Bears Ears and lend a hand, and a voice, where you can.

SIGNATURE ACTIVITY: GAIN A LITTLE KNOWLEDGE!

WHY GO?
A talk with the locals, then a visit to Bears Ears for a hike, a mountain bike ride, an ATV ride, a rock-climbing expedition, or a little camping is the best way to educate ourselves on the values and controversies of an incredible outdoor museum.

SPECS
ACTIVITY TYPE: Talk first, then hike, bike, ride, climb, sit, and contemplate
TRAILHEAD/PUT-IN/ETC.: Bears Ears Education Center, 567 Main Street, Bluff, UT 84512, 435–414–0343, http://bearsearsmonument.org; Blanding Visitor's

Center, 12 North Grayson Parkway, Blanding, UT 84511, 435–678–3662; Edge of the Cedars State Park Museum, 660 W 400 N, Blanding, UT 84511, 435–678–2238, https://stateparks.utah.gov/parks/edge-of-the-cedars; Canyon Country Discovery Center, 1117 North Main Street, Monticello, UT 84535, 435–587–2156, ccdiscovery.org

DISTANCE/LENGTH: Whatever you think you can handle!

AVERAGE TIME REQUIRED: One day to one lifetime!

CONTACT/MANAGING AGENCY: Bears Ears Educational Center, 435–414–0343; Bureau of Land Management, 365 North Main Street, Monticello, UT, 435–587–1500

DIFFICULTY: Easy to strenuous. You choose!

SPECIAL CONSIDERATIONS: The best seasons to visit are spring and fall, although winter is fabulous in this country since there's no one else here. Some roads may be impassable, however. You'll have the place to yourself in the summer too, since it gets pretty hot! Beware!

GETTING THERE

SHORT DESCRIPTION: Find the Bears Ears Education Center, Blanding Visitor's Center, Edge of the Cedars State Park Museum, and Canyon Country Discovery Center. Their addresses are listed in the "Specs" section above.

OVERVIEW

I'm pretty opinionated until someone convinces me I'm full of myself. Surprisingly, that happens a lot. That's why it's good to talk to people and gain a different perspective. Talking to someone at the Blanding Visitor's Center about Bears Ears, for example, may elicit an entirely different point of view than talking to someone at Bluff's new Bears Ears Education Center. Likewise, you may get a different perspective about the incredible artifacts—and where they came from—at Edge of the Cedars State Park Museum than you would from someone in town who was busted for theft of antiquities. Some antiquities recovered after the big federal crackdown in Blanding in 2009 are now on display at the museum. But if you talk about it in town, beware. People are still quite sensitive, feeling that these antiquities were simply found in their backyard and the heavy hand of the federal government was, at the very least, inappropriate.

Go find out for yourself by talking to these people. Then head into the wilderness.

Which way? Any way at all! As Professor Gulliford would say, "You can't make a wrong turn in the Southwest."

CHAPTER 29
VALLEY OF THE GODS

SIZE—22,863 acres
YEAR ESTABLISHED—The land was purchased by the United States in 1848 as part of the Treaty of Guadalupe Hidalgo that ended the Mexican-American War. It was managed by the General Land Office until the creation of the Bureau of Land Management in 1946.
MANAGING AGENCY—Bureau of Land Management, Monticello, UT
DOG-FRIENDLY?—Dogs are allowed under control at all times. It is illegal for pets to chase wildlife!
FEES AND PERMITS—No entrance fees are charged; no services are provided!
NEAREST CITIES—Mexican Hat, Bluff, Blanding, and Monticello, UT; Kayenta, AZ
NEARBY PUBLIC PROPERTY—Goosenecks State Park, Cedar Mesa and Grand Gulch, what's left of Bears Ears National Monument, La Sal National Forest, Natural Bridges National Monument, Glen Canyon National Recreation Area, Cedar Mesa State Park Museum
SPECIAL CONSIDERATIONS—You're on your own out here. There are no services and only two roads—Utah Highway 261 and San Juan County Road 242, the 17-mile gravel road that winds around and through the spires and pinnacles of the valley.

OVERVIEW

Valley of the Gods, like nearby Monument Valley, is a land of isolated buttes, statuesque pinnacles, and wide-open spaces. From the Moki Dugway on the edge of Cedar Mesa at the northwestern end of the valley, panoramic views extend for 50 miles into Monument Valley. It's like viewing all of Rhode Island without seeing any people, cars, or trees. Really! Rhode Island is 37 miles east to west and 48 miles north to south. Most days, you can easily see that far from here!

In 2016, this was all part of Bears Ears National Monument. Then, in 2018, it wasn't. Poof. President Trump downsized this monument as well as the Grand Staircase–Escalante National Monument on December 4, 2017, and while the action has been challenged in court, the Utah state office of the BLM printed maps with the new/disputed boundaries before ink was dry on the proclamation. The new map boundaries correspond directly with existing oil, gas, and uranium mining claims that, in the industry's own estimation, could not logistically be utilized for two or more decades. That's because it is remote, difficult to access, and has low-price commodities. (See chapter 37, "Grand Staircase–Escalante National Monument.")

Located north of Monument Valley across the San Juan River, between Mexican Hat (population 31) and Bluff, Utah (population 260), Valley of the Gods remains protected as an Area of Critical Concern and is managed by the BLM. A 17-mile

Isolated red and rust-colored pinnacles and buttes dot the landscape in the Valley of the Gods.

dirt road—San Juan County Road 242—loops through the valley. It is graded with a gravel and clay surface and crosses several washes. It usually is accessible by passenger vehicle but could become impassable for any vehicle when wet.

This road can be accessed from either Utah Highway 261, 10 miles northeast of Mexican Hat, or U.S. Highway 163, 15 miles west of Bluff. There are numerous pull-outs for dispersed camping (no campfires are allowed) and plenty of spots to simply pull over and stare in awe at the openness. You can wander to your heart's content and hike anywhere out here. There are no established trails. You're on your own.

Erosional remnants of the Cedar Mesa Sandstone have brick-red Halgaito Shale bases here. These remains of coastal sand dunes were deposited about 250 million years ago. They often display a red-and-white–banded appearance as a result of periodic floods that carried and deposited iron-rich sediments. Following the original uplift of the Colorado Plateau about 70 to 40 million years ago, wind and water erosion, along with freezing and thawing, created the spectacular spires, bluffs, and arroyos that continue to change shape today.

DOGS IN THE WILD!

When the BLM says dogs are allowed "under voice command" or "under control at all times," that does not mean you can just yell at the top of your lungs, "He's friendly!"

My dog is not. He hates all other dogs, and his dogfights are dangerously ugly. My friend is emotionally scarred from a dog attack when she was young. She runs from your dog. The mule my buddy rides does not differentiate between a wolf or coyote, his only predators, or a dog. He hates them all. One kick and your dog is dead. I saw a cute little beagle get run down by a speeding mountain bike. The beagle broke her hip and was crippled. So was the bicycle rider.

Let's face it: Very few people in this world actually have "voice command" over their dog. The rabbit ran from the coyote half the night, now he has to run from your dog too. His energy resources will soon be depleted. Maybe that coyote will catch him tonight!

Another thing to consider: Doggie doo-doo bag dispensers now appear at many of our trailheads across the Colorado Plateau. That doesn't mean you can deposit those bags, when full, along the trail to be retrieved later. By whom? You forgot it. Again. It's not my job to pick up after you or your dog. It's not the job of the BLM ranger who patrols about 120,000 acres all by himself. It's your job. WHEN you pick it up, pack it out! That's your responsibility as a pet owner. If you can't do that, maybe you should keep a small garden trowel in your backpack and bury your dogs' excrement. That's better than littering the trail with little turd-bomb baggies.

One final note on dogs out here: It's hot in the desert! Really hot! Deathly hot! For the most part, dogs are allowed in the forest or on BLM property, but there are only a few national monuments or national parks that allow dogs. That means you have to leave your dog in the vehicle. That's a great way to kill your dog! It's TOO HOT! Really.

I have always loved dogs and have had dogs since I was a small child. They don't get to go to the desert. They have to stay home. That's how much I love them!

Each chapter here tells you whether the area is dog-friendly or not. Beware of that if you're planning a trip.

The Moki Dugway is a well-graded dirt switchback road carved into the cliff edge of Cedar Mesa. From the valley floor to the top of Cedar Mesa, motorists travel 1,200 feet up 3 miles of steep (11 percent grade), unpaved switchbacks. Scenic views open at every turn—at least for passengers. Drivers better keep their eyes on the road! This dugway—a term used to describe a roadway carved into a hillside—was built in the

1950s to haul ore from the Happy Jack Mine on Cedar Mesa to a mill in Halchita, near Mexican Hat. How hauling trucks made it up and down this road is worth pondering. The State of Utah now prohibits any vehicle here that is more than 28 feet in length or over 10,000 pounds.

Once you're on top of the mesa, you may want to take the first left turnout leading west to Muley Point. Here, you'll spy a fantastic vista and allow your vehicle driver to relieve him- or herself after the white-knuckle drive up the dugway. It also offers the driver a glimpse of what he or she missed—an incredible panoramic view of the Goosenecks of the San Juan River and the vast desert valley below.

From Muley Point, you're now on paved Utah Highway 261, which takes you through the heart of Cedar Mesa into Grand Gulch Primitive Area and up to Utah Highway 95. Only a few miles to the west is Natural Bridges National Monument. Blanding lies 30 miles to the east.

Like Valley of the Gods, Cedar Mesa once lay within the boundaries of Bears Ears National Monument, and the Bears Ears themselves are clearly visible along most of the road across Grand Gulch to the Kane Gulch Ranger Station. Grand Gulch Primitive Area actually lies west of this road and inside the Bears Ears boundary, while much of the major Cedar Mesa archeological sites lie east of the road and outside the new Bears Ears boundary. (See chapter 28, "Bears Ears National Monument," and chapter 31, "Grand Gulch/Cedar Mesa Special Recreation Management Area.")

SIGNATURE ACTIVITY: BLUFF INTERNATIONAL BALLOON FESTIVAL—THIS IS NOWHERE NEAR KANSAS, DOROTHY!

WHY GO?

Hot air balloons flying over the Valley of the Gods? How cool is that? From Navajo taco night at Bluff Elementary, to the magical "Glow-In," to the spectacle of 15 to 20 hot air balloons floating gracefully around the majestic spires in Valley of the Gods at sunrise, you can't help but love this event!

SPECS

ACTIVITY TYPE: Hot air balloon festival
TRAILHEAD/PUT-IN/ETC.: It all starts at Bluff Elementary School.
DISTANCE/LENGTH: It's about 20 miles to Valley of the Gods from Bluff.
AVERAGE TIME REQUIRED: A weekend affair, usually the third weekend in January
CONTACT/MANAGING AGENCY: Bluff Chamber of Commerce
DIFFICULTY: Easy
SPECIAL CONSIDERATIONS: This balloon festival is held in mid-January. It's a beautiful time of year to watch hot air balloons float gracefully across Valley

The Bluff International Hot Air Balloon Festival is usually held the third week in January each year.

of the Gods, but it can be really cold! Dress appropriately. Also, call for room reservations well in advance. This is the one time of year when all rooms fill in Bluff!

GETTING THERE
SHORT DESCRIPTION: Drive to Bluff, UT, on U.S. Highway 191.
GPS COORDINATES: 37°17'00.60"N, 109°33'05.99"W

OVERVIEW
Jennifer Davila, who went to high school in Bluff, Utah (population 260), moved to Flagstaff, Arizona, for college and swore she'd never come back. Yet she recently admitted, "I wasn't in Flag for three months before I was completely overwhelmed and homesick." She graduated from Northern Arizona University "in Flag," as she called it, married, and soon returned home to Bluff. "This is where I'm at peace. Red Rock country is where I have to be."

The Bluff International Balloon Festival has been in existence since 1998. "That first year," Jennifer laughed, "we had one pilot, one balloon, and 17 chase vehicles. After that, we got bigger and bigger." And Jennifer has been involved in all of them.

While not the size of the Albuquerque Balloon Fiesta, which draws more than 550 balloons annually, the Bluff International draws about 20 pilots each year. Every now and again, a pilot from out of the country will come just to fly here, providing that

Takeoff is at sunrise!

international flare. The festival is sponsored by the business owners of Bluff, of which Jennifer is one. She and her husband own and operate La Posada Pintada Boutique Inn, a sweet little establishment with private patios for each room and homemade breakfasts.

She's proud of those breakfasts, but she really got excited about the balloons coming to town. "We use the proceeds from the balloon festival to perform community service projects," she said. The festival also benefits Bluff Elementary School.

Cookie See, from Elephant Butte, New Mexico, is the balloon-meister. She's been corralling balloon pilots since the second year of this festival. Cookie not only directs the pilots, she and her husband Glen fly one of the balloons and spend a day prior to the festival making replica tissue-paper balloons with 60 kids at the elementary school. Then the paper balloons are inflated and flown above school grounds while the kids chase them down. "It gets the entire community involved. Native American children and Anglo children can commingle, and they're all engaged. That cultural mix is really important here," Cookie said.

The festival is usually held the third weekend in January. There's a Navajo taco benefit at the elementary school on Friday, and all proceeds go to the school. Local Navajo schoolchildren dress in traditional garb and perform native dance and song. There's a chili and ice-cream social on Saturday, prior to the "Glow-In." You can't miss that! It happens after dark when ALL the balloons inflate and, while staked to the ground, ignite their burners, resulting in a magical dance of light and fire. Onlookers are encouraged to wander and talk to the various pilots. It's also a good time to hook up with a pilot who may need an extra hand unfolding a balloon the following morning when everyone travels to Valley of the Gods for a spectacular sunrise liftoff. Every now and then, lucky bystanders may catch a free ride!

"The school kids design the posters, we build the paper tissue hot air balloons and launch from the elementary school, [and] we launch the big balloons from the elementary school," Jennifer said. "I've seen an entire generation grow up here. They love it."

You will too!

CHAPTER 30
NATURAL BRIDGES NATIONAL MONUMENT

SIZE—12 square miles; 7,636 acres; 6,505-foot elevation
YEAR ESTABLISHED—1908, by President Theodore Roosevelt, following extensive publicity about the natural bridges generated by a 1904 *National Geographic* magazine article
MANAGING AGENCY—National Park Service, U.S. Department of the Interior
DOG-FRIENDLY?—Pets are allowed on paved trails and roads but must be leashed at all times. Pets are not allowed on hiking trails or in the backcountry.
FEES AND PERMITS—$20 per vehicle, $15 per motorcycle, $10 per individual (walk-in or bicycle). Campgrounds: A 13-site campground is open year-round on a first-come, first-served basis. Fee is $15 per night ($7 if you have a Senior National Parks and Federal Recreation Pass). Sites will accommodate up to 8 people and 1 vehicle. There is a 26-foot length limit (vehicle and camper/trailer combined). Overflow camping is available outside Natural Bridges on Forest Service or BLM property, including Valley of the Gods and Bears Ears.
NEARBY PUBLIC PROPERTY—Goosenecks State Park, Cedar Mesa and Grand Gulch, what's left of Bears Ears National Monument, La Sal National Forest, Valley of the Gods, Glen Canyon National Recreation Area, Cedar Mesa State Park Museum
NEAREST CITY—Blanding, UT
SPECIAL CONSIDERATIONS—Cell service? Forget about it!

OVERVIEW

What's the difference between a natural bridge and an arch? The Natural Arch and Bridge Society offers this: "A natural arch is a rock exposure that has a hole completely through it formed by the natural, selective removal of rock, leaving a relatively intact frame. A natural bridge is a type of natural arch where a current of water, such as a stream, clearly was a major agent in the formation of the opening (hole)."[22]

What draws us to natural bridges and arches? Why do we admire them? Is it their singular strength in resisting the earth's crushing pressure from all sides? Is it that they connect one side to the other, or that they gap a wide schism between their buttresses?

These particular bridges have attracted human visitors periodically at least as far back as 9,000 years ago. Rock art and tools found near ancient ruins here are all that remain of cultures and civilizations that have come before.

From 1,200 to 700 years ago, a number of single-family dwellings near the deepest, best-watered soils were built here. Some, such as Horse Collar Ruins, still remain in various stages of collapse.

By 1300, however, Ancestral Puebloans migrated southward and away from this arid land. Some speculate a terrible drought drove them away. Some believe they'd cut

Sipapu in Hopi means "gateway through which souls may pass to the spirit world."

down all the trees and had nothing to burn. Others hypothesize some kind of disease drove them out or they became weary of too many wars with other tribes.

No matter. It is clear these Ancient Ones simply migrated away from here. They left their homes, their fortresses, their granaries, and their kivas intact. They left numerous vessels as large as watermelons, intricately painted with geometrical designs. They left finely made trinkets of stone, bone, and wood. They left stories painted on the canyon walls.

Navajo and Paiutes and Hopi all lived here after that, at times in harmony, at other times not. Navajo oral tradition has early Navajo living among those early Puebloans. And while the Navajo had again been displaced by the mid-1800s, so were the Hopi and the Paiutes. Both indigenous tribes continue to struggle for recognition, even within the much larger Navajo Nation.

The Hopi today live on or near three mesas in northeastern Arizona. In the past they lived other places as well. Their history is a story of many migrations—the movements of clans and villages. The ancestors of the Hopi, called Hisatsinom, once inhabited many parts of the American Southwest, including the Natural Bridges area. Archeologists often refer to them as Ancestral Puebloans. Throughout their migrations the Hisatsinom clans left markers (pictographs and petroglyphs) to show where they had been. Often they left artifacts from special religious societies in place and they left markings on walls to indicate that particular ceremonies had been performed before the people left. Religious society leaders gave permission for such sacred symbols to be put on the walls. These images make up much of the 'prehistoric' rock art now enjoyed by visitors to the Southwest.

—Walter Hamana, Hopi elder (1992 visit to Natural Bridges rock art sites)

So it is that beneath and between these bridges lie archeological sites that have fascinated mankind for eons, and modern man since at least 1883. That's when a gold prospector named Cass Hite wandered up White Canyon from the Colorado River and found these three magnificent bridges that water carved from stone. In 1904, *National Geographic* magazine featured this area, and four years later, in 1908, President Theodore Roosevelt proclaimed Natural Bridges a national monument. It was the state of Utah's first National Park System area.

Sipapu Bridge, one of the three famed bridges, is the second-largest natural bridge in this area. The largest is Rainbow Bridge in Glen Canyon, only a few miles from here as the raven flies.

The other two famous bridges here—Kachina Bridge and Owachomo Bridge—are as impressive as Sipapu. All three may be viewed from above, along the scenic, paved nine-mile Bridge View Drive. It's a lovely single-lane loop drive in a vehicle, made even lovelier when viewed from the seat of a bicycle.

Hiking trails lead visitors beneath all three bridges and past a number of intriguing ancient Puebloan ruins and pictographs. The shortest hike of about 0.4 mile (0.6 kilometer) leads to Owachomo Bridge. The longest hike is a loop of about 8.6 miles (13.8 kilometers), passing all three bridges. The trails receive a fair amount of humanoid traffic in the spring and fall, but not too much, because trails leading into both White and Armstrong Canyons are steep and difficult.

In Hopi mythology, Sipapu is a "gateway through which souls may pass to the spirit world." A hike through this gateway remains soulful, even after descending a steep Park Service–provided staircase and three wooden ladders to reach the canyon floor

RESPECTING ARCHEOLOGICAL SITES

If you find an archeological site, please be kind. The Park Service reminds us that once an artifact is taken or defaced, no fine or jail term can replace or repair it. Its spiritual, scientific, and educational value is lost to all of us forever.

1. Don't touch, chalk, or make rubbings of rock art. Skin oils will destroy it.
2. Don't enter rooms or sit, stand, or lean on walls. Most are not stabilized. Enjoy sites from a distance.
3. Leave everything exactly as you found it. Interesting artifacts should be left as found and reported to park rangers.
4. Watch children and other visitors, and tactfully explain these rules if they seem unaware of them.
5. Leave each sacred site as you would like to find it. Your children will thank you!

beneath this tremendous bridge. Early visitors to this area climbed down nearby trees and logs to reach the bottom, much the same as Ancestral Puebloans who lived in this area 1,200 years ago. Once down, you're in the labyrinth called White Canyon, its pale meanders continuing to erode the soft sandstone that was deposited and then slowly uplifted as part of the Colorado Plateau.

Plant communities have varied over time in this canyon, and scientists believe this area was once a spruce-fir forest. There are, in fact, pockets of Douglas fir remaining along the cooler, moist, north-facing cliffs near Sipapu Bridge. "Microclimates are created here by canyon shade or slope aspect, north and south, being in a wetter spot, or near some sort of spring," says ecologist John Toolen, who has worked for the BLM, NPS, USFWS and Colorado Division of Wildlife during his long and distinguished career. In those microclimates, Toolen recently found green gentian, Douglas fir, ponderosa pine, and even oak brush. "Oak is usually found at about 7,000 feet and up," Toolen said. "Here, they grow at about 5,700 feet," although he noted some oak growth near Moab, Utah, below 5,000 feet.

These cool, shaded places with moisture are also what the ancient Puebloans sought as they made a living in this arid country. "Some of the places in White Canyon, for example, are really shaded in the U-shaped meanders facing north, and they don't get a lot of sun, even in the summer," Toolen explained.

Whether hiking into White and Armstrong Canyons beneath the bridges or riding along the top, one can easily see the continually eroding Cedar Mesa Sandstone, formed about 250 million years ago on the edge of an inland sea. This loosely cemented sandstone erodes easily, creating incredibly intricate tributaries into the main canyons.

Erosion from wind, as well as freeze/thaw cycles, continues to affect these canyons. Yet the predominant agent of change here remains water and its relentless action against cross-bedded sandstone. Very infrequent rainstorms create flash floods that scour the sandstone streambed. This scouring comes from rushing water, for sure, but also from the rocks, sand, gravel, trees, and other detritus swept along in a flash flood.

Fresh piles of debris stuck in 200-year-old Fremont cottonwood trees in the bottom of White Canyon, for example, can be found 10 to 12 feet above the streambed. In fact, it's wise to query the rangers at the visitor center about the possibility of flash floods before you venture down into the canyons from Bridge View Drive.

SIGNATURE ACTIVITY: WANNA SEE STARS?

WHY GO?

No, really! Do you want to see stars? Away from the light-polluted population centers of the world, the light-polluted centers of your state, the light-polluted centers of your mind?

SPECS

ACTIVITY TYPE: Nighttime photography
TRAILHEAD/PUT-IN/ETC.: Owachomo Trailhead
DISTANCE/LENGTH: 0.4 mile
AVERAGE TIME REQUIRED: 1 to 2 hours, but it's in the middle of the night!
CONTACT/MANAGING AGENCY: Natural Bridges National Monument
DIFFICULTY: Tough. It's in the dark of night!
SPECIAL CONSIDERATIONS: Take a flashlight! Be careful. Watch out for wildlife and other photographers creeping down this trail doing the same thing you're doing.

GETTING THERE

SHORT DESCRIPTION: Take Bridge View Drive to the Owachomo Overlook and Trailhead. It's the last of the three bridge overlooks on the drive, 6.2 miles from the start of the loop.
GPS COORDINATES: 37°35'06.34"N, 110°00'49.46"W

OVERVIEW

As one ranger put it, "Even on a full moon, you can see more stars here than any city in America!"

Being at Natural Bridges at night is very special indeed.

Those stars are very special. They're what guided man across this plateau for eons. They've guided man around the world, across the seas, through the cosmos, to the moon and beyond.

Yet most of us would not know the North Star—Polaris—from the Polar Express if the conductor hit us in the head with it.

They say a person gazing at the night sky on a clear night in the city may see about 500 stars. In the most undisturbed areas of the Colorado Plateau, however, some 15,000 stars are on display—as is the sprawling Milky Way. Here, at the first night sky park in the United States designated by the International Night Sky Association, your senses will be staggered by the sight of that many stars.

The number of twinkling lights in the sky is so dizzying that you'll have to sit down to look up. The entire Milky Way appears as a soft, shadowy belt behind the ancient natural

Approximately 4,000 tons of sandstone fell from the inside of Kachina Bridge in 1992, enlarging the opening and proving the canyon is dynamic rather than static.

bridges in this ancient canyon in the crack of the earth where the Colorado Plateau uplifted and flash floods through White Canyon, a tributary of the once mighty Colorado River, cut down and carved through layers of time and stone.

Now the trick is to photograph this magnificent spectacle so you can show it to all your city-dwelling friends who will never believe you otherwise. Before you go, be prepared. Read. There's a great book by Jennifer Wu and James Martin called *Photography: Night Sky*.[23] It's excellent. Then get a camera that will work at night. Next, figure out how to use it. Then figure out how to mount it to a good tripod, because you can't just hand-hold these long-exposure shots, and if you try to set it up on the hood of the car, you can bet it will slide off and you'll wreck your fancy camera. Trust me on this!

Here are the settings I used with my new Nikon D500 and 18mm lens: ISO 3200 at f/6.3, 19-second exposure. Weird, but it worked. I also had the white balance set at bright sunny, and I taped the focus ring at infinity so I wouldn't move it while I was setting everything up.

I also went back to Natural Bridges four times in a year to get the shot I was looking for—and it still wasn't as good as Jennifer Wu's. Nighttime photography, it seems, takes a little persistence.

CHAPTER 31
GRAND GULCH/CEDAR MESA SPECIAL RECREATION MANAGEMENT AREA

SIZE—400 square miles

YEAR ESTABLISHED—Cedar Mesa has been under federal control since the Treaty of Guadalupe Hidalgo ended the Mexican-American War in 1848; it was managed by the General Land Office (GLO) until 1946, when the GLO and Grazing Service merged to create the BLM. It has remained under BLM management since then. (See chapter 37, "Grand Staircase–Escalante National Monument.") Grand Gulch became a Wilderness Study Area in 1982 under Section 603 of the Federal Land Policy and Management Act (FLPMA).

MANAGING AGENCY—Bureau of Land Management, Monticello, UT

DOG-FRIENDLY?—Pets are not allowed in Grand Gulch, Slickhorn, or tributary canyons, nor are they allowed in any archeological site. You must pick up after your dog and treat its waste the same as you would human waste! Read on, dear reader. It's an issue!

FEES AND PERMITS—Overnight backpacking requires a permit. Reservations are accepted from 3 days to 3 months in advance through recreation.gov. Overnight use is limited to 20 people per trailhead. Unreserved permits are available at Kane Gulch Ranger Station. A permit for a day hike to Moon House Ruins is required. This trail is limited to 20 people per day. The ranger station is located on Highway 261, 4 miles south of Highway 95, and is open from 8 a.m. to noon, March 1 to June 15 and September 1 to October 1.

NEAREST CITIES—Blanding, Bluff, and Monticello, UT

NEARBY PUBLIC PROPERTY—Bears Ears National Monument, Natural Bridges National Monument, Valley of the Gods, Edge of the Cedars State Park Museum, Manti–La Sal National Forest, Canyonlands National Park, Glen Canyon National Recreation Area

SPECIAL CONSIDERATIONS—This area is not recommended for beginner backpackers. It is very rugged, and trails may be difficult to follow.

OVERVIEW

At an average 6,500 feet in elevation, the 400-square-mile Cedar Mesa plateau dominates the northern skyline of Valley of the Gods, which sits 1,500 to 2,300 feet below. It's a bit cooler in the evenings, yet it remains humble in the shadow of the twin flat-top peaks known as the Bears Ears—at 8,929 feet and 9,058 feet, respectively.

Cedar Mesa is sacred country to ancestors of the Ancient Ones. Navajo from as far away as Monument Valley timbered here, made pilgrimages here, held sacred ceremonies in reverence of the abundance of resources found here. (See chapters 25 through 30.) Bare rocks, high mesas, sheer cliffs, and deep canyons characterize Cedar Mesa, a phenomenal outdoor museum featuring thousands of Ancestral Puebloan ruins and

View from inside Moon House Ruins looking into McCloyd Canyon in Cedar Mesa

rock art. The area remains under BLM control even if it's not now within the official Bears Ears National Monument boundary and, for the most part, it remains protected. Popular with hikers and backpackers, this remote, primitive setting provides boundless opportunities to enjoy the scenery and wildlife as well as the solitude of desert canyons that have been inhabited for 13,000 years.

Grand Gulch Canyon, composing most of its namesake wilderness study area, cuts into Cedar Mesa's western flank, eventually draining into the San Juan River to the south. Fish Creek Canyon spills off the east side of Cedar Mesa to Comb Ridge. The southeast flank of Cedar Mesa lies within the Road Canyon Wilderness Study Area. Valley of the Gods is directly to the south of that. All of this area once existed within the boundaries of Bears Ears National Monument. Now only Comb Ridge, up to the Bears Ears, lies within the monument, pending legal action. (See chapter 28, "Bears Ears National Monument.") Comb Ridge is the prominent hogback of eastward-dipping rocks that trends north as THE significant topographic feature between the towns of Blanding and Bluff on the east and Cedar Mesa on the west.

Geologists have studied the phenomenon of Comb Ridge for more than a hundred years. It's surrounded by incredible red-rock scenery found nowhere else in the world. One of the oldest known archeological sites here was discovered at Lime Ridge, on the south end of Cedar Mesa near the San Juan River. Distinctive "Clovis points," fluted projectiles usually fastened to wooden spears, were discovered here. They were radiocarbon-dated to 13,000 years ago, indicating that Clovis people hunted on Cedar Mesa. Clovis people are considered to be the ancestors of many indigenous cultures of America.

Ancient Puebloans inhabited Cedar Mesa between 700 and 2,000 years ago, with many archaic dwellings, farming areas, and rock art sites still remaining to be explored. If you visit, please treat everything you find with care and respect, and leave no trace of your visit. Most of these fragile canyons and cultural sites can only be reached by hiking or backpacking.

Native Ancestral Puebloans proved they were quite self-reliant, remaining in this arid, high-altitude desert for 1,300 years while farming, hunting, and gathering native plants for food and medicinal use. Skilled in the art of basket weaving, they also domesticated turkey, wove cotton, and irrigated crops, and they were adept potters and exceptional stone masons.

Modern visitors should be self-reliant as well. This is a remote area. There are no facilities except for a few sites along State Route 95 between Blanding and Natural Bridges National Monument; the Kane Gulch Ranger Station on State Route 261, which runs directly up the center of the mesa between U.S. Highway 191 and State Route 95; the Bullet Canyon Trailhead; and Fish and Owl Trailheads.

There is limited seasonal drinking water available during business hours at the ranger station, and there are no trash receptacles. Phone reception is sketchy at best anywhere out here, and there are no campgrounds on the mesa. Dispersed camping is allowed, and car camping is primitive and often is accessed along roads requiring high-clearance vehicles. Hiking occurs on slickrock canyon ledges and along wash bottoms with primitive footpaths. There are no constructed trails or directional signs along the hiking routes, only an occasional rock cairn.

In other words, you're on your own.

Access to the area is from State Route 95 (SR 95) between Blanding and Hite or on SR 261 between SR 95 and Mexican Hat. The Kane Gulch Ranger Station is open spring through fall and is located on SR 261 about four miles south of the junction with SR 95. The Grand Gulch Trailhead is adjacent to the Kane Gulch Ranger Station. There's a great hike here, down Kane Gulch to Grand Gulch. You will find a paved parking lot and restroom at the ranger station before heading out on a grand trek. Dirt roads lead to many trails at the heads of canyons on both sides of Comb Wash. Most are recommended for high-clearance vehicles only and may be impassible when wet.

Because of the primitive nature of this area and the sensitivity of its archeological resources, a permit is required year-round for day use and overnight backpacking in most Cedar Mesa canyons and their tributaries. They all have great names like Grand Gulch, Slickhorn Canyon, Fish Canyon, Owl Canyon, North and South Forks of Mule Canyon, Road Canyon, and Lime Creek. Each and every one of them is worth exploring. A day-use permit also is required to visit Moon House Ruins. (See "Signature Activity: Hiking to Moon House Ruins.")

On the back wall, there was a whitewashed line with white dots above it marking the moons, thus the name—Moon House Ruin.

No permits are required for mesa-top car camping on Cedar Mesa. With the exception of Moon House Ruins, day-use permits must be obtained at self-pay fee tubes at trailheads and other kiosk locations on the mesa top. No reservations are required. A maximum of 20 visitors are permitted per day to hike to the Moon House Ruins. Permits may be reserved online at recreation.gov and must be picked up in person at the Kane Gulch Ranger Station.

During high-use season (March 1 through June 15 and September 1 through October 31) reservations for overnight backpacking permits are available at recreation.gov. Reservations for low-use season (June 16 through August 31 and November 1 through February 28) may be obtained at the trailheads and other kiosk locations on Cedar Mesa. No reservations are required. For more detailed information, visit the Utah Bureau of Land Management Cedar Mesa permits web page at blm.gov/programs/recreation/permits-and-passes/lotteries-and-permit-systems/utah/cedarmesa.

OK, did you get all that? Good. Take a deep breath and we'll continue.

Why all the rules? Too many people and too few BLM rangers to patrol this huge area. All water sources are intermittent and should not be counted on; the use of rock-climbing equipment to access archeological sites is not allowed, and moving or disturbing cultural artifacts from any location is unlawful. No camping is allowed at any ruins, rock art sites, or alcoves. Use an established campsite and avoid impacting undisturbed areas. No wood or charcoal fires are allowed in any of the Cedar Mesa canyons.

One last tip, because too many people can really mess the nest: Disposal of human waste is not permitted within 200 feet of a water source, trail, or campsite. Please don't wash, bathe, or swim in streams or potholes. Duh! It's disgusting to have to write about this because it's becoming a big problem in some areas. This is a sacred area to ancestors of ancient Puebloans. It's a sacred area to most of us. Revel in that, not in human waste.

SIGNATURE ACTIVITY: HIKING TO MOON HOUSE RUINS

WHY GO?

A well-preserved and restored site, Moon House consists of three separate dwellings with a total of 49 rooms. You can actually walk through this one, thanks to the excellent restoration. Also, this funnels most people here (only 20 people per day, maximum) instead of trampling other fragile ruins.

SPECS

ACTIVITY TYPE: Hike to Moon House Ruins

TRAILHEAD/PUT-IN/ETC.: Trailhead at the end of Snow Flat Road

DISTANCE/LENGTH: 0.52 mile one way from the lower parking area (high clearance required); 2.3 miles from the upper parking area

AVERAGE TIME REQUIRED: 20 minutes one way from the lower parking area; 1 hour and 40 minutes one way from the upper parking area

CONTACT/MANAGING AGENCY: BLM; permits may be reserved online at recreation.gov and must be picked up in person at the Kane Gulch Ranger Station. Only 20 permits per day allowed.

DIFFICULTY: Strenuous, with a total descent of 351 feet from the lower parking area (497 feet from the upper parking area) and a vertical (31 percent) ascent of 69 feet up to the ruins

SPECIAL CONSIDERATIONS: You need a four-wheel-drive, high-clearance vehicle to reach the lower parking area. You may need that just to reach the upper parking area. Check on road conditions at the Kane Gulch Ranger Station, since that's where you have to pick up your permit after having first reserved it at recreation.gov. It's hot in the desert. You'll think you've hiked much farther than a half mile. Take lots of water!

GETTING THERE

SHORT DESCRIPTION: From the Kane Gulch Ranger Station, drive south 6 miles on Utah SR 261, then turn left (east) on Snow Flat Road. Continue another 8 miles to the two-wheel-drive trailhead. The four-wheel-drive trailhead is another 1.2 miles away.

GPS COORDINATES: 37°25'58"N, 109°47'49"W

OVERVIEW

Holy Saturday, the day before Easter 2018, I'm with my old buddy Geoff Tishbein and his new mate Kate in the Grand Gulch–Cedar Mesa area of the Colorado Plateau between Valley of the Gods to the south and Bears Ears to the north.

Moors and McCombers play acoustic Irish tunes on the CD player.

> Some days you feel the struggle,
> Some days you don't feel it at all.
> Today is one of those days. I feel the struggle, and I don't feel it at all.
> All the angry voices filling up the air . . .
> That ain't no way to live.

Jesus returned from 40 days in the desert to save humanity. I remain in the desert. I don't feel as if I'm going to save humanity today. Or tomorrow. But I'll try to do my part.

We're camping a few miles from Moon House Ruins. We witnessed a full moon last night. We planned it that way. The moon will be pretty full tonight, although a thin veil of nimbostratus clouds has floated in, obscuring the sky. Nighttime photography may be difficult. It's almost sunset. The sand displays a soft, reddish-brown hue across the cedar-filled mesas and canyons that stretch from here to Bears Ears.

Cedar Mesa is a grand outdoor museum of cultural significance. Moon House Ruins is only one of hundreds of ancient Puebloan establishments that remain from a significant population of people who made a living on the plateau around AD 1200.

They knew how to keep cool in the torrid heat of summer and obviously knew how to keep warm in the bone-chilling winters found in this high-desert plateau at 5,800

Kate Kellogg from Ouray, Colorado, checks out the structure known as six windows at Moon House Ruin.

feet in elevation. Those ruins were so cool—not just in the "like, cool" sense. They were really cool, almost chilly, in the hot afternoon. They were layered into the side of a cliff, 20 feet deep, 90 feet long, separated by sandstone walls, some with small windows that provided shaded ventilation along the hot cliff face of McCloyd Canyon.

Incredible.

On the back wall, there was a whitewashed line with white dots above it marking the moons, thus the name. These people had it together. They knew when to plant, when to harvest, when to store water, and apparently when to leave.

Visiting this place can be a spiritual experience, if you've got the mind for it.

Panorama of Coral Pink Sand Dunes

PART 8
ARIZONA STRIP

OVERVIEW

The Arizona strip lies north of the Colorado River. Most of the remainder of Arizona lies on the south side of the river—on the other side of the Grand Canyon. It's kind of hard to get from one side to the other. Thus, the strip has a greater association with people and culture from the areas in southern Utah and Nevada than the rest of Arizona.

The largest cities along the strip are Colorado City and Fredonia, and you couldn't call them metropolises. Fredonia, population 1,314, bills itself as the gateway to the North Rim of the Grand Canyon. The Fredonia Historical Park chronicles the lifestyles of early pioneers and includes a look at the timber and mining history of the area. Less than a mile east of town is a rock formation locally known as the Clamshell. Here you'll find ancient petroglyphs similar to the ones found in Grand Canyon–Parashant National Monument and Kodachrome Basin State Park.

Thirty-one miles west of Fredonia is Colorado City, Arizona, and its sister city, Hildale, Utah. They straddle the border, with a combined population of about 8,000. You can get gas on either side. You can get liquor on the Arizona side. These twin cities were settled in 1913 by a splinter group from the Mormons of the Church of Jesus Christ of Latter-Day Saints. The goal of the splinter group was to continue the practice of plural marriage, which had been publicly abandoned by the LDS Church in 1890. For the next century, the sect practiced polygamy and encouraged multiple marriages between close relatives.

Fundamentalist leader Warren Jeffs put Colorado City/Hildale in the news by being one of the FBI's Ten Most Wanted in 2005. He was arrested in 2006 for rape and aggravated sexual assault against a child, for which he is serving a life sentence. Prior to Jeffs's conviction, the Colorado City/Hildale area had been ravaged by a rare disease called fumarase deficiency. It causes a buildup of fumaric acid in the system that can cause encephalopathy and severe intellectual disabilities. Only 13 cases were known worldwide in 1990. By the late 1990s, neurologists at St. Joseph's Hospital in Phoenix and the University of Arizona College of Medicine in Tucson had found 20 cases of fumarase deficiency in this community alone. They attributed this to the prevalence of "cousin marriages" between descendants of two of the town's founders, Joseph Smith Jessop and John Y. Barlow.

Two excellent state parks are featured in this section. Both Kodachrome Basin and Coral Pink Sand Dunes are a photographer's dream. Make sure you're there at sunrise and sunset. Grand Canyon–Parashant is one of the largest national monuments in the Lower 48, and there are NO PAVED ROADS! Gas up and be prepared. You're going to love it. On the other hand, Pipe Spring is one of the nation's smallest national monuments, but it looms large in the history and development—or lack thereof—of the entire Arizona Strip. Read on and you'll see why.

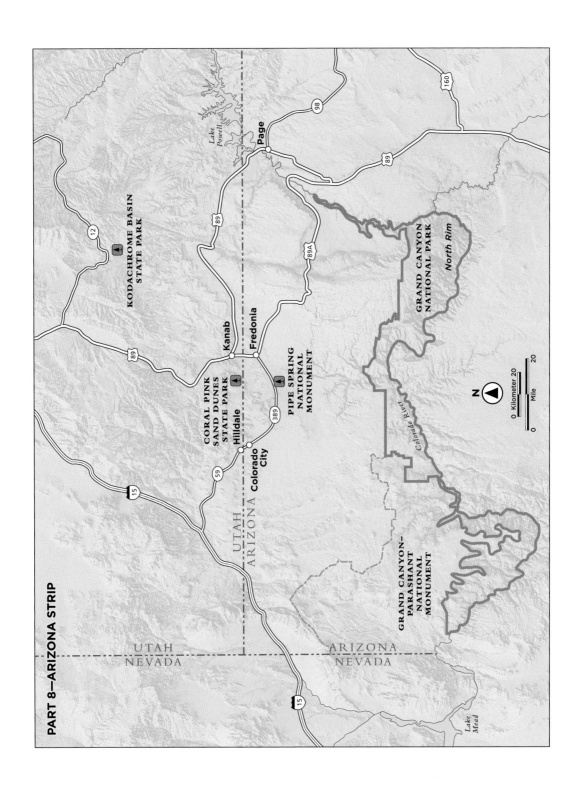

PART 8—ARIZONA STRIP

CHAPTER 32
GRAND CANYON–PARASHANT NATIONAL MONUMENT

SIZE—1,048,321 acres (208,449 acres NPS; 812,581 acres BLM; 27,291 acres non-federal)

YEAR ESTABLISHED—Designated a national monument in 2000 by President Bill Clinton following an Interior Department review ordered by Congress that reported the area was, indeed, deserving of this special designation.

MANAGING AGENCY—Jointly managed by the BLM and National Park Service, Public Lands Information Center, St. George, UT

DOG-FRIENDLY?—Pets should be on-leash in developed areas and campgrounds. They are not required to be leashed in the backcountry but must be under voice control. (See "Dogs in the Wild!" sidebar in chapter 29.)

FEES AND PERMITS—None, but a permit system is in place for motorized travel to Kelly Point during the winter. It is dependent upon road and weather conditions. Contact the Public Lands Information Center in St. George for more information.

NEAREST CITY—St. George, UT

NEARBY PUBLIC PROPERTY—North Rim of the Grand Canyon, Pipe Springs National Monument, Kodachrome Basin State Park, Coral Pink Sand Dunes State Park, Lake Mead National Recreation Area

SPECIAL CONSIDERATIONS—There are more than 1,200 miles of dirt roads out here. There are 0 miles of paved roads. Be forewarned. Also, in order to use an ATV/UTV on roads here, it must be registered and meet Arizona street-legal (on-highway use) requirements, including appropriate insurance and mandatory equipment.

OVERVIEW

The Antiquities Act of 1906 was the first law passed by Congress to protect public lands as valuable and important public resources. It specifically authorized the president to set aside "historic landmarks, historic and prehistoric structures, and other objects of historic or scientific interest" as national monuments.

Concerns about protecting prehistoric ruins and artifacts on the Colorado Plateau—antiquities—prompted the legislation. In the late 1800s and early 1900s, places like Mesa Verde, Canyon de Chelly, Hovenweep, Wupatki, and even the Grand Canyon were being looted and destroyed daily.

President Theodore Roosevelt first used this power to create 18 national monuments, 9 of which were expanded into national parks by Congress. President Jimmy Carter used the act to protect important ecosystems in Alaska. However, according to some Arizonans, politicians, and the extractive minerals industry, President Bill Clinton's designation of Grand Canyon–Parashant and Agua Fria National Monuments in Arizona pushed the envelope. They characterized this as anti-growth, anti-business,

"In the confrontation between the stream and the rock, the stream always wins . . . not through strength but by perseverance." —H. Jackson Brown

and anti-American. While a 1999 editorial in the *Arizona Republic* supported the act, then Arizona governor Jane Hull denounced the proposal as "lacking input from affected Arizonans."

Congress intended to expand Grand Canyon National Park in 1975 but instructed the Department of the Interior to study this area further. In 1998, Interior Secretary Bruce Babbitt visited the area three times, held two large public meetings, and held more than 59 other meetings with concerned local governments, Native American tribes, and various groups regarding the future of these lands.

His report stated that the areas contained geologically significant exposures of rock formations and fossil beds, important watersheds for the Colorado River and Grand Canyon, archeological sites, historical resources, and biological riches.

Grand Canyon–Parashant is located at the very southwestern edge of the Colorado Plateau. Agua Fria National Monument, southeast of Prescott, Arizona, on the north edge of the Sonoran Desert, contains a network of late-prehistoric pueblos, petroglyphs, and other ruins of significant archeological interest. They both lie in an invaluable transition zone between two great geologic provinces.

The Antiquities Act is a matter of perspective. According to James Peck, an Arizona attorney practicing environmental law, it can be viewed "as a powerful land conservation tool that empowers the President to unilaterally protect lands that are threatened as a result of congressional inaction or from proposed congressional actions," he wrote in July 2000. "The Act provides a mechanism for decisive executive action, yet the

BOB

Want to get away? Grand Canyon–Parashant offers one million acres of public property to get lost in. According to BLM statistics, about 18,200 people visit this area per year, so your chances of being found, if you don't want to be found, are slim to none.

You're alone with the Kaibab squirrels, northern goshawks, Steller's jays, Great Basin rattlesnakes, and mule deer.

And Bob.

Bob is a volunteer for the National Park Service at Tuweep Ranger Station. It's on the way to Toroweap Overlook on the North Rim of the Grand Canyon, inside national park boundaries. If you drive all the way through Grand Canyon–Parashant National Monument, southeast from St. George, Utah, for about 90 miles on dirt roads, you'll eventually drive past Bob's outpost—and you'll probably meet Bob.

He's the nicest guy you'd ever want to meet.

He lost his wife about five years ago to cancer.

He's 58 years old, pale Omaha skin slightly darkened by the Arizona desert, 6'1", 215-ish pounds. He wears a National Park Service baseball cap, hiding the thinning gray hair that matches his sparse gray beard, both slightly disheveled yet gracefully offsetting his light blue eyes, with those gentle wrinkles beneath them that smile as he tells his story.

It's as old as the Grand Canyon.

Navy vet. Loves serving. Pensioned. Alone. Looking west.

Says he doesn't like people but doesn't like anything more than talking to them. Entertaining them. Even feeding them.

There's no cell phone service out here. No services to speak of at all, other than Bob.

There's a barn that was built at the turn of the last century that Bob calls HQ. It stores a couple old hand crosscut saws, used in a foregone age to cut through the incredible trunks of fallen ponderosa pine that succumbed to the ravages of time in the desert, although it took some of those ponderosas 700 years to live and die.

There's also a handful of shovels in Bob's HQ, a couple Forest Service signs, a bunch of maps, and miscellaneous other farming implements. It's got a file cabinet where Bob keeps more maps, books, references, and other "important" info.

There's a refrigerator and a table with an electric burner to boil water for herbal tea or a cup of hot chocolate that Bob is eager to offer his visitors. There's also a two-burner propane stove that cooks whatever Bob wants to cook.

"You know," he said, "one of the benefits I had as a vet was that I could go back to school. I chose culinary school." One day at Tuweep, he cooked a spaghetti dinner for about 85 ATV riders who thought they could get into the park without special permits—like everyone else.

Go figure.

The overlook was full. It can only handle 30 vehicles, or 85 visitors at a time. That includes the people at the reserved campsites: There are 9 small campsites for 1 to 6 people (up to 2 vehicles each) and 1 larger group campsite for 7 to 11 people (up to 4 vehicles). Advance permits are required for camping and overnight use at Tuweep Campground. (Obtain permits at nps.gov/grca/planyourvisit/backcountry-permit.htm.)

They have composting vault toilets here. Way cool. Bob has to turn them a couple times a week, but it doesn't seem to be a problem. What a wonderful solution to a nasty outdoor problem, especially as more people discover this sensitive part of our planet next to one of the seven natural wonders of the world, the Grand Canyon of the Colorado River.

Anyway, back to the 85 ATVers. They weren't happy they'd driven for hours over rough dirt roads, sucking each other's dust, only to be stuck waiting until someone else left the park and another vehicle could enter.

Bob settled their nerves, mellowed their attitudes, and cooked spaghetti for all of them.

He loved it. They loved it.

What a guy.

Bob likes to cook. And apparently he's good at it.

You can get good at a lot of things when you're all alone and 90 miles from nowhere. You have time to listen to the wind, pay heed to the cry of the wren, or watch the Kaibab squirrel, with its bushy white tail and dark-colored body, streak across the desert landscape where there are open lands, open skies, open hearts, open minds, and no constraints.

Bob locks the gate about three quarters of a mile from the barn an hour after sunset and opens it at sunrise every day while he's here. He walks up and back every morning and every evening. If he's not here, someone like him takes his place.

"I love that walk," he says.

This year, he's been here since the first of March. He's on his way out now, at the end of March, and my friends Diane and JT have volunteered to take his place.

They will be here until the first of May, and they're just as friendly as Bob. That's how they hire 'em here!

Last year, Bob volunteered for March, April, and May, and then again for October and November. There was one stretch during which Bob didn't see anyone for 27 days.

There are other days when he has to turn around dozens of people because Toroweap Overlook is full.

You've seen those gorgeous photos from the South Rim of the Canyon. Miles and miles of multicolored mesas, canyons, clouds, sky. You know the Colorado

River carved this canyon, but there are very few places on the rim where you can actually see it.

Toroweap Overlook (just beyond the campground) is one of the few places anywhere along the plateau where you can actually see the river. That's how immense the Grand Canyon really is.

And this is where Bob works, er, volunteers.

Bob likes to volunteer. He likes to serve.

Maybe it keeps his mind off his wounded heart.

The Grand Canyon and Grand Canyon–Parashant National Monument are great places to contemplate the important things in life.

public is protected from abuse by Congress which can legislatively alter or revoke any national monument designation."[24]

However, Peck noted that President Clinton's designations "can be viewed as an abuse of the intent of the Antiquities Act and as inconsistent with principles of modern land use planning and management." Peck believes the original intent of the act did not include national monuments as large as the million-acre Grand Canyon–Parashant.

"Both perspectives are consistent with the stated policy of FLPMA (Federal Land Policy and Management Act of 1976)" that "the Congress exercise its constitutional authority to withdraw or otherwise designate or dedicate Federal lands for specified purposes and that Congress delineate the extent to which the Executive may withdraw lands without legislative action."

"Should public policy support the use of the Antiquities Act for conservation purposes," wrote Peck, "Congress should refrain from legal reform and recognize the executive's delegated authority. Should Congress feel it is necessary to restrain the use of the Antiquities Act for conservation purposes, it is the prerogative of Congress to revise the Antiquities Act."

As Peck wrote, there's no doubt that Grand Canyon–Parashant is a national scientific treasure. Its ancient lava flows, desert sand dunes, sandstones, shales, and limestones create a kaleidoscopic landscape containing diverse communities of plants and animals through desert, shrubland, and montane habitats. However, this geologic wonder also holds deposits of minerals that have enticed miners for 150 years—specifically, coal, copper, and uranium.

The uranium frenzy, in particular, first struck here in the 1950s. Prospectors flocked to the Colorado Plateau and mined millions of tons of uranium ore from tribal and public lands during this atomic era. They left behind a toxic legacy that continues to pollute the land, water, and air today. In addition, those miners who worked with uranium either died prematurely or have been inordinately inflicted with lung cancer and other diseases after being exposed to radon gas and mining dust.

A spike in the uranium market in the mid-2000s renewed interest in the region, with numerous proposals to mine within the Grand Canyon itself. In 2012, Interior Secretary Gale Norton issued a 20-year ban on new uranium mines on one million acres of public lands surrounding the Grand Canyon. This would give scientists time to study the risks and potential impacts on scarce groundwater sources and communities of plants and animals.

The Trump administration, however, is loath to accept anything that was created by the Obama administration. Thus, it issued a presidential order to identify "regulations hindering domestic energy production." The Forest Service has now set a three-year timeline for "revising the ban"—from October 2017 to October 2020—despite the fact that large swaths of public property here are managed by the National Park Service and Bureau of Land Management and not the Forest Service.

Stay tuned.

Signs to Bundyville, not far from Mount Trumbull

In the meantime, explore this fairyland of scientific wonder. At its lower levels in the Grand Wash between Pakoon Springs and Tassi Ranch, you may spot a roadrunner racing across the desert landscape. In upper Whitmore Canyon, you'll find desert paintbrush and barrel cactus. The steppe country east of Mount Trumbull is home to rabbitbrush, sagebrush, and coyotes. The piñon-juniper woodlands attract Steller's jays and noisy ravens, while the ponderosa pine forest in the highest regions of this monument is home to mule deer, mountain lion, and the rare and elusive Kaibab squirrel, found here and on the North Rim of the Grand Canyon, and nowhere else in the world.

SIGNATURE ACTIVITY: KAIBAB SQUIRREL SAFARI (WITH YOUR CAMERA!)

WHY GO?

If you really want to get away, this is the place. One million acres, 1,200 miles of dirt roads, no pavement. And it's home to the rare and elusive Kaibab squirrel. If you're into wildlife, that's pretty cool! Even if you're not, this is beautiful country!

ACTIVITY: Photo safari

TRAILHEAD/PUT-IN/ETC.: No trailhead. You just have to drive around the Mount Trumbull loop until you find 'em. (See "Getting There" below.)

DISTANCE/LENGTH: Hard to say, but make sure you have plenty of gas in the tank.

AVERAGE TIME REQUIRED: It could take a day or two, or you could get lucky in an hour or two.

CONTACT/MANAGING AGENCY: Comanaged by the Bureau of Land Management and the National Park Service; Public Lands Information Center, 345 East Riverside Drive, St. George, UT 84790, 435–688–3200, nps.gov/para; blm.gov

DIFFICULTY: You have to be quick!

SPECIAL CONSIDERATIONS: You need a camera with a long, fast lens. These guys are quick. They don't sit still very long!

GETTING THERE

SHORT DESCRIPTION: Arizona Highway 5, the Mount Trumbull loop, between Mount Trumbull and Mount Logan—18 to 20 miles north of Tuweep Ranger Station; 60 miles southeast of St. George, UT; 56 miles south of Colorado City, AZ (along the Arizona-Utah border). Elevation: 6,453 feet.

GPS COORDINATES: 36°22'53.00"N, 113°07'32.77"W (This will get you close, anyway!)

OVERVIEW

Here and the North Rim of the Grand Canyon are the only two places on earth where one may find the elusive Kaibab squirrel.

Slowly we crept, as quietly as possible, probing, scanning, turning our heads from left to right, right to left, slowly peering through the trees, squinting through our binoculars and long-lensed cameras.

There, 40 yards to the right, halfway up a 100-foot ponderosa, a flash of tail.

Click.

Click. Click. Click.

Nothing.

The camera worked fine. The squirrel was gone.

This is only one of two places in the world where you can find the Kaibab squirrel—here and the North Rim of the Grand Canyon, which is usually only open from May 15 to October 15 each year.

This tassel-eared squirrel's habitat is confined to ponderosa forests, where it builds its nest from pine needles and twigs of the mighty ponderosa. It lives on the seeds

Claret cup, agave, and red-rock desert

of ponderosa pinecones, as well as the fungi (an underground truffle) found at the base of the tree. It's considered a subspecies of Abert's squirrel (*Sciurus aberti*).

And it's really cool. But it's quick. Nonetheless, in a few hours we had spotted eight or nine of them. At one point, near the old Forest Service Fire Training Center along the dirt road known as the Mount Trumbull loop, on Arizona Highway 5 in the middle of nowhere, we spotted three of them, racing through the trees, gleefully eluding my camera lens. I snapped one shot and got all three of them in one frame, but they were blurry.

They're quick little buggers. You have to be ready.

CHAPTER 33
PIPE SPRING NATIONAL MONUMENT

SIZE—40 acres

YEAR ESTABLISHED—May 31, 1923, by proclamation from President Warren G. Harding as a "fascinating" bus stop between Zion National Park and the North Rim of the Grand Canyon.

MANAGING AGENCY—National Park Service, Pipe Spring National Monument

DOG-FRIENDLY?—Dogs allowed on a leash. Please remain on the sidewalks with your pet. Pets are not allowed in historic buildings or on the ridge trail. Pick up after your pet.

FEES AND PERMITS—$10 per person for 7 days (includes a $3 per person tribal use fee). Children 15 years old and under are admitted free. Annual pass, senior pass, access pass, and active duty military passes also accepted.

NEAREST CITIES—Fredonia, AZ; Hurricane, UT

NEARBY PUBLIC PROPERTY—Kodachrome Basin State Park, Grand Canyon–Parashant National Monument, North Rim of the Grand Canyon, Lake Mead National Recreation Area, Zion National Park, Grand Staircase–Escalante National Monument, Vermillion Cliffs National Monument, Coral Pink Sand Dunes State Park

SPECIAL CONSIDERATIONS—The Kaibab Indian Reservation offers occasional cultural programs and hiking tours on its 120,000 acres of plateau and desert grassland surrounding the national monument. The Southern Paiute Nation, Kaibab Band, also operates a campground adjacent to the monument.

OVERVIEW

A reliable water source is a rare and sacred thing in the arid desert. For eons, waters flowing from what is now Pipe Spring National Monument provided an oasis in this desert for plants and animals. The first indication of human occupation here was around 300 BC. These Ancient Ones lived in pithouses, hunted with bow and arrow, gathered edible plants, wove baskets, and traded for salt, turquoise, and seashells.

Eventually they became less nomadic, sticking closer and closer to the natural springs in the area. Here, permeable sandstone aquifers to the north held water from rain and snowmelt. That water slowly percolated down to the impermeable layers. It then flowed south to the base of the Vermilion Cliffs, where it was forced to the surface at places like Pipe Spring.

This diminutive 40-acre national monument, the least visited of 24 national park units in Arizona, lies on what is now known as the Arizona Strip. It is a vast, hot, high desert between the boundless Grand Canyon gorge to the south and the colorful escarpments of the Vermilion Cliffs to the north.

It's a long way from anywhere. Always was. Still is.

Covered wagon

SCARED MEN, RUTHLESS TIMES

The Mountain Meadows Massacre, which began on September 7 and culminated on September 11, 1857, occurred not far from Pipe Spring. It resulted in the slaughter of 120 men, women, and children, members of the Baker-Francher emigrant wagon train from Arkansas, bound for California. Seventeen children below the age of seven were spared. They were adopted by local Mormon families and raised in that religion.

According to historians, the massacre was a manifestation of mass hysteria, part of the excesses of hyperbolic Mormon teachings against outsiders during the Mormon Reformation Period. Local Mormon militias were worried about the possible invasion of Mormon territory. One of the key instigators was a local militia leader named John D. Lee. He used Pipe Spring as a supply depot.

Prior to the massacre, Lee wrote to Brigham Young seeking guidance. Young's reply of restraint came too late.

Lee and his cohorts actually tried to make the scene appear as if native Paiutes instigated it. They succeeded—for a while.

Lee eventually became Washington County's judge and gave a land certificate for the spring to James Montgomery Whitmore, a Mormon from Texas, in 1863. (Whitmore was later killed in raids by Navajo, and his wife retained the deed until she sold it to Brigham Young in 1870.)

The American Civil War interrupted investigations into the massacre. Following the war, however, those investigations proved that the story of a Paiute uprising was not true. Lee was one of nine men indicted in 1874. He was the only one tried in a court of law. He was found guilty, sentenced to death, and executed by a Utah firing squad on March 23, 1877—30 years following the massacre.

The Arizona Strip was used as a cross-country travel and trade route for thousands of years. Prehistoric petroglyphs attest to the presence of these ancient people, whom the Kaibab Paiute called "E'nengweng." John Wesley Powell, one of the first to explore this area, said the native peoples called the spring Yellow Rock Water because of the surrounding yellow-colored cliffs.

Pipe Spring got its current moniker when, in 1858, William "Gunlock Bill" Hamblin bet he could shoot a target from a distance of 50 yards. He used Dudley Leavitt's tobacco pipe as that target, and he blasted the pipe off a rock—hence the name Pipe Spring. (Leavitt was the great-grandfather of three-time Utah governor Mike Leavitt, who served as Utah's 14th governor from 1993 to 2003.)

The Kaibab Band of Paiutes still lived, hunted, and raised crops near these natural springs until the great Mormon migration to the West in the mid-1800s.

This westward migration—not just of Mormons but of all Anglo-Americans—was "Manifest Destiny," according to John L. O'Sullivan, editor of the influential *United States Magazine and Democratic Review*, who coined the term in 1845.

In advocating the annexation of Texas, he wore that "other nations have undertaken to intrude themselves . . . for the avowed object of thwarting our policy and hampering our power, limiting our greatness and checking the fulfillment of our manifest destiny to overspread the continent allotted by Providence for the free development of our yearly multiplying millions."

O'Sullivan had captured the expansionist movement's philosophy: It was both America's duty and divine mission to expand liberty and democratic institutions across the continent. Anglo-Americans felt it was their natural right to expand, bringing with them "the blessings of self-government and Protestantism."

As one historian put it, however, "the Mormons took Manifest Destiny to the Nth degree."

The persecution of Joseph Smith and his Church of Jesus Christ of Latter-Day Saints gave rise to some of those feelings. Smith, who founded the religion, was killed by a mob in Carthage, Illinois, in 1844. This helped push his followers to the Western frontier. This expansion is what brought "Gunlock Bill" to the spring in 1858.

Twelve years later, in September 1870, Brigham Young himself, president of the Church of Jesus Christ of Latter-Day Saints following Smith's death, walked off the rough outlines of a fortified ranch house to be built over the spring. It was dubbed Winsor Castle for Anson Winsor, who was appointed by Young to run the Winsor Castle Stock Growing Company. The stock came from "tithing" to the church, and at its height in 1879, the herd numbered 2,200 head of cattle.

At least some of those cattle had descended from stock seized at the Mountain Meadows Massacre, according to journalist J. H. Beadle, who claimed that Winsor showed him the stock. The massacre had occurred not far from here in 1857—the year before Gunlock Bill shot the pipe. (See "Scared Men, Ruthless Times" sidebar.)

Winsor Castle eventually covered the two main natural springs, those same life-giving springs that had supported Native Americans for more than a thousand years. The Kaibab Paiutes struggled to survive as new Mormon settlements displaced them from their traditional lands and overgrazing by livestock reduced their native foods.

Their tribe had been greatly decimated already. European diseases introduced in the 1500s, combined with Navajo and Ute slaving raids, reduced their numbers to around 1,200 by the time Brigham Young designed his new castle.

The Winsor Castle Stock Growing Company thrived between 1871 and 1879. It boasted the first telegraph line in the territory. It also became a hideout for polygamous wives. Polygamy—the early Mormon practice of men taking more than one wife—became a felony in America in 1862. An 1890 manifesto officially terminated the practice of polygamy within the Mormon Church. Yet the region remains one of the last outposts of polygamy as practiced by breakaway groups of the Mormon Church, especially in the twin cities of Hildale, Utah, and Colorado City, Arizona, 17 miles northwest of Pipe Spring National Monument.

The livestock preferred by the Winsor Castle Stock Growing Company were Texas longhorns. These large creatures astounded the native Paiutes. Horses had been introduced in the 1500s, but they had never seen anything like these creatures. They were used to local game—rabbits, pronghorn, and deer.

However, the cattlemen were drawn here by the high-desert grasses, which they felt were the best in the entire country. It took only nine dry years for the range to become overgrazed and depleted.

Pipe Spring continued as a church ranch and way station until it became a national monument.

Today, the spring has been reduced to a trickle.

SIGNATURE ACTIVITY: VISIT THE PAST!

WHY GO?
Writer/philosopher George Santayana once wrote: "Those who cannot remember the past are condemned to repeat it!" This may be true, but as humans we're often susceptible to fear and mass hysteria. Even knowing our own history, we still repeat past mistakes over and over.

SPECS
ACTIVITY TYPE: Visit the past
TRAILHEAD/PUT-IN/ETC.: Visitor center at Pipe Spring National Monument
DISTANCE/LENGTH: Less than 1 mile
AVERAGE TIME REQUIRED: 3 hours max
CONTACT/MANAGING AGENCY: National Park Service, Pipe Spring National Monument
DIFFICULTY: Easy
SPECIAL CONSIDERATIONS: Ranch livestock are not tame; keep a safe distance. There are rattlesnakes and other desert wildlife in the area.

GETTING THERE
SHORT DESCRIPTION: U.S. Alt 89 via AZ 389, 14 miles southwest of Fredonia, AZ. From Interstate 15 (I-15), Utah 9 and 17 connect with Utah 59 at Hurricane, UT, which leads to AZ 389.
GPS COORDINATES: 36°51'46.4"N, 112°44'22.9"W

OVERVIEW

This national monument was established in 1923 when Steven Mather, first director of the National Park Service, proposed adding it to the National Park System. Mather was "fascinated" by the old fort and Pipe Spring's history. He also felt Pipe Spring would be a good stopping point for the busloads of tourists who were shuttling between Zion National Park and the North Rim of the Grand Canyon.

The official proclamation said that the monument was to "commemorate pioneer and Indian life on the southwestern frontier," and it has been restored to excellent condition.

What it really does, however, is make us reflect on our own history.

I speak my own sins; I cannot judge another. I have no tongue for it.
—American playwright Arthur Miller

It takes about an hour to view the exhibits in the NPS/Tribal museum. You can take another 45-minute tour of the historic Winsor Castle. It's a short five-minute walk from the visitor center.

If you amble around the grounds, you'll visit the orchard, a seasonal garden, the east and west cabins, the ponds, and the corrals. That'll take about 30 minutes.

The half-mile hike along Ridge Trail allows for views of the Arizona Strip, which takes another 30 minutes. By then, you'll get a feel for what life was like back in the 1870s and how we displaced the native Paiutes by controlling their water.

CHAPTER 34

CORAL PINK SAND DUNES STATE PARK

SIZE—3,730 acres

YEAR ESTABLISHED—Purchased by the Utah Parks and Recreation Commission in 1963 because of its unique formation and scenic beauty, as well as to entice out-of-state visitors to visit Kane County.

MANAGING AGENCY—Utah State Parks and Recreation, Coral Pink Sand Dunes State Park, Kanab, UT, 435-648-2800, e-mail: coralpink@utah.gov, or visit state parks.utah.gov

DOG-FRIENDLY?—Pets are allowed on a maximum 6-foot leash.

FEES AND PERMITS—Day use: $15 per vehicle up to 8 people; senior day use (for seniors 62 and up): $10 per vehicle up to 8 people; walk-in: $5 per person; annual pass: $75, available for purchase at the entrance gate; senior adventure pass (annual): $35, available for purchase at the gate

NEAREST CITY—Kanab, UT

NEARBY PUBLIC PROPERTY—Pipe Spring National Monument, Veremillion Cliffs National Monument, Kodachrome Basin State Park, Grand Canyon–Parashant National Monument, North Rim of the Grand Canyon, Lake Mead National Recreation Area, Zion National Park, Grand Staircase–Escalante National Monument

SPECIAL CONSIDERATIONS—The park is a popular destination for OHV (off-highway vehicle) riders. Ninety percent of the dunes are open for riding, but all of the dunes are open for hiking and playing in the sand.

OVERVIEW

Beneath the giant skyscrapers of modern downtown cities, the wind blowing around you is stronger than elsewhere as air squeezes through narrow spaces. That's a function of the Venturi effect, named for the physicist Giovanni Battista Venturi (1746–1822), the bright Italian who was the first to figure it out.

Carburetors, paint guns, and "inspirators"—those little things that mix air and flammable gas in gas grills—all function according to the Venturi effect.

You could ask your middle-school nephew about the Venturi effect in passing a different type of natural gas. Really, it's all the same thing: A fluid's velocity increases and its static pressure decreases when surging through a constricted area. It could be air or paint or gas—or even sand.

Sand dunes are created by sand, high winds, and, according to Utah State Parks, "a unique influence upon the wind." It's the Venturi effect.

There's a notch between the Moquith and Moccasin Mountains just west of these coral pink sand dunes that provides this influence. The phenomenon has been occurring for at least 10,000 to 15,000 years here. Wind from the west is funneled through

Tall grass

Fence in sand

the notch. This increases wind velocity to a point where it can carry sand grains from the eroding Navajo Sandstone.

Wind decreases once it passes through the notch, and the sand is deposited, in this case creating uniquely spectacular pink-colored sand dunes.

Located in the extreme southern portion of Utah, 22 miles northwest of Kanab and just 1 mile north of the Utah-Arizona state line, Coral Pink Sand Dunes State Park covers 3,730 acres. The dunes, however, cover another 1,500 acres of the BLM's Moquith Mountain Wilderness Study Area (WSA), to the northeast.

This is one giant, colorful, pink playground of sand. Here and there, you'll find six-foot-tall dune grasses, puddles you may pretend are a mirage in the desert, and Welsh's milkweed (*Asclepias welshii*), a federally listed threatened species. Most of the planet's remaining specimens of this rare plant live here at Coral Pink Sand Dunes.

Deep pockets of ponderosa pine have formed in the cavities of this massive sand dune. One particularly large and old ponderosa stands out, and if you find it in your wanderings through this intriguing ecosystem, you'll also find a sign that tells you that this tree began growing in 1562: "Kissing in public was banned in Naples, Italy, Sir Francis Bacon was one year old, and religious wars were rampant in France."

A rare insect species, the Coral Pink Sand Dunes tiger beetle (*Cicindela albissima*), is endemic to these dunes, being found here and nowhere else in the world. A 265-acre conservation parcel protects the beetle and its habitat.

The sand is coral pink–colored and originates from Navajo Sandstone beds to the south. The color is the result of a high concentration of iron oxide (rust) and other elements found in the sandstone. This type of sand is seen throughout much of the Four Corners region. This, however, is the only true dune on the Colorado Plateau.

The wind here is pretty selective. Particles of sand that are too small blow away as dust. Particles too large can't be moved very far by the wind, which moves sand grains in three ways: surface creep, suspension, and saltation.

Have you ever wondered about ripples in the sand?

"If you watch the flowing sand, you might see time itself riding the granules," wrote Vera Nazarian in *The Perpetual Calendar of Inspiration*. At Coral Pink Sand Dunes, you can actualize that bit of inspiration.

Saltating sand grains form those ripples across the dunes. In fact, saltation creates about 75 percent of all movement of sand grains on this dune. The average space between ripples is equal to the average bounce of the saltating sand grain. When a sand grain hits the ground, it often dislodges another grain, and the process continues.

Larger grains move by surface creep. This happens when a light wind exists and causes the grains to roll across the surface of the dune.

Suspension occurs when the wind is strong enough to pick up the sand and carry the grains through the air.

> In every outthrust headland, in every curving beach, in every grain of sand there is the story of the earth.
> —Rachel Carson, American marine biologist, conservationist, and author of *Silent Spring*, advancing the global environmental movement

This all creates a living, breathing, moving sand dune—and an incredible outdoor sandbox for the terminally young. Bring your sandbox toys, grab an old snowboard, a piece of plywood, or even a sheet of cardboard, and get playing!

Be aware that this is a very popular area for OHV enthusiasts, as 90 percent of the area is open to motorized play. They're pretty polite around here though. They won't run you over, and there's plenty of room.

Adjacent to the dunes is a 22-site campground with restrooms, hot showers, and a sewage disposal station. There's a half-mile nature trail and a wheelchair-accessible walkway that extends onto the dunes.

The visitor center offers information about the park and surrounding areas and, just to prove all sand is not created equal, it has an interesting display of sand specimens from around the world.

The Utah Parks and Recreation Commission's $9,325 ($2.50 per acre) purchase of this piece of wonderland back in 1963 was made through the BLM's Recreation and Public Purchases Act (RP&P). Passed by Congress in 1954 and signed into law by Dwight D. Eisenhower, any land purchased through this act must be maintained for public recreation purposes.

SIGNATURE ACTIVITY: SANDBOARDING!

WHY GO?

Want to feel like a kid again? Oh, you already are? Well, sliding down a huge sand dune here will make you feel young and exhilarated and alive. And, yeah, you may get a little sand in your pants, but you can always shake that out!

SPECS
ACTIVITY: Sand shredding

TRAILHEAD/PUT-IN/ETC.: Hike to a dune just beyond the parking area behind the visitor center!

DISTANCE/LENGTH: 600 feet to 1 mile

AVERAGE TIME REQUIRED: What's time to a shredder?

CONTACT/MANAGING AGENCY: Utah State Parks and Recreation, Coral Pink Sand Dunes State Park, Kanab, UT, 435–648–2800, e-mail: coralpink@utah.gov, or visit stateparks.utah.gov

DIFFICULTY: As easy as falling downhill (after the hike up, of course)

SPECIAL CONSIDERATIONS: The park is situated at 6,000 feet in elevation, and you have to climb up these somewhat steep sand dunes before sliding down them, so it's a little challenging.

GETTING THERE

SHORT DESCRIPTION: Drive 7.5 miles north on Highway 89 from Kanab, then turn left onto Hancock Road. Continue for 9.5 miles until you get to the Coral Pink Sand Dunes Road at the entrance of the park.

GPS COORDINATES: 37°2′16″N, 112°43′13″W

Sandboarding

OVERVIEW

Have you been having severe withdrawal since the last ski season? Can't wait to get back on the board?

Well, check out sand shredding. It's gnarly, dude!

Here you can bring your old, retired snowboard and your own boots. Then, shred away. Or you can rent a board at the state park for $20. Just slip your own shoes into the simple open-toed bindings and away you go. That's what many people prefer, rather than shredding their own board on the sand.

If you're really into shredding though, you'll want to feel that level of precision and control you get with your own equipment.

A third option, and one most people go for, however, is a piece of cardboard under your butt.

Slide, baby, slide!

You'll feel like a kid again, running up a sand hill, jumping, sliding, somersaulting down a huge sand dune.

Weeeeee . . .

It's just too much fun.

And a piece of cardboard is much cheaper than a new ATV! Quieter too!

CHAPTER 35
KODACHROME BASIN STATE PARK

SIZE—2,240 acres
YEAR ESTABLISHED—The Utah Parks and Outdoor Recreation Commission, fearing repercussions from Kodak for using the name Kodachrome, christened this Chimney Rock State Park in 1963. It was renamed Kodachrome Basin a few years later with Kodak's permission.
MANAGING AGENCY—Utah State Parks and Recreation, Kodachrome Basin State Park
DOG-FRIENDLY?—Dogs are allowed on-leash only.
FEES AND PERMITS—DAY USE FEES: $10 per vehicle (maximum 8 people per vehicle); Utah residents 62 and older, $6 per vehicle; **CAMPING FEES:** Standard site (no hookups), $25/night (maximum 8 people, 1 vehicle); full hookup site, $35/night
NEAREST CITIES—Cannondale, Escalante, and Boulder, UT
NEARBY PUBLIC LAND—Grand Staircase–Escalante National Monument, Canyonlands National Park, Dixie National Forest, Glen Canyon National Park and Lake Powell, Bryce Canyon National Park, Zion National Park, Vermillion Cliffs National Monument, Coral Pink Sand Dunes State Park

OVERVIEW

Utah's parks, in general, are fine facilities. This comfortable state park is no exception. There are miles of scenic trails to hike, and the mountain biking and horseback riding are outstanding here. The campgrounds are quiet and semi-secluded in piñon-juniper woodlands with clean restrooms, swank showers, wash stations, hookups for trailers and RVs, and level, sanded areas for tent campers. What really makes this a great state park, however, is the scenery. It lives up to its name.

Maybe some of you are too young to know Kodachrome. Back in the pre-digital dark ages, there was a thing known as photographic film. One of the best was Kodak's Kodachrome slide film, although quite often, here in the West—with BIG blue skies—I preferred Ektachrome. Anyway, this basin was—is—picture-perfect, offering Kodak moments all over the place. In fact, a National Geographic Society expedition dubbed it Kodachrome in 1948. Naturally, the State of Utah had to ask Kodak's permission to name this state park, but the name is appropriate. While Ektachrome film was great for the blue-hued light spectrum, it would have been hard to pronounce. Also, Kodachrome film was much richer in the yellow-brown tones. That's perfect around here, where rock formations from the Middle Jurassic period (180 million years ago) to the Cretaceous period (95 million years ago) expose multicolored layers of reddish-brown and yellow sandstone and rock.

Sunset in Kodachrome Basin lives up to its name.

The 180-million-year-old Carmel Formation, for example, displays solid layers of gypsum, the mineral that forms white striations in the red-colored cliffs at lower elevations of the park. The red-colored layer was deposited here about 180 million to 140 million years ago. It displays the fine-grained Entrada Sandstone, along with gypsum, shale, quartz, and clay. This is the ubiquitous "slickrock" that southern Utah and this part of the Colorado Plateau are known for. This red rock is rich in iron oxide, producing the red color.

At Kodachrome Basin, most of its unique and picturesque sedimentary pipes are found in the Entrada Formation. However, you'll notice a number of cylindrical cones of a much lighter color. According to geologists, these are boiling cones of sand that were forced to the earth's surface and eventually became even harder than the Entrada Sandstone overlaying it. The reddish Entrada eventually eroded away, leaving the hard, white pipes standing.

Erosion is the great sculptor here, constantly changing landforms. A single raindrop may move a few particles of soil in this fragile environment, while a summer

PHOTO TIPS FOR BEGINNERS

- For most outdoor photography, early morning and late afternoon are ideal because of the beautiful, diffused lighting and long, graceful shadows. They're also the best times of day to capture wildlife.
- Don't shoot toward the sun. Your images will be washed out and your focal point may be completely dark. Try to shoot with the sun at your back. This will result in a well-illuminated landscape.
- Always have a focal point—a point of interest that demands the most attention and to which the viewer's eye is drawn. While point-and-shoot cameras are great, you need to think about your focal point and compose your photo around that. Don't just point and shoot!
- Unless you're using your cell phone or point-and-shoot camera, use a polarizing filter, especially here in the West. They work by letting light in from certain angles. Rotate the filter to improve color saturation or remove unwanted surface glare. These filters also cut through atmospheric haze, making distant mountains or canyons appear more clear and in focus.
- Pay attention to the position of the horizon. You can move it lower to include more sky or raise it to capture more foreground.
- Don't always have your subject—or focal point—in the center of the photo. That's boring.
- Don't be afraid to try different things. After all, you can delete it if you don't like it, and you just never know—you may just take the best photo ever!

thunderstorm moves mountains of soil and carries it to a new place. Wind also picks up soil and dust and carries it miles away. Just look at Coral Pink Sand Dunes to the south of here (see chapter 34, "Coral Pink Sand Dunes State Park").

The effects of water and wind, and the constant movement of sand and particles, scour rock faces and create interesting spires, pillars, and hoodoos. It's so dramatic in some places that it carves Grand Canyons. These changes are imperceptible to us, but over millions of years the effects of a rain shower or a windy day have radically changed the landscape of the Colorado Plateau.

The uppermost formation in the park was deposited approximately 95 million years ago when a vast seaway covered much of North America. That's the white-and-tan Henrieville Sandstone. Only 11 miles south of the park, it shines even more brightly at Grosvenor Arch in the Grand Staircase–Escalante National Monument, one of the more unique arches in an area loaded with arches.

Kodachrome Basin is surrounded by unique places like Grand Staircase–Escalante National Monument and Bryce Canyon National Park. Just east lie Lake Powell and Glen Canyon National Recreation Area, and to the south lie the Grand Canyon and Grand Canyon National Park. Just north of Bryce is Dixie National Forest, stretching for nearly 2 million acres and 170 miles across southern Utah. It straddles the divide between the Great Basin province and the Colorado Plateau.

The finest workers of stone are not copper or steel tools, but the gentle touches of air and water working at their leisure with a liberal allowance of time.

—Henry David Thoreau

There also are two other state parks nearby—Coral Pink Sand Dunes State Park and Escalante Petrified Forest State Park, where designated campgrounds exist. If you want to get off the grid, however, go to one of the nationally managed areas.

There's plenty to see and do on this edge of the Colorado Plateau because of the plethora of public property here. Kodachrome Basin offers a great base for hiking, photography, mountain biking, horseback riding, or simply soaking up the scenery and listening to the wind. It can't help but revive our aching souls. As Rachel Carson once wrote, "Those who contemplate the beauty of the Earth find reserves of strength that will endure as long as life lasts."

SIGNATURE ACTIVITY: KODAK MOMENTS!

WHY GO?

"Look deep, deep into nature," said Albert Einstein, "and then you will understand everything better."

This place is called Kodachrome Basin for a reason. Taking pictures here allows us to contemplate nature a little deeper, a little longer, a little more—especially as time marches on and memories fade.

SPECS

ACTIVITY TYPE: Outdoor photography
TRAILHEAD/PUT-IN/ETC.: Panorama Trail
DISTANCE/LENGTH: 200 yards to 6 miles
AVERAGE TIME REQUIRED: Usually a half hour before sunrise and a half hour after; then a half hour before sunset and a half hour after
CONTACT/MANAGING AGENCY: Utah State Parks and Recreation, 435-679-8562
DIFFICULTY: Easy, if you have the patience to wait for the right shot at the right time of day!
SPECIAL CONSIDERATIONS: You'll need a camera that works, and you'll need to know how to operate it! Otherwise, pull out the cell phone. It takes

A boiling cone of sand was forced to the earth's surface here, and it eventually became harder than the Entrada Sandstone overlaying it. The reddish Entrada eventually eroded, leaving the hard white pipe standing.

phenomenal photos. Don't forget the tripod for night photography. This is an International Night Sky Park, and the stargazing is phenomenal.

GETTING THERE

SHORT DESCRIPTION: From UT Highway 12 in Cannonville, turn south onto Cottonwood Canyon Road (the Cottonwood Canyon Scenic Backway) toward Kodachrome Basin. Proceed 7.4 miles to the end of the pavement on Cottonwood Canyon Road. Turn left, stay on the paved road, and enter the state park. In 0.9 mile, stop at the visitor center to pay the day-use fee, then continue north 0.6 mile to the signed parking area for Panorama Trail, Grand Parade Trail, and Picnic Area. The trailhead is located on the left (west) side of the road.

GPS COORDINATES: 37°31'21"N, 111°59'31"W

OVERVIEW

"The best time to take a photo is when you have a camera hanging around your neck."

That was solid advice from my first really tough photography professor in journalism school at the University of Colorado eons ago.

The next best advice I received was from an outdoor photographer years later, after I bored him to death with some of "my best": "These suck. You need to get up before noon, and you need to be sober before dark. Shoot outdoor photos at sunrise and sunset."

The third and most valuable piece of photographic advice I received was from my old buddy Bud Smith, an information/education specialist for the Colorado Division of Wildlife, who said, "Make sure there's a kid or a critter in the photo."

Bud was right. (Check out the "Carrot Top meets triceratops" photo in chapter 2. Cute as hell.) However, as an outdoor photographer in Kodachrome Basin, you don't even need a kid or a critter. Your eyes and heart are drawn to this scenery.

I used to love black-and-white photography here. That's how long ago I started to learn the art and craft of photography. I progressed from Plus-X and Tri-X black-and-white film to Kodacolor and Kodachrome and Ektachrome slide film. Now I'm into digital.

You know why?

$$$$$

Also, the world has gone digital—and that's OK. I used to be really happy with one good photo from a 36-exposure roll of film. That was expensive. Now? Delete. Delete. Delete if you don't like 'em. Keep the one good one.

Be outside at sunrise and sunset and you'll be amazed at what the sun will do for you—and your photography. Then, monkey around. I shot a couple shots at sunset the other day, one at 125th of a second at f/8, one at f/11, and one at f/16. The one at f/8 was very clear, but the one at f/16 was really dramatic.

The most important thing is to get outside. Be there. Be present.

What kind of camera should you use? Use the kind that's hanging around your neck, or the one in your pocket. Point-and-shoot cameras are excellent these days, as are cell phones. (Full disclosure: The cover photo of this book was taken with my cell phone!) Of course I'm in love with my Nikon D-500 and Nikkor 18–300mm lens. I ALWAYS use a protective UV filter and usually have a polarizing filter on that lens as well. It pops the color like Kodachrome!

Also, when you download your digital photos, find a good editing tool, such as Adobe Lightroom or Photoshop, Skylum Luminar, Canva, Capture One, or even the editing program that comes with your iPhone. Editing your photos will help bring focus to an image and highlight your subject, whether it's a kid in the foreground or a rock spire in the background. It may transform an average picture into a stunning photograph.

Or not.

Even in the middle of the day, this is a great place to take photographs!

You have to work at it. But the more you do it, the better you'll get—and the better your photos will look. That will make everyone around you happy they don't have to look at any more of your boring, out-of-focus, poorly composed, overexposed photos of your kids and pets—in nature.

Hikes around Sandstone
Mountain are fun and challenging.

OVERVIEW

In the late 1870s, geologist Clarence Dutton first conceptualized the idea of a grand staircase, "ascending from the bottom of the Grand Canyon northward, with the cliff edge of each layer forming giant steps." From a satellite, Dutton's concept runs true. This portion of the Colorado Plateau certainly resembles a grand staircase. On top of the stairs are the pink cliffs of Bryce Canyon at 10,000 feet. The lowest step is at 3,000 feet on the North Rim of the Grand Canyon. Eons of time lie between. The sedimentary rock layers that create the stairs stretch south from Bryce Canyon National Park and Grand Staircase–Escalante National Monument, through Zion National Park, and into the Grand Canyon National Park.

Dutton didn't have a clue about satellites. He knew his rocks though. He saw this land firsthand after joining John Wesley Powell in his 1875 survey of the region for the U.S. Geographical Survey. He spent 10 years exploring the plateaus of Utah, Arizona, and New Mexico and divided this area into five steps, or layers, of the earth's history. He named them quite scientifically: Pink Cliffs, Grey Cliffs, White Cliffs, Vermillion Cliffs, and Chocolate Cliffs.

Those Pink Cliffs at the top of Bryce Canyon are the youngest known units in the Grand Staircase, and the oldest exposed formation in Bryce—the Dakota Sandstone—is the youngest formation seen in the Zion area. In turn, the oldest exposed formation in Zion National Park is the youngest exposed formation in the Grand Canyon—the 240-million-year-old Kaibab Limestone.

The beauty and majesty of the Grand Canyon, Zion, and Bryce are undeniable. By purposefully shifting the focus away from these national parks, however, I invite readers to the various public lands and protected areas that are as exciting and wonderful as any of the major parks. Well, OK, nothing beats the Grand Canyon. Nonetheless, you'll be blown away by what exists in Dixie National Forest just outside Bryce and Zion. Sandstone Mountain and the area known as Red Cliffs will amaze you. Goblin Valley, not far from here, will restore your faith in your own imagination, with gnomes, hoodoos, and goblins by the thousands marching across a dry, barren desert, with children climbing and hooting and hollering to their hearts' delight. Then there's the Grand Staircase–Escalante itself. I can do no better than to let you read the proclamation that President Bill Clinton signed when he dedicated this magnificent area as a national monument. His words still ring true today in calling for the preservation of a grand staircase!

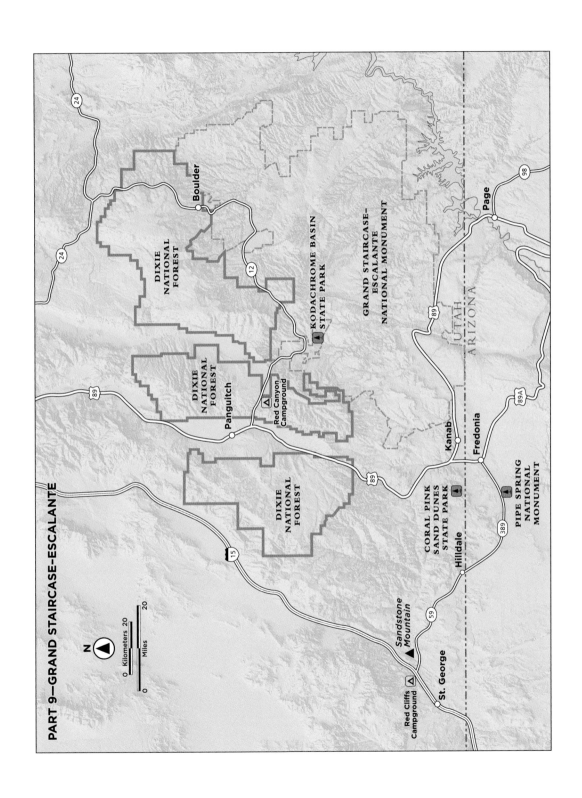

PART 9—GRAND STAIRCASE-ESCALANTE

N

0 Kilometers 20

0 Miles 20

Boulder

DIXIE
NATIONAL
FOREST

24

24

12

KODACHROME BASIN
STATE PARK

GRAND STAIRCASE-
ESCALANTE
NATIONAL MONUMENT

Page

98

DIXIE
NATIONAL
FOREST

89

Panguitch

Red Canyon
Campground

89

UTAH
ARIZONA

89A

DIXIE
NATIONAL
FOREST

15

89

Kanab

Fredonia

CORAL PINK
SAND DUNES
STATE PARK

PIPE SPRING
NATIONAL
MONUMENT

389

Hilldale

59

Sandstone
Mountain

St. George

Red Cliffs
Campground

CHAPTER 36

DIXIE NATIONAL FOREST/RED CLIFFS DESERT RESERVE AND SANDSTONE MOUNTAIN

SIZE—Dixie National Forest includes 2 million acres across 170 miles of southern Utah; Red Cliffs Desert Reserve adds another 62,000 acres at the merging point of three great physiographic regions—the Colorado Plateau, the Mojave Desert, and the Great Basin.

YEAR ESTABLISHED—Dixie Forest Reserve was established on September 25, 1905, "for the protection of watersheds for communities, and so the land would be managed in perpetuity for multiple uses." It became a national forest in 1907. The western part of Sevier National Forest was added in 1922, and all of Powell National Forest was added in 1944; Redcliffs Desert Reserve was established in 1996 to protect endemic wildlife species, such as the desert tortoise, that occur nowhere else in the world.

MANAGING AGENCY—Dixie is managed by the National Forest Service, Dixie National Forest, Cedar City, UT; Red Cliffs is managed by the Washington County, UT, Habitat Conservation Program, in conjunction with the U.S. Fish and Wildlife Service and Bureau of Land Management.

DOG-FRIENDLY?—Pets are allowed in all national forests but must be kept on a 6-foot leash while in developed recreation areas and on interpretive trails. It is illegal for dogs to chase wildlife! Pets are allowed on-leash only at Red Cliffs Desert Reserve. (Hunting dogs are allowed off-leash during hunting season with a licensed hunter. Don't worry. They don't hunt where you'll be hiking!)

FEES AND PERMITS—The forest is fee-free, but you'll have to pay for designated campgrounds, generally from $9 to $18 per campsite. Go to recreation.gov or call 877–444–6777 for reservations. The Red Cliffs Desert Reserve also is fee-free, although you must pay at campgrounds located at the Red Cliffs Recreation Area and in Snow Canyon State Park. Contact the BLM (435–688–3200) or Snow Canyon State Park (435–628–2255) for further information.

NEAREST CITIES—Cedar City, Escalante, St. George, Hurriane, La Verkin, and Panguitch, UT

NEARBY PUBLIC PROPERTY—Bryce Canyon National Park, Zion National Park, Capitol Reef National Park

SPECIAL CONSIDERATIONS—Be prepared for changing weather. In springtime, it could easily snow in the morning and turn sunny and 50 degrees in the afternoon.

OVERVIEW

All right! Get ready to travel. We're about to cover a lot of ground in a few short pages.

Interstate 15 (I-15) runs through Red Cliffs National Conservation Area—a major component of the Red Cliffs Desert Reserve. North of St. George, Utah, most of the NCA is located on the northwest side of I-15, at the merging point of three

Red Cliffs NCA is broad and spectacular in the setting sun.

great physiographic regions—the Colorado Plateau, the Mojave Desert, and the Great Basin. It is home to an unusual mix of plants and animals, including the threatened Mojave Desert tortoise. Its unique geologic features, such as red rock cliffs, basalt lava flows, rugged canyons, and windblown sand dunes, are mind-boggling.

Dixie National Forest straddles the divide between the Great Basin and the Colorado River. The towering Pine Valley Mountains and Dixie National Forest form the northern boundary of Red Cliffs. You could spend years stomping around the two-million-acre Dixie National Forest. It's spread across about 170 miles in Utah. Dixie surrounds Zion National Park and abuts Capitol Reef and Bryce Canyon National Parks. As the largest forest in Utah, it also creates the eastern boundary of Grand Staircase–Escalante National Monument and encompasses Cedar Breaks National Monument.

It is divided into four geographically distinct plateaus. Gently rolling hills of high-altitude forests spread across three of them—the Aquarius, Pansaugunt, and Markagunt Plateaus. Boulder Mountain, the fourth geographic area, is one of the largest

Swirling patterns in red rock

high-elevation plateaus in the United States, dotted with hundreds of small, sparkling lakes at 10,000 to 11,000 feet above sea level.

The forest features 83,000 acres of wilderness in Pine Valley, Box-Death Hollow, and Ashdown Gorge, yet developed facilities and roads abound. There are 26 campgrounds and 5 picnic areas in the forest. You can hike or fish or hunt in very primitive conditions or enjoy vehicle-based activities in other areas.

About 15 percent of the forest is used to produce timber. After all, that's part of the Forest Service management for "multiple use." The Forest Service notes that "many of the roads developed to remove timber from the land also provide opportunities for gathering firewood, hunting, driving for pleasure, or snowmobiling and cross-country skiing in the winter."

Red Cliffs also is a multiple-use area, although some areas are more restricted than others. It's been collaboratively managed by a number of agencies—led by Washington County's Habitat Conservation Plan (HCP). Since its inception in 1996, the HCP has protected populations and habitat of the threatened Mojave Desert tortoise. The reserve also contains the most northern populations of the Gila monster, a venomous lizard that can grow up to two feet long; and chuckwalla, a flat, chunky lizard that puffs itself up by gulping air and wedging tightly in a rock crevice when disturbed.

Cool.

These reptiles are typically associated with hotter and more southerly deserts like the Mojave. However, the habitat here consists of shrubs such as blackbrush that are more commonly found in the cooler Great Basin desert. In fact, there are a number of at-risk native plant and animal species that occur here and nowhere else in the world. In the face of rapid development in and around St. George and Hurricane, Utah, along the I-15 corridor, Washington County officials entered into this rare cooperative agreement more than two decades ago. Good on them!

A wildfire threatened the reserve a few years back. A bill to expand the reserve by 6,865 acres was introduced into Congress by Utah Republican representative Chris Steward in 2018. Representative Steward's expansion bill, supported by the Washington County commissioners, would have created a zone not connected to the remainder of the reserve, ensuring that one event—for example, a wildfire—would not affect the entire reserve. Congress never acted.

Welcome to Kanab, Utah.

Recent scientific studies have shown that the proposed expansion area exhibited tortoise densities higher than previously thought. Yet it may be a moot point. The Turkey Farm Road Fire destroyed nearly 12,000 acres north of St. George, Utah, in July 2020. Much of that fire raced across this tortoise range. Biologists continue to investigate. Some tortoises may have escaped or managed to stay underground as the blaze passed overhead. But life will be difficult for a live tortoise lingering in this burned-out landscape.

Red Cliffs NCA is divided into Upland and Lowland Zones. Recreation in the Lowland Zone is more restrictive since this area is more biologically sensitive and less durable. There are fewer recreation use restrictions in the Upland Zone.

There are literally hundreds of miles of hiking and horseback trails in the desert reserve, from about 80 trailheads, but none more fun than the hikes around Sandstone Mountain in the Babylon/Hurricane section of the area. Located between the towns of La Verkin, Hurricane, Leeds, and Toquerville, Sandstone Mountain is way cool! A remote and steep backcountry hike provides fabulous views, with arches, sand coves, and hidden formations found throughout.

Yet there is so much to do and so much to see around here, it would take years. So grab a good map and start plotting. To get you going, Utah's Scenic Byway 12 is a great way to see the red everything, from Dixie to Bryce to Capitol Reef. Zion and Capitol Reef get the brunt of tourism traffic out here, and Grand Staircase is also well discovered. However, Red Cliffs NCA and Dixie deserve recognition as well, for their outstanding geological, archeological, scenic, and pristine qualities.

SIGNATURE ACTIVITY: HIKE IT BABY!

WHY GO?

Time outside is good for babies too! It helps ward off illness and creates healthy sleep patterns. It lays a foundation for learning, improves physical development, and jump-starts language skills, according to a 2014 study published in the *European Journal of Social Sciences Education and Research*.

SPECS

ACTIVITY TYPE: Hike with a baby!
TRAILHEAD/PUT-IN/ETC.: The trailhead closest to you
DISTANCE/LENGTH: Start slowly, with short walks and hikes.
AVERAGE TIME REQUIRED: 15 minutes to an hour or so. You don't want to overdo it!
CONTACT/MANAGING AGENCY: Your spouse, your brain, your neighbor
DIFFICULTY: It's as easy as a stroll in the park!
SPECIAL CONSIDERATIONS: ALWAYS carry wet wipes, snacks, and water! Stay out of direct sunlight and dress in appropriate layers. Make sure your baby is warm, dry, and fed.

GETTING THERE

SHORT DESCRIPTION: Pack the baby and head out the front door!
GPS COORDINATES: You don't really need any!

OVERVIEW

My grandmother intuitively knew this: Fresh air and sunshine are good for kids. Scientific discoveries within the past two decades have expanded our understanding of experience (stimulation) in early brain development. Taking babies outside has now been "scientifically" proven to aid in early childhood language development. Babies have more sensory information to absorb and process when they're outside as opposed to in a controlled indoor environment. Turns out, it's good for Mom and Dad too. One of the official recommendations from the March of Dimes is to get outside. It helps prevent postpartum depression, improves self-esteem, and decreases anger and tension.

Raz, the bad-ass adventure dog, enjoys a break in the shade of a small arch.

So why don't more people do it? Perhaps they're not comfortable outside themselves, or they need a little help. Well, Shanti Hodges has just the thing for you: Hike it Baby! Hike it Baby is a national nonprofit group that gets kids and parents outside. Hike it Baby provides tools, information, and community "inspiring all families with babies and young children to get outside and connect with nature," according to its website at hikeitbaby.com.

The site offers tips on hikes and trails across the nation, how to connect to a community of like-minded outdoor enthusiasts, and how to safely and enjoyably take your child into the great outdoors. "Start by helping get families and families with disabilities and people of color onto the trail. Then, amplify younger children so you aren't introducing people to the outdoors at sixth grade. Introduce them at a younger age while recognizing getting to the great outdoors isn't easy for all," said Hodges. She founded the group in 2013 after looking for a way to get outside with her baby son, Mason, and other parents in her area. It started as a hike with three new friends and

This double arch is found on the hike around Sandstone Mountain.

three new babies. Hike it Baby now includes more than 125,000 families in 277 cities across the United States, with 3,600 free nature walks every month.

Hodges agrees that transportation and intimidation prevent people of color and other cultures from getting outdoors. That's why, she says, "we start with making it easier for groups like Hike it Baby, with strong urban presences, to get to the parks and amplifying that energy. Getting companies (such as Patagonia and REI) to support these 'meet-up' style groups and help work out the details of getting people outdoors really helps."

Turns out, Grandma was right all along.

CHAPTER 37
GRAND STAIRCASE–ESCALANTE NATIONAL MONUMENT

SIZE—Originally 1.7 million acres; proposed reduction to 1.003 million acres, a 47 percent reduction. Stay tuned. It's still in court!

YEAR ESTABLISHED—September 1996 by President Bill Clinton, because its "vast and austere landscape embraces a spectacular array of scientific and historic resources."

MANAGING AGENCY—Bureau of Land Management, Kanab, UT

DOG-FRIENDLY?—Dogs are allowed on-leash. Keep pets away from all archeological sites.

FEES AND PERMITS—Free permits are required for dispersed backcountry camping. They are available at visitor centers in Kanab, Escalante, Cannonville, Big Water, Aztec State Park Museum in Boulder, and at all trailheads. Fees are charged for camping at Calf Creek, Deer Creek, and White House campgrounds. In addition, use fees are charged in the Paria Canyon–Vermillion Cliffs Wilderness area.

NEAREST CITIES—Glendale, Kanab, and Boulder, UT

NEARBY PUBLIC PROPERTY—Red Canyon, Bryce Canyon National Park, Zion National Park, Capitol Reef National Park, Kodachrome Basin State Park, Escalante State Park, Calf Creek Recreation Area, Aztec State Park Museum, Dixie National Forest, Glen Canyon National Recreation Area, Boulder Mountain

SPECIAL CONSIDERATIONS—Because of all the controversy, it's getting crowded out here on designated roads, which become VERY dusty. Like most public property on the Colorado Plateau, however, if you get a half mile from the vehicle or a trailhead, you'll have a very solitary experience.

OVERVIEW

Controversy surrounding the Grand Staircase–Escalante National Monument and Bears Ears National Monument is as blustery as a huge, mad dust devil in the desert. On occasion, these vertically rotating columns of hot air grow large enough to raise a real stink. The politics of these two areas is intensely polarizing, yet this land is geologically mesmerizing to anyone who has ever stepped up its geologic flight of cliffs.

The Grand Staircase consists of five tilted escarpments called stairsteps, all facing south. They rise 5,500 feet from the North Rim of the Grand Canyon to the rim of Bryce Canyon. For millions of years, sediments were deposited here, eventually forming layers of sandstone, shale, and mudstone. Then came the slow lift of the Colorado Plateau, exposing layer after colorful layer: chocolate, vermillion, white, gray, and pink. The bottom chocolate layer along the North Rim of the Grand Canyon is the oldest layer. It consists of Kaibab Limestone, formed 200 to 225 million years ago. The vermillion layer along the reddish or vermillion-colored cliffs is about 165 to

Spooky Gulch and slot canyon is located off the Hole-in-the-Rock Road within the Grand Staircase–Escalante National Monument.

200 million years old, while the magnificent white towering Navajo Sandstone cliffs seen in Zion National Park occupy the white layer. The gray cliffs between Zion and Bryce consist of soft Cretaceous shale and sandstone deposited around 130 million years ago. The youngest layer consists of the pink cliffs of Bryce Canyon, exposing the 50- to 60-million-year-old sandstone found in Bryce, Red Canyon, and Cedar Breaks.

President Bill Clinton's Presidential Proclamation establishing Grand Staircase–Escalante as a national monument on September 18, 1996, stated:

> *The Grand Staircase–Escalante National Monument's vast and austere landscape embraces a spectacular array of scientific and historic resources. This high, rugged, and remote region, where bold plateaus and multi-hued cliffs run for distances that defy human perspective, was the last place in the continental United States to be mapped. Even today, this unspoiled natural area remains a frontier, a quality that greatly enhances the monument's value for scientific study. The monument has a long and dignified human history: it is a place where one can see how nature shapes human endeavors in the American West, where distance and aridity have been pitted against our dreams and courage. The monument presents exemplary opportunities for geologists, paleontologists, archeologists, historians, and biologists.*
>
> *The monument is a geologic treasure of clearly exposed stratigraphy and structures. The sedimentary rock layers are relatively undeformed and unobscured by vegetation, offering a clear view to understanding the processes of the earth's formation. A wide variety of formations, some in brilliant colors, have been exposed by millennia of erosion. The monument contains significant portions of a vast geologic stairway, named the Grand Staircase by pioneering geologist Clarence Dutton, which rises 5,500 feet to the rim of Bryce Canyon in an unbroken sequence of great cliffs and plateaus. The monument includes the rugged canyon country of the upper Paria Canyon system, major components of the White and Vermilion Cliffs and associated benches, and the Kaiparowits Plateau. That Plateau encompasses about 1,600 square miles of sedimentary rock and consists of successive south-to-north ascending plateaus or benches, deeply cut by steep-walled canyons. Naturally burning coal seams have scorched the tops of the Burning Hills brick red. Another prominent geological feature of the plateau is the East Kaibab Monocline, known as the Cockscomb. The monument also includes the spectacular Circle Cliffs and part of the Waterpocket Fold, the inclusion of which completes the protection of this geologic feature begun with the establishment of*

Capitol Reef National Monument in 1938 (Proclamation No. 2246, 50 Stat. 1856). The monument holds many arches and natural bridges, including the 130-foot-high Escalante Natural Bridge, with a 100-foot span, and Grosvenor Arch, a rare double arch. The upper Escalante Canyons, in the northeastern reaches of the monument, are distinctive: in addition to several major arches and natural bridges, vivid geological features are laid bare in narrow, serpentine canyons, where erosion has exposed sandstone and shale deposits in shades of red, maroon, chocolate, tan, gray, and white. Such diverse objects make the monument outstanding for purposes of geologic study.

The monument includes world-class paleontological sites. The Circle Cliffs reveal remarkable specimens of petrified wood, such as large unbroken logs exceeding 30 feet in length. The thickness, continuity and broad temporal distribution of the Kaiparowits Plateau's stratigraphy provide significant opportunities to study the paleontology of the late Cretaceous Era. Extremely significant fossils, including marine and brackish water mollusks, turtles, crocodilians, lizards, dinosaurs, fishes, and mammals, have been recovered from the Dakota, Tropic Shale and Wahweap Formations, and the Tibbet Canyon, Smoky Hollow and John Henry members of the Straight Cliffs Formation. Within the monument, these formations have produced the only evidence in our hemisphere of terrestrial vertebrate fauna, including mammals, of the Cenomanian-Santonian ages. This sequence of rocks, including the overlaying Wahweap and Kaiparowits formations, contains one of the best and most continuous records of Late Cretaceous terrestrial life in the world.

Archeological inventories carried out to date show extensive use of places within the monument by ancient Native American cultures. The area was a contact point for the Anasazi and Fremont cultures, and the evidence of this mingling provides a significant opportunity for archeological study. The cultural resources discovered so far in the monument are outstanding in their variety of cultural affiliation, type and distribution. Hundreds of recorded sites include rock art panels, occupation sites, campsites and granaries. Many more undocumented sites that exist within the monument are of significant scientific and historic value worthy of preservation for future study.

The monument is rich in human history. In addition to occupations by the Anasazi and Fremont cultures, the area has been used by modern tribal groups, including the Southern Paiute and Navajo. John Wesley Powell's expedition did initial mapping and scientific field work in the

Grand Staircase–Escalante is a land of immense beauty.

area in 1872. Early Mormon pioneers left many historic objects, including trails, inscriptions, ghost towns such as the Old Paria town site, rock houses, and cowboy line camps, and built and traversed the renowned Hole-in-the-Rock Trail as part of their epic colonization efforts. Sixty miles of the Trail lie within the monument, as does Dance Hall Rock, used by intrepid Mormon pioneers and now a National Historic Site.

Spanning five life zones from low-lying desert to coniferous forest, with scarce and scattered water sources, the monument is an outstanding biological resource. Remoteness, limited travel corridors and low visitation have all helped to preserve intact the monument's important ecological values. The blending of warm and cold desert floras, along with the high number of endemic species, place this area in the heart of perhaps the richest floristic region in the Intermountain West. It contains an abundance of unique, isolated communities such as hanging gardens, tinajas, and rock crevice, canyon bottom, and dunal pocket communities, which have provided refugia for many ancient plant species for millennia. Geologic uplift with minimal deformation and subsequent downcutting by streams have exposed large expanses of a variety of geologic strata, each with unique physical and chemical characteristics.

These strata are the parent material for a spectacular array of unusual and diverse soils that support many different vegetative communities and numerous types of endemic plants and their pollinators. This presents an extraordinary opportunity to study plant speciation and community dynamics independent of climatic variables. The monument contains an extraordinary number of areas of relict vegetation, many of which have existed since the Pleistocene, where natural processes continue unaltered by man. These include relict grasslands, of which No Mans Mesa is an outstanding example, and pinyon-juniper communities containing trees up to 1,400 years old. As witnesses to the past, these relict areas establish a baseline against which to measure changes in community dynamics and biogeochemical cycles in areas impacted by human activity. Most of the ecological communities contained in the monument have low resistance to, and slow recovery from, disturbance. Fragile cryptobiotic crusts, themselves of significant biological interest, play a critical role throughout the monument, stabilizing the highly erodible desert soils and providing nutrients to plants. An abundance of packrat middens provides insight into the vegetation and climate of the past 25,000 years and furnishes context for studies of evolution and climate change. The wildlife of the monument is characterized by a diversity of species. The monument varies greatly in elevation and topography and is in a climatic zone where northern and southern habitat species intermingle. Mountain lion, bear, and desert bighorn sheep roam the monument. Over 200 species of birds, including bald eagles and peregrine falcons, are found within the area. Wildlife, including neotropical birds, concentrate around the Paria and Escalante Rivers and other riparian corridors within the monument.

. . . The Federal land and interests in land reserved consist of approximately 1.7 million acres, which is the smallest area compatible with the proper care and management of the objects to be protected.

In his proclamation modifying the Grand Staircase–Escalante National Monument on December 4, 2017, President Donald Trump declared that most of the important geological, paleontological, archeological, historical, and biological aspects of the area were already protected. Therefore, the areas he outlined in his proclamation "are the smallest compatible with the proper care and management of the objects to be protected." He eliminated 861,974 acres of land from the national monument "that I find are no longer necessary for the proper care and management of the objects to be protected."

BLM UTAH HISTORY

In 1812, Congress established the General Land Office (GLO) to administer the public lands, with the primary purpose of passing public lands into private ownership. While most of the accessible land east of the Mississippi River had been settled and developed by the mid-19th century, the land to the west was largely unaltered by modern human influence until the first Mormon pioneers entered the Salt Lake Valley in 1847.

At the time, the area was claimed by Mexico until the Mexican-American War of 1848. Unlike prior land transfers, from public domain to private interests, Utah was unusual due to conflicts between the Mormon Church and the United States over issues such as polygamy and separation of church and state. Early Utahans were not permitted to enjoy the benefits of the Preemption Act of 1830, nor could they take up land under the Homestead Act of 1862. Near the end of 1856, most surveyors and the surveyor general were asked to leave the Territory of Utah and the General Land Office was moved to Denver, Colorado. In 1868, the General Land Office returned to Utah, and in 1869 U.S. law became applicable in Utah Territory. As a result, Utah was the last area in the continental United States where the public domain was open to private ownership.

In 1934, Congress passed the Taylor Grazing Act, which provided regulation of livestock grazing on public lands, and the Grazing Service was established. In 1946, the GLO and the Grazing Service merged to create the Bureau of Land Management (BLM). Cadastral workers began school land township surveys in 1956, which identified sections 2, 16, 32, and 36 for transfer to the State of Utah. To this day, state land can be seen in these sections across Utah.

The BLM's multiple-use mission was recognized when the Classification and Multiple Use Act was passed in 1964. In 1976, Congress enacted the Federal Land Policy and Management Act (FLPMA), which established a coherent legislative mandate for managing the public lands and made the BLM a true multiple-use agency and involved the public in decision making. Today, the BLM in Utah manages almost 23 million acres, or 42 percent of the state's land area, for a variety of uses. There are BLM offices in 13 Utah communities, including the BLM's first and largest national monument, the Grand Staircase–Escalante National Monument.

Prior to federal status, the land managed by the BLM in Utah had a long history of ancient cultures and immigration into and through the state. Rich cultural heritage that dates back to 11,000 BP (years before the present) and represents eight current American Indian tribes, include ancient rock art, irreplaceable pueblo homes, and countless artifacts. In addition to ancient cultures, the BLM in Utah is home to early homesteads, hideouts for notorious criminals, and historic immigration and trade routes. The lands managed by the BLM in Utah also represent a vast paleontological history dating back to 510 million years ago, when trilobites thrived in the seas that covered western Utah.

Source: blm.gov/about/history/history-by-region/utah

The eventual size of this national monument may ultimately be decided by the courts, since numerous groups immediately sued the Trump administration following the signing of Trump's 2017 proclamation.

There are really two issues here: One issue is energy development; the second issue is power politics and who controls federal land that we all own. Protection of antiquities seems have been swept aside in this debate.

Gnarly ancient pine ekes out an existence in Grand Staircase–Escalante National Monument.

Concerning energy, the Kaiparowits Plateau coalfield is the largest in Utah. It's located directly in the heart of the original Grand Staircase–Escalante National Monument. A 1997 report by the Utah Geological Survey noted this area might contain 11.4 billion tons of recoverable coal. The "downsized" national monument boundary correlates with this belt of coal streaking through it.

In Bears Ears (see chapter 28), the oil and gas industry has its eyes on 90,000 acres of oil and gas leases along the eastern boundary of the original Bears Ears National Monument. Meanwhile, the BLM has expedited environmental review processes for the possible expansion of the Daneros Uranium Mine from 4.5 acres to 46 acres. This would allow Canadian mining company Energy Fuels Resources to increase uranium ore production to 500,000 tons over the next 20 years, even though Energy Fuels says the price of uranium is so low they can't afford to mine it. The Bears Ears reduction also is directly correlated with an obvious belt of past producing uranium mines.

The second real issue here is power politics: Who controls the land? The State of Utah believes it should control all public land in Utah, even though it has never owned or controlled that land since Utah became the 45th state in 1896. This public land has remained under federal control since the Treaty of Guadalupe Hidalgo ended the Mexican-American War in 1848. The treaty added 525,000 square miles to U.S. territory, including land that makes up all or parts of present-day Arizona, California, Colorado, Nevada, New Mexico, Utah, and Wyoming. Mexico relinquished all claims to Texas and recognized the Rio Grande as America's southern boundary. In return, the United States paid Mexico $15 million and settled all claims of U.S. citizens against Mexico. The reason Utah was never given control of the land was because of a little issue between the United States and the Mormon Church concerning separation of church and state. (See "BLM Utah History" sidebar.) Yet 164 years later, in

Sunset over Harris Wash

Devil's Garden at Sunset

2012, Governor Gary Herbert and the Utah state legislature demanded the U.S. government relinquish control over some 30 million acres of public land in Utah. They complained that federal control over vast tracts of Utah's territory kept too much land off-limits to commercial activities such as energy development.

It was my small pickup truck that brought me to the Grand Staircase. I, too, rely on fossil fuels to get around. So I just don't know what to write, or what is right! But I know what the signature activity is here: Visit Grand Staircase–Escalante National Monument and see it for yourself. Drive, camp, hike, ride. Explore any way you can, and do it soon—while you still own it!

CHAPTER 38
GOBLIN VALLEY STATE PARK

SIZE—4.686 square miles

YEAR ESTABLISHED—August 24, 1964, when it was apparent the area needed protection from vandalism

MANAGING AGENCY—Utah State Parks and Recreation, 435-275-4584, stateparks.utah.gov

DOG-FRIENDLY?—Pets are allowed in Utah state parks, but they must be on a maximum 6-foot leash.

FEES AND PERMITS—$20 per day per vehicle day-use fee; $30 campground fee ($15 extra per vehicle). This is a state park. National Recreation Area cards do not apply.

NEAREST CITIES—Hanksville and Green River, UT

NEARBY PUBLIC PROPERTY—San Rafael Swell, Capitol Reef National Park, Fish Lake National Forest, Canyonlands National Park

SPECIAL CONSIDERATIONS—It's very hot and dry in the desert. Make sure you have enough water to drink, and hide behind a hoodoo for shade.

OVERVIEW

Competition for camp spots was fierce on this Easter Sunday.

The official campground at southeast Utah's Goblin Valley State Park was full—30 spaces, 1 group site, and 2 yurts—$30 per vehicle per night to camp.

The park was near capacity with about 400 to 500 visitors that day. The kind woman at the entrance smiled patronizingly when I asked for the old-guy break. She then assured me that free camping on BLM property surrounding this small state park along the San Rafael Swell was allowed.

She was correct, yet behind every hint of shade on that public property was a camper/trailer, with dozens of tents speckled in between.

This is a big area. You can see for a mile across. And there were campers behind every goblin and hoodoo.

Is it worth it? The hundreds of miles driving to get here? The planning, the packing, the maps. Yes, maps. There's no cell service. Google Maps won't get you there unless you downloaded it first.

The kids whine for hundreds of miles, fight in the back seat.

Do I have to stop this car?

They even get bored with their electronic devices.

Yet I'm observing an incredible sunset, not knowing whether to take pictures; write about the unexpected quiet, solitude, and experience; or just sit here with my jaw dropped, in awe of the incredible beauty.

Two-hundred-foot-tall hills, multilayered and multicolored with deep rusty sandstone, the Entrada, then a layer of dirty white siltstone and shale beds about a third as thick as the red base, then another layer of red, topped with a jaggedly brilliant reddish-yellow hard-cap of the Curtis Formation

Looking east, I see rabbitbrush poking through the sand, not yet bloomed. The sweep of its branches creates artful lines of soft, wavy Navajo sand. It sways gracefully in the breeze beneath incredibly steep 200-foot-tall hills, multilayered and multicolored with deep rusty sandstone, the Entrada, then a layer of dirty white siltstone and shale beds about a third as thick as the red base, then another layer of red, topped with a jaggedly brilliant reddish-yellow hard-cap of the Curtis Formation.

And, oh my, the pastel colors of a desert sunset glow behind me to the west.

Incredible.

The challenge of finding a good camping spot around here is actually pretty passive compared to anything I've seen at Arches or Zion or some of the more well-known jewels of public ownership.

There's a reason for so many people out here. We're escaping, finding a little peace and serenity in nature, even out here in the hot and dry desert, where there's sand everywhere. It's in your sleeping bag and in your socks and in your eye sockets. It's in your ears and all other orifices of your body.

Yet these become minor inconveniences for the joys of getting away.

Maybe it's only for one ride on a motorized side-by-side Razor OHV, the latest in off-road technology. Maybe it's just for one hike in this incredible canyon country. Maybe it's only for one mountain bike ride down a dirt road, like the two kids who flew by here a little while ago just before sunset, heading home to the campsite around the corner and their parents' tent. They were grinning ear to ear.

Maybe it's the anticipation of hiking through your first slot canyon. Is it Little Wild Horse and Bell Canyons? Or are you going into Ding Canyon and out Dang Canyon, or into Crack Canyon and out Chute Canyon? That's a long way, but if you're into nature's art at its finest, with swirls and narrows and color changes and soft sand and hard rock and thrills and awe-striking views, maybe it's worth it.

And the biggest allure of all are the goblins themselves. They are 170-million-year-old remnants of a shallow inland sea. They continue to erode and change and evolve.

"We saw swirls and cracks and long patience of the desert scape as it stood to hold its shape against water and rain and heat and ice and wind, and as old goblins dissolve, new ones are formed. Yet, we must be careful to preserve them so human activity doesn't push nature's paintbrush faster than it's designed to paint."

I read that somewhere. I wish I could remember where so I could give proper credit.

I'm thinking it was Arthur Chaffin, owner and operator of the Hite Ferry, who shuttled people across the Colorado River not far from here. He and two companions viewed this valley in the late 1920s, searching for an alternative route between Green River and Cainsville. They were blown away.

In 1949, Chaffin came back to photograph the area he called Mushroom Valley. Publicity attracted more people to this area, even with its remoteness, and by 1954, locals were clamoring to protect the area from vandalism.

> We must preserve them so human activity doesn't push nature's paintbrush faster than it's designed to paint.
> —Author unknown

"We must preserve them so human activity doesn't push nature's paintbrush faster than it's designed to paint."

The area directly in front of the observation/picnic area is open to climbing and scrambling, and that's where most people stay for their visit here. There are, however, acres of other hoodoos and layered deposits here. Three trails lead through the area: the Carmel Canyon Trail, a 1.5-mile moderately strenuous loop around Carmel Canyon; Curtis Bench Trail, an easy 2.1-mile out-and-back trail; and the moderately

Dad needs to stretch it out too!

strenuous 1.3-mile one-way trail from the camp-ground into Entrada Canyon. They all offer less-crowded glimpses of the weathering and erosion that created these incredible goblins.

You really don't even need a trail, however. Meander through what's known as Valley 1 in front of the observation point, into Valley 2 or Valley 3, and you lose all the people.

Two guys you probably won't see out here anymore are the ex–Boy Scout "leaders" who shoved over a delicate hoodoo in 2013. They claimed it was in danger of falling over and hurting someone, yet they pleaded guilty to criminal mischief.

In fact, the goblins are made of Entrada Sandstone. The average rate of erosion is approximately 2 to 4 feet every 100 years. The hoodoos were of no danger to anyone.

This sandstone was created when debris eroded from former highlands and redeposited here on a tidal flat. You can see the alternating layers of sandstone, then siltstone and shale. The ebb and flow of tides, tidal channels, and coastal sand dunes also can be observed here, if you can imagine what that was like 170 million years ago.

Multicolored hues of sandstone shine brightly in the setting sun.

The Utah Parks and Recreation Division is, in fact, looking at environmental changes due to the use that Valley 1 actually receives. They are compiling their information and comparing it to what's happening in other parts of the park that don't receive this pressure.

As with everything here on the Colorado Plateau, time will tell.

SIGNATURE ACTIVITY: GOBLIN HOPPING

WHY GO?

The stone shapes of Goblin Valley drew me in like a moth to the camping lantern. Soon, I was peering from behind a 12-foot-tall goblin, feeling like "an overfed, long-haired leaping gnome" (apologies to Eric Burdon). I was a kid again, laughing with the other kids, although *their* knees still worked.

SPECS

ACTIVITY TYPE: Goblin hopping/sandstone scrambling

TRAILHEAD/PUT-IN/ETC.: Observation point at the end of the road, where you'll find a covered picnic area and restrooms
DISTANCE/LENGTH: It's up to you!
AVERAGE TIME REQUIRED: Depends on how long you can last
CONTACT/MANAGING AGENCY: Utah State Parks and Recreation, 435–275–4584, stateparks.utah.gov
DIFFICULTY: From easy to as hard as you want to make it
SPECIAL CONSIDERATIONS: This sandstone is slick, so be careful. You can easily fall and scrape yourself up! Also, it's hot out here. So drink lots of water and carry Band-Aids.

GETTING THERE

SHORT DESCRIPTION: Go west from Green River on I-70 to the Hanksville exit, Highway 24. Turn south on Highway 24 and travel 24 miles to the Temple Mountain Junction; follow signs 12 miles to the park. Once through the state park entrance station, continue a short distance and turn left, southeast. (To the right are campgrounds and an OHV staging area.) Continue to the observation point and covered picnic area. Get out, gander, gawk, then get going.
GPS COORDINATES: 38°33'50.0"N, 110°42'13.0"W

OVERVIEW

"Do I get to climb here?" asked one wide-eyed seven-year-old as he darted out of the car and up to the rail at the Goblin Valley Observation Point. There were dozens of other kids already out there, in this wide valley of strange rock/dirt structures that looked like giant mushrooms or gnomes or goblins or ducks.

"Yes, you do," said his pleased mother.

It's not really rock climbing. It's more like dirt scrambling.

This is a kid's climbing paradise. Any kid can see faces in this goblin-forming Entrada Sandstone. Any adult can too. I found Donald Duck, a zebra, and a rabbit carrying a bundle on its back being chased by the Travelocity gnome. There was a javelina and a dog and a hedgehog.

Another family—Mom and Dad with two small boys—passed us deeper in the valley. The younger boy, perhaps six years old, said, "We just went to the king and queen's castle, and we got to sit on the king's throne." His eight-year-old brother said, "Yeah, and it was an air throne."

"What's an air throne?" I asked.

"You sit in it and your feet dangle in the air."

"Way over the air," his father said.

"Yeah, way over the air," said the six-year-old.

There are inherent dangers to climbing around here. You can get too much air. Sometimes the best thing a parent can do is turn her back and not watch.

Get the kids out of the vehicle and let 'em climb!

Did I mention this is kid-climbing heaven?

"Don't you just love it out here?" said the mother of another family of six.

"It's great to get the kids out here and climbing around," I noted.

"Wear 'em out," said Dad with a huge smile and a double fist pump.

"They'll be quiet on the ride home, that's for sure," Mom grinned.

As the sun shifts through Goblin Valley, the hoodoos and voodoos and goblins and ducks and javelina and rabbits turn into saddles and stagecoaches and the bobbing heads of passengers on a bus.

"Do I STILL get to climb?" quizzed the youngster a good 45 minutes later.

"Yes, you do," she told him.

"Until he wears out," she grinned at me.

Notes

1. *Desert Cabal: A New Season in the Wilderness*, Amy Irvine, Torrey House Press, 2018. Irvine admires the nature writer Edward Abbey as the man who influenced her life and work while challenging some of his outdated theories and at times offensive diatribes.

2. Rick Moore, Grand Canyon Trust on tourism, 2018, grandcanyontrust.org. Founded in 1985, the trust works to safeguard the wonders of the Grand Canyon and the Colorado Plateau while supporting the rights of its Native peoples.

3. *Desert Solitaire: A Season in the Wilderness*, Edward Abbey, McGraw-Hill, 1968. Recognized as an iconic work of nature writing, this book brought Abbey critical acclaim and popularity; based on Abbey's activities as a park ranger at Arches National Monument (now Arches National Park) in the late 1950s.

4. *Divine Dog Wisdom Cards,* Barb Horn and Randy Crutcher, 2017; enlightenup.biz. A dog's honesty teaches us about life. This deck of 62 cards and a guidebook with exceptional color drawings of dogs and puppies portray universal themes such as Passion, Purpose, Balance, Cooperation, and more.

5. *The Black Canyon of the Gunnison: In Depth*, Wallace Hansen, first published as U.S. Geological Survey Bulletin 1191; published by Southwest Parks & Monuments Association, 1987. A scholarly view of the geologic forces that created the Black Canyon of the Gunnison.

6. *Best Easy Day Hikes, Canyonlands and Arches National Parks* and *Hiking Canyonlands and Arches National Parks,* Bill Schneider; FalconGuides, 2017. Veteran hiker, author, and photographer Bill Schneider explores the canyonlands area extensively in these two books, providing precise maps, exact descriptions, and great photography.

7. "History and Intent of the Proclamation for Canyons of the Ancients National Monument," Kristina L. Woodall, online at: npshistory.com/publications/blm/canyons-of-the-ancients/history-intent.pdf. National parks historian Woodall traces the history of the area and defines the reasons for elevating Canyons of the Ancients to national monument status.

8. "Colorado Prehistory: A context for the Southern Colorado River Basin," Colorado Council of Professional Archaeologists, Denver, CO, 1999, W.D. Lipe, M. Varien and R. Wilshusen (editors).

9. Project WILD, 1983, Western Association of Fish and Wildlife agencies and Western Regional Environmental Education Council. Project WILD is an interdisciplinary, supplementary environmental and conservation education program for educators of kindergarten through high school–age young people.

10. *New Mexico,* Nancy Harbert, Compass American Guides/Fodor's Travel Publications Inc., 1992. The veteran Albuquerque-based journalist/writer covers the history, culture, and character of one of America's most spectacular—and sparsely populated—states.

11. *Chaco Canyon: Archaeology and Archaeologists*, Robert and Florence Lister, University of New Mexico Press, 1981. The first complete account of Chacoan archeology, from the discovery of the ruins by Spanish soldiers in the 17th century through the scientific analyses of the 1970s.

12. *A Study of Southwestern Archaeology*, Steven Lekson, University of Utah Press, 2018. Renowned archeologist Lekson argues that Southwestern archeology got the history of the ancient Southwest wrong. He advocates a new approach to study that separates archeological thought in the Southwest from its anthropological home and moves to more historical ways of thinking.

13. *Chaco Canyon: Archaeologists Explore the Lives of an Ancient Society*, Brian Fagan, Oxford University Press, 2005. Fagan (anthropology emeritus, University of California, Santa Barbara) aims to tell a story of Chaco Canyon as a historical narrative based on archeological research.

14. *Marietta Wetherill: Life with the Navajos in Chaco Canyon,* Kathryn Gabriel, University of New Mexico Press, 1992. Based on interviews from 1953, a year before her death, Marietta Wetherill told the story of her life to a newspaper reporter who recorded it on 75 reels of tape. In Marietta's own words, the book vividly portrays the beauty and tragedy of life with the Navajo in the turn-of-the-20th-century Southwest.

15. "Early National History," Sean P. Harvey, from Oxford Research Encyclopedias, April 2016. Harvey's dissertation on "Native Tongues: Colonialism and Race from Encounter to the Reservation" provides focused attention on religion, material culture, and language.

16. *Abstract: Wupatki National Monument: Archeology and Tourism, 1900–1956,* Tyson Pendery, University of Northern Arizona, circa 2003. Pendery inves-

tigates the movement to preserve Wupatki National Monument through archeological work and through tourism.

17. "Hopi History, Culture, and Landscape," Ferguson and Loma'omvaya, *Sunset Crater Archaeology: The History of a Volcanic Landscape*, Center for Desert Archaeology, Tucson, 2005. This was part of the 2011 Synthesis and Conclusions section Anthropological Papers No. 37, US89 Archaeological Project, Northern Arizona; academia.edu/11686455/ Sunset_Crater_Archaeology_The_History_of_a_Volcanic_Landscape._ Prehistoric_Settlement_in_the_Shadow_of_the_Volcano_2011_Synthesis_ and_Conclusions_Anthropological_Papers_No._37_US89_Archaeological_ Project_Northern_Arizona_.

18. *House of Rain: Tracking a Vanished Civilization across the American Southwest*, Craig Childs, Back Bay Books/Little, Brown and Company, 2006. Award-winning author Childs considers conventional thinking concerning the disappearance of the Anasazi, now known as Ancestral Puebloans. He then walks his way through time, covering an amazing amount of the Colorado Plateau in his search for this vanished civilization, adding his own suppositions to the narrative.

19. *The Navajo Political Experience*, David Wilkins, Rowman & Littlefield, 1999. Wilkins notes the Navajo Nation is the largest of more than 560 federally recognized indigenous entities in the United States today. Thus, Navajo history and politics serve as a model for understanding current Native American issues, from tribal-federal relationships to taxation policies and casino gaming challenges.

20. "Largest coal plant in the West Shuts Down . . . ," *USA Today*, November 18, 2019; usatoday.com/story/money/2019/11/18/navajo-generating -station-coal-plant-arizona-closes/4232386002/.

21. "Could Oil Demand Peak in Just Five Years?" Sarah Kent, *Wall Street Journal*, September 10, 2018; wsj.com/articles/debate-heats-up-over-when-era -of-oil-will-end-1536620460. The era of oil may be coming to an end, but experts disagree about just when that will happen.

22. Natural Arch and Bridge Society, a nonprofit all-volunteer society supporting the study, appreciation, and preservation of natural arches and bridges. The society's website explains the difference between an arch and a natural bridge; naturalarches.org/archinfo/faq.htm#bridge.

23. *Photography: Night Sky: A Field Guide for Shooting After Dark*, Jennifer Wu and James Martin, Mountaineers Books, 2014. Award-winning photographers Wu and Martin share tips for taking stunning photographs in the dark and overcoming the unique issues that come with nighttime photography.

24. *Monuments: The Controversy Over President Clinton's New Designations Under the Antiquities Act,* James Peck, 2000; myazbar.org/AZAttorney/Archives/July00/monuments.pdf. The environmental law attorney writes that the Antiquities Act is a matter of perspective, yet believes the original intent of the act did not include monuments as large as the million-acre Grand Canyon–Parashant.

About the Author

Bill Haggerty is a Colorado native, an avid outdoorsman and hiker, and author of *Hiking Colorado's Western Slope* (FalconGuides, 2017); *Best Easy Day Hikes Grand Junction and Fruita* (FalconGuides, 2015); and *Haggerty's Hikes in a Bottle* (H3J Publications/GJ Daily Sentinel, 2007), a collection of the 52 top hikes on the Colorado Plateau chosen from 13 years of weekly hiking columns that Haggerty penned for the *Grand Junction Daily Sentinel*.

Haggerty was also a contributing author to the nationally recognized Project WILD, an interdisciplinary environmental education program for K–12, and a contributing author to *Monumental Majesty: 100 years of Colorado National Monument*, published by Grand Junction Media in 2011. He hosted the popular *Bill's Backyard* on Grand Junction television for 18 years, a weekly program that documented wildlife in western Colorado. He also taught journalism and mass media at Mesa State College (now Colorado Mesa University).

Haggerty has roamed the Colorado Plateau for more than four decades as a reporter, photographer, Colorado Division of Wildlife information/education specialist, outdoor columnist, conservationist, naturalist, wildlife enthusiast, and public lands advocate. He sincerely hopes future generations will have as much foresight as our forefathers in preserving and enhancing our natural resources.